T0321944

Machine Learning
for Healthcare

Machine Learning for Healthcare

Handling and Managing Data

Edited by
Rashmi Agrawal
Jyotir Moy Chatterjee
Abhishek Kumar
Pramod Singh Rathore
Dac-Nhuong Le

CRC Press
Taylor & Francis Group
Boca Raton London New York

CRC Press is an imprint of the
Taylor & Francis Group, an **informa** business
A CHAPMAN & HALL BOOK

First edition published 2021
by CRC Press
6000 Broken Sound Parkway NW, Suite 300, Boca Raton, FL 33487-2742

and by CRC Press
2 Park Square, Milton Park, Abingdon, Oxon, OX14 4RN

ISBN: [978-0-367-35233-2] (hbk)
ISBN: [978-0-429-33013-1] (ebk)

Typeset in Palatino
by Deanta Global Publishing Services, Chennai, India

Contents

Preface.. vii
Acknowledgments xi
Editors... xiii
List of Contributors... xvii

1. **Fundamentals of Machine Learning** 1
   Rashmi Agrawal

2. **Medical Information Systems**..17
   Uday Sah, Abhushan Chataut, and Jyotir Moy Chatterjee

3. **The Role of Metaheuristic Algorithms in Healthcare** 25
   G. Uma Maheswari, R. Sujatha, V. Mareeswari, and E. P. Ephzibah

4. **Decision Support System to Improve Patient Care** 41
   V. Diviya Prabha and R. Rathipriya

5. **Effects of Cell Phone Usage on Human Health and Specifically
   on the Brain**..53
   *Soobia Saeed, Afnizanfaizal Abdullah, N. Z. Jhanjhi, Mehmood Naqvi
   and Shakeel Ahmed*

6. **Feature Extraction and Bio Signals** 69
   A. Mary Judith, S Baghavathi Priya, N. Kanya, and Jyotir Moy Chatterjee

7. **Comparison Analysis of Multidimensional Segmentation Using
   Medical Health-Care Information** 81
   *Soobia Saeed, Afnizanfaizal Abdullah, N. Z. Jhanjhi, Memood Naqvi,
   and Azeem Khan*

8. **Deep Convolutional Network Based Approach for Detection
   of Liver Cancer and Predictive Analytics on Cloud**...............................95
   Pramod H. B. and Goutham M.

9. **Performance Analysis of Machine Learning Algorithm for
   Healthcare Tools with High Dimension Segmentation** 115
   *Soobia Saeed, Afnizanfaizal Abdullah, N. Z. Jhanjhi, Memood Naqvi
   and Mamoona Humayun*

10. **Patient Report Analysis for Identification and Diagnosis of Disease**...129
    Muralidharan C., Mohamed Sirajudeen Y., and Anitha R.

11. **Statistical Analysis of the Pre- and Post-Surgery in the Healthcare Sector Using High Dimension Segmentation** 159
    Soobia Saeed, Afnizanfaizal Abdullah, N. Z. Jhanjhi, Memood Naqvi, and Mamoona Humayun

12. **Machine Learning in Diagnosis of Children with Disorders** 175
    Lokesh Kumar Saxena and Manishikha Saxena

13. **Forecasting Dengue Incidence Rate in Tamil Nadu Using ARIMA Time Series Model**.. 187
    S. Dhamodharavadhani, R. Rathipriya

Index...203

Preface

The key objective of publishing this book is to explore the concepts of machine learning, along with recent research developments in healthcare sectors. The book includes chapters by authors who are experts in this area and have experience of the recent research developments in the field of healthcare using machine learning technology. It will provide in-depth information about the applications and utilizations of machine learning in healthcare. It will provide a better understanding of the processing of big data from the healthcare sector as used in machine learning processes, and it will highlight the links between machine learning and computer science in healthcare applications from many perspectives.

Machine learning (ML) is currently causing quite a buzz, and is having a huge impact on healthcare. Payers, providers, and pharmaceutical companies are today seeing applicability in their spaces and are taking advantage of ML. A machine learning model is created by feeding data into a learning algorithm. The algorithm is the place where the magic happens. There are algorithms to determine a patient's length of stay based on diagnosis, for example, and that algorithm all began when someone decided to write it and train it with true and reliable data. Over time, the model can be re-trained with newer data, increasing the model's effectiveness. Machine learning is defined as when a computer has been taught to recognize patterns by providing it with data and an algorithm to help understand that data. We call the process of learning "training" and the output that this process produces is called a "model". A model can be provided with new data and it can reason with this new information based on what it has previously learned.

Machine learning models determine a set of rules using vast amounts of computing power that a human brain would be incapable of processing. The more data a machine learning model is fed, the more complex the rules – and the more accurate the predictions. Whereas a statistical model is likely to have an inherent logic that can be understood by most people, the rules created by machine learning are often beyond human comprehension because our brains are incapable of digesting and analyzing enormous datasets.

Deep learning is another buzzword we often hear a lot about but it is often misunderstood. In reality, it is just a special case of machine learning algorithm through artificial neural networks. A neural network is an algorithm that was inspired by the ways a brain works and it involves many nodes (or "neurons") that are often connected together in layers to form a network. A neural network must have at least two layers – a layer of inputs and a layer of outputs. There may be many "hidden" layers between the input layer and output layer, and these are used to extract more information by exploiting structure in the data. A network is considered "deep" if it has more than one hidden layer (see the diagram opposite which illustrates the complexity of a neural network). Neural networks are great at solving problems where the data is highly structured – like an image of a brain scan – but are also "black box" algorithms. In other words, it is hard for humans to comprehend the patterns they find. Despite being around for over 50 years, neural networks have only become popular and feasible in the last ten years thanks to advances in both algorithm design and computing power. While the healthcare sector is being transformed by the ability to record massive amounts of information about individual patients, the enormous volume of data being collected is impossible for human beings to analyze. Machine learning provides a way to automatically find patterns and reasons behind data, which enables healthcare professionals to move towards more personalized care – known as precision medicine. There are many possibilities for how machine learning can be used in healthcare settings, and all of them depend on having sufficient data and permissions to use it. Previously, alerts and recommendations for medical practice have been developed based on external studies, and hard coded into their software. However, that can limit the accuracy of the data because they might be from different populations and environments. Machine learning, on the other hand, can be refined using data that is available in that particular environment. For example, anonymized patient record information from a hospital and the area in which it serves.

One further example of how healthcare providers can take advantage of machine learning is utilizing it in order to predict the likelihood of hospital re-admission for chronically ill patients. Identifying the patients who are most at risk of being re-admitted means they can be given greater support after they have been discharged. By lowering the rate of re-admission, not only are the lives of those most at risk improved, but it also helps save precious healthcare funds, which can then perhaps be used for wellness and prevention programs instead.

The main research issues and important concepts relating to machine learning technology in the healthcare industry are covered in more detail throughout this book. It will provide in-depth information about handling and managing healthcare data with machine learning methods. Throughout this book we will try our best to show readers about the links between machine learning and computer science applications in healthcare sector more broadly

---

What You'll Learn

1. A deeper understanding of various machine learning uses and their implementation within wider healthcare.
2. The ability to implement machine learning systems, such as cancer detection, and enhanced deep learning.

3. How to select learning methods and tuning for use in healthcare.

4. How to recognize and prepare for the future of machine learning in healthcare through best practices, feedback loops, and intelligent agents.

Who This Book Is For

Machine intelligence for the healthcare industry is the need of the hour. It requires adopting both new and better ways to the healthcare providers who can take advantage of these techniques in order to improve the health of human beings. The machine learning techniques enable healthcare providers to garner and operationalize new insights efficiently as a by-product of an organization's day-to-day operations. This is becoming vital to hospitals and health systems' ability to persist and flourish. This book will provide in-depth information about handling and managing healthcare data with machine learning methods. It will discuss the long-standing challenges in healthcare informatics and provide rational ideas of how best to navigate them.

Rashmi Agrawal (Haryana, India)
Jyotir Moy Chatterjee (Kathmandu, Nepal)
Abhishek Kumar (Himachal Pradesh, India)
Pramod Singh Rathore (Rajasthan, India)
Dac-Nhuong Le (Haiphong, Vietnam)

MATLAB® is a registered trademark of The MathWorks, Inc. For product information, please contact:

The MathWorks, Inc.
3 Apple Hill Drive
Natick, MA 01760-2098 USA
Tel: 508 647 7000
Fax: 508-647-7001
E-mail: info@mathworks.com
Web: www.mathworks.com

Acknowledgments

I would like to acknowledge the most important people in my life, my uncle Mr. Moni Moy Chatterjee, my father Aloke Moy Chatterjee, and my late mother Nomita Chatterjee. This book has been my long-cherished dream – one which could not have been turned into a reality without the support and love of these amazing people. They have continuously encouraged me despite my failing to give them the proper time and attention. I am also grateful to my friends, who have encouraged and blessed this work with their unconditional love and patience.

Jyotir Moy Chatterjee
Department of IT
Lord Buddha Education Foundation
Kathmandu, Nepal

Editors

Rashmi Agrawal is a Professor in the Department of Computer Applications in MRIIRS, Faridabad. Dr. Agrawal has a rich teaching experience of more than 17 years. She is UGC-NET(CS) qualified, and has completed a PhD, M. Phil, M. Tech, MSc, and MBA(IT). Her PhD focused on the area of machine learning, and her areas of expertise include Artificial Intelligence, Machine Learning, Data Mining, and Operating Systems. She has published more than 30 research papers in various national and international conferences and journals, and has authored many published books and chapters. She has organized various faculty development programs and has also directly participated in workshops and faculty development programmes. She is actively involved in research activities, and is a lifetime member of Computer Society of India. She has been a member of the technical programme committee of various reputable conferences.

Jyotir Moy Chatterjee is an Assistant Professor at the IT Department of Lord Buddha Education Foundation (Asia Pacific University of Technology and Innovation), Kathmandu, Nepal. Prior to this he has worked as an Assistant Professor at the CSE Department of GD Rungta College of Engineering and Technology (CSVTU), Bhilai, India. He has completed an M. Tech in Computer Science and Engineering from Kalinga Institute of Industrial Technology, Bhubaneswar, Odisha and a B. Tech in Computer Science and Engineering from Dr. MGR Educational and Research Institute, Chennai. He has published 40 international research papers, two international conference papers, authored four books, edited eight books, written 11 book chapters and has one patent to his account. His research interests include cloud computing, big data, privacy preservation, data mining, the Internet of Things, machine learning, and blockchain technology. He is a member of various professional societies and international conferences.

Abhishek Kumar has a PhD in computer science from University of Madras and an M. Tech in computer science and engineering from Government Engineering College Ajmer at Rajasthan Technical University, Kota, India. He has over eight years of experience in academic teaching and has been published more than 55 times in reputed, peer-reviewed national and international journals, books and conferences (such as by Wiley, Taylor & Francis, Springer, Elsevier, Science Direct, Inderscience, Annals of Computer Science, Poland, and IEEE). His research areas include: Artificial Intelligence, image processing, computer vision, data mining, and machine learning. He has also been on the international conference committees of many international conferences, and is currently serving as a reviewer for IEEE and Inderscience journals. He has authored six internationally published books and has edited 11 books with Wiley, IGI GLOBAL, Springer, Apple Academic Press, CRC, and more. He is also member of various national and international professional societies in the field of engineering and research including being a member of IEEE, ISOC (Internet Society)); IAIP (International Association of Innovation Professionals), ICSES (International Computer Science and Engineering Society) IAENG (International Association of Engineers); an associate member of IRED (Institute of Research Engineers and Doctors; a life member of ISRD (International Society for research & Development); and an editorial board member of IOSRD. He has received the national Sir CV Raman lifetime achievement award in 2018 in the young researcher and faculty category.

Pramod Singh Rathore is currently pursuing his PhD in computer science and engineering at Bundelkhand University and is conducting ongoing research on networking. He has an M. Tech in computer science and engineering from Government Engineering College Ajmer, at Rajasthan Technical University, Kota, India. He has been working as an Assistant Professor of the Computer Science and Engineering Department at Aryabhatt Engineering College and Research Centre, Ajmer, Rajasthan and is also a visiting faculty at Government University MDS Ajmer. He has over eight years of experience in academic teaching and has been published more than 45 times in reputed, peer-reviewed national and international journals, books and conferences (such as Wiley, IGI GLOBAL, Taylor & Francis, Springer, Elsevier, Science Direct, Annals of Computer Science, Poland, and IEEE). He has co-authored and edited many books with many reputed publishers like Wiley, and CRC Press, USA. His research areas include: NS2, computer networks, mining, and DBMS.

 **Dac-Nhuong Le** has a PhD and is Deputy-Head of the Faculty of Information Technology at Haiphong University, Vietnam and Vice-Director of Information Technology at the Apply Center of the same university. He is a research scientist at the Research and Development Center of Visualization & Simulation in (CSV), Duy Tan University, Danang, Vietnam. He has more than 45 publications in the reputed international conferences, journals, and online book chapter contributions (indexed by: SCI, SCIE, SSCI, Scopus, ACM, and DBLP). His areas of research include: evaluation computing and approximate algorithms, network communication, security and vulnerability, network performance analysis and simulation, cloud computing, and biomedical image processing. His core work is in network security, wireless, soft computing, mobile computing and biomedical technology. Recently, he has been on a technical program committee, a technical reviewer, and the track chair for international conferences such as: FICTA 2014, CSI 2014, IC4SD 2015, ICICT 2015, INDIA 2015, IC3T 2015, INDIA 2016, FICTA 2016, IC3T 2016, ICDECT 2016, IUKM 2016, INDIA 2017, FICTA 2017, CISC 2017, ICICC 2018, ICCUT 2018 under the Springer-ASIC/LNAI/CISC Series. Presently, he is serving on the editorial board of international journals and he has authored six computer science books (published by Springer, Wiley, CRC Press, Lambert Publication, VSRD Academic Publishing, and Scholar Press).

List of Contributors

Mary Judith A.
Assistant Professor (CSE)
Loyola-ICAM College of
    Engineering & Technology
Chennai, India

Afnizanfaizal Abdullah
Department of Software
    Engineering
UniversitiTeknologi Malaysia-UTM
Johor Bharu, Malaysia

Rashmi Agrawal
Manav Rachna International
    Institute of Research and Studies
Faridabad, India

Shakeel Ahmed
College of Computer Sciences
    and IT
King Faisal University
Hofuf, Saudi Arabia

Anitha R.
Department of Computer Science
    and Engineering
Sri Venkateswara College of
    Engineering
Sriperumbudur, India

Abhushan Chataut
Lord Buddha Education Foundation
Kathmandu, Nepal

Jyotir Moy Chatterjee
Lord Buddha Education Foundation
Kathmandu, Nepal

S. Dhamodharavadhani
Department of Computer Science
Periyar University
Salem, India

E. P. Ephzibah
School of Information Technology
    and Engineering
Vellore Institute of Technology
Vellore, India

Goutham M.
Department of Computer Science
    and Engineering
NIE Institute of Technology
Mysuru, India

Mamoona Humayun
Department of Information Systems
Jouf University
Al-Jouf, Saudi Arabia

N. Z. Jhanjhi,
School of Computer Science and
    Engineering (SCE)
Taylor's University
Selangor, Malaysia

Mary Judith A.
Loyola-ICAM College of
    Engineering & Technology
Chennai, India

N. Kanya
Dr. M.G.R Educational and Research
    Institute
Chennai, India

Azeem Khan
American Degree Program ADP
Taylor's University
Selangor, Malaysia

G. Uma Maheswari
School of Information Technology
and Engineering
Vellore Institute of Technology
Vellore, India

V. Mareeswari
School of Information Technology
and Engineering
Vellore Institute of Technology
Vellore, India

Muralidharan C.
Department of Computer Science
and Engineering
Sri Venkateswara College of
Engineering
Sriperumbudur, India

Mehmood Naqvi
Faculty of Engineering Technology
Mohawk College
Hamilton, Canada

V. Diviya Prabha
Department of Computer Science
Periyar University Salem
Salem, India

Pramod H. B.
Department of Computer Science
and Engineering
Rajeev Institute of Technology
Hassan, India

S. Baghavathi Priya
Rajalakshmi Engineering College
Chennai, India

R. Rathipriya
Department of Computer Science
Periyar University Salem
Salem, India

Soobia Saeed
Department of Software
Engineering
UniversitiTeknologi Malaysia-UTM
Johor Bharu, Malaysia

Uday Sah
Lord Buddha Education Foundation
Kathmandu, Nepal

Lokesh Kumar Saxena
Department of Mechanical
Engineering
Faculty of Engineering and
Technology
Jamia Millia Islamia
New Delhi, India

Manishikha Saxena
Department of Education
Government of Delhi
Delhi, India

Mohamed Sirajudeen Y.
Department of Computer Science
and Engineering
Sri Venkateswara College of
Engineering
Sriperumbudur, India

R. Sujatha
School of Information Technology
and Engineering
Vellore Institute of Technology
Vellore, India

1

Fundamentals of Machine Learning

Rashmi Agrawal

CONTENTS

1.1 Introduction...1
1.2 Data in Machine Learning...2
1.3 The Relationship between Data Mining, Machine Learning, and
    Artificial Intelligence...4
1.4 Applications of Machine Learning 5
    1.4.1 Machine Learning: The Expected 5
    1.4.2 Machine Learning: The Unexpected..5
1.5 Types of Machine Learning...6
    1.5.1 Supervised Learning..6
          1.5.1.1 Supervised Learning Use Cases 9
    1.5.2 Unsupervised Learning...9
          1.5.2.1 Types of Unsupervised Learning 10
          1.5.2.2 Clustering...11
          1.5.2.3 Association Rule...11
          1.5.2.4 Unsupervised Learning Use Case.............................13
    1.5.3 Reinforcement Learning (RL) 13
1.6 Conclusion 14
References...15

1.1 Introduction

Machine learning is a discipline in which algorithms are applied to help mine knowledge out of large pools of existing information. It is the science that gives power to computers to perform without being openly programmed. "It is defined by the ability to choose effective features for pattern recognition, classification, and prediction based on the models derived from existing data" (Tarca and Carey 2007). According to Arthur L Samuel (1959), "machine learning is the ability of computers to learn to function in ways that they were not specifically programmed to do". Many factors have contributed to making machine learning a reality. These include sources of data that are generating vast information, improved computational control for

1

processing large amounts of information in fractions of time, and algorithms which are now more reliable and efficient.

Machine learning is one of the most exciting technologies one could come by. As is apparent from its name, machine learning offers the computer *the ability to learn*, meaning it can become more like a human. It is being vigorously used today, perhaps in many more ways than one would expect.

1.2 Data in Machine Learning

The data required for analysis is gathered from various sources such as web pages, emails, IoT sensors, text files, etc. This data serves as the input needed for machine learning algorithms to generate insights. Without data, we can't train any models and all contemporary research and automation would be ineffective. Large initiatives are spending masses of money just to collect as much specific data as possible. Data uncertainty is common in real-world applications. Various factors like physical data generation and collection processes, unreliable data transmission, transmission bandwidth, measurement errors, and decision errors contribute to the uncertainty in data. This may apply for both numerical data and categorical data (Agrawal and Ram 2015).

After collecting data, it is preprocessed and used for extracting information and knowledge (Figure 1.1).

Now the question of how the data is used in machine learning arises. As shown in Figure 1.2, the data is split into three parts – testing, training, and validation data.

FIGURE 1.1
Data, information and knowledge.

FIGURE 1.2
Types of data.

Training data is applied to train machine learning models and, after completion of the training part, testing data is used for unprejudiced valuation of the model. Validation data is used for frequent evaluation of the model thereafter. Thus, the data plays an important role in the model building and selection. Data has a lot of potential for organizations and almost all large- and mid-level organizations are therefore continuously looking for ways to utilize it (Agrawal 2020). Some of the important dimensions of big data are described here:

1) **Volume:** the main characteristic feature or dimension of big data is its sheer volume. The term volume refers to the amount of data an organization, or an individual, collects and/or generates. Currently, to qualify as big data, a minimum of 1 terabyte is the threshold for big data which stores as much data as would fit on 1,500 CDs or 220 DVDs, (or enough to store approximately 16 million Facebook images). The vast amounts of data are generated every second. E-commerce, social media, and various sensors produce high volumes of unstructured data in the form of various audio, images, and video files. Today big data is also generated by machines, networks, and human interaction on systems and the volume of data to be analyzed is massive.

2) **Variety:** is one of the most attractive dimensions in technology, as almost all information is digitized nowadays. Traditional data types or structured data include information (such as date, amount, and time) in a structured way which can easily fit neatly in a relational database. Structured data is augmented by unstructured data. Modern day data sources include Twitter feeds, YouTube videos, audio files, MRI images, web pages, web logs, and anything else that can be captured and stored and does not require any meta model for its structure to access it later on.

   Unstructured data is an essential concept in big data. To understand the difference between structured and unstructured data, we can compare these two types of data and see that a picture, a voice recording, or a tweet are all different in their function and usage, but both express ideas and thoughts based on human understanding. One of the major goals of big data is to make sense from this unstructured data.

3) **Velocity:** refers to the frequency of incoming data that is needing to be processed. The flow of data is massive and continuous. The velocity of data increases over time. In 2016, approximately 5.5 million new devices were connected every day for collecting and sharing data. The improved data streaming potential of linked devices will continue to gather speed in the future. Streaming applications like Amazon Web Services Kinesis is an example of an application that handles the velocity of data.

4) **Veracity:** refers to the reliability of the data. Given the increasing volume of data being generated at an unparalleled rate, it is common that the data must contain noise. Veracity refers to the trustworthiness of the data that needs to be analyzed. Uncertainty and unreliability arise due to incompleteness, inaccuracy, latency, inconsistency, subjectivity, and deception in data.

In addition to these four dimensions, there are two additional dimensions which are key for operationalizing data.

5) **Volatility:** this big data dimension refers to the length of time that this data will remain valid and for how long it should be stored.

6) **Validity:** the validity dimension in big data means that data in use should be correct and accurate. If one wants to use the results for decision making, validity of big data sources and subsequent analysis must be accurate.

1.3 The Relationship between Data Mining, Machine Learning, and Artificial Intelligence

Figure 1.3 represents the relationship among data mining, Artificial Intelligence (AI), data science, and machine learning. Artificial Intelligence can be defined as the study of training computers in such a way that computers can accomplish tasks which, at present, can be done better by humans. Machine learning is a sub-field of knowledge science that focuses on the development of algorithms that may be learned from in order to generate likelihoods based on the given information.

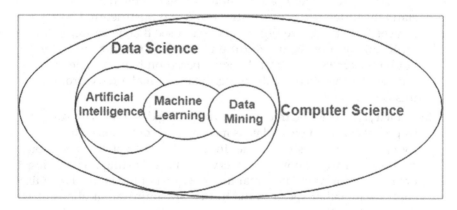

FIGURE 1.3
Relationship in AI and machine learning.

TABLE 1.1

Difference between Machine Learning and AI

Artificial Intelligence (AI)	Machine Learning (ML)
Focus is given to increasing success and not the accuracy.	Main focus is to get the maximum accuracy.
The goal of AI is to imitate human intelligence which will be used to solve complex problems.	In ML, the primary goal is to be trained from data on a definite task to make the most of the performance of the machine on this task.
AI leads to intelligence.	ML leads to knowledge.
It progresses to build up an arrangement to imitate humans and to behave similarly in a particular circumstance.	It involves developing self-learning algorithms which can learn independently.

The difference between machine learning and AI is represented by the Table 1.1 below.

1.4 Applications of Machine Learning

Each and every time the word machine learning is used, people generally think of "AI" and "Neural networks that can simulate human brains", Self-Driving Cars, and more. But machine learning is much different. Below we expound on anticipated and unexpected aspects of contemporary computing where machine learning is enacted.

1.4.1 Machine Learning: The Expected

1. Speech Recognition
2. Computer Vision (Facial Recognition, Pattern Recognition, and Character Recognition Techniques belong to Computer Vision)
3. Google's Self-Driving
4. Web Search Engine
5. Photo Tagging Applications
6. Spam Detector
7. Database Mining for Growth of Automation
8. Understanding Human Learning

1.4.2 Machine Learning: The Unexpected

1. YouTube/Netflix
2. Data Mining/Big Data

3. Amazon's Product Recommendations
4. Stock Market/Housing Finance/Real Estate

1.5 Types of Machine Learning

We can define machine learning as learning from some past experiences based on some task, and it may have one of the following types as shown in Figure 1.4.

1.5.1 Supervised Learning

This is the most popular paradigm for machine learning, which learns from labeled data. A function is inferred from the data that maps the input, output pair to the target, h: f(x,y) → y, where f is the function learned from input and output pairs x and y, respectively. It is further of two types: classification and regression. Classification predicts categorical answers and function acquires the class codes of different classes, that is, (0/1) or (yes/no). Naïve Bayes, decision tree (Batra and Agrawal 2018), k nearest neighbor (Agrawal 2019), and support vector machines (SVM) are frequently used algorithms for classification. Regression predicts the numerical response, e.g. predicting the future value of stock prices. Linear Regression, neural networks, and regularization are algorithms used for regression. Table 1.2 (A and B) shows the difference between classification and regression.

Table 1.2A represents the classification task by showing the dataset of a shopping store with input variables as user ID, gender, age, and salary.

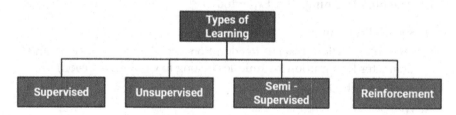

FIGURE 1.4

Types of machine learning.

TABLE 1.2A

Classification

User ID	Gender	Age	Salary	Buy Product (Yes/No)
101	M	42	15k	Yes
102	M	65	55k	No
103	F	65	50k	Yes
105	F	35	20k	Yes

TABLE 1.2B

Regression

Temp	Pressure	Relative Humidity	Wind Direction	Wind Speed
17.70	988.11	39.11	192.92	2.973
24.23	988.24	19.74	318.32	0.32
22.54	989.56	22.81	44.66	0.264

Based on these input variables, the machine learning algorithm will predict whether the customer will buy a product or not (0 for no, 1 for yes). Table 1.2B here shows the data of a meteorological department with input variables of temperature, pressure, relative humidity, and wind direction; after applying regression techniques, wind speed is determined.

In classification, the goal is to predict discrete values going to a specific class and calculate them on the basis of accuracy. This can be 0 or 1 (yes or no) in binary classification, but in the case of multi-class classification, it is more than one class. In regression, the output has continuous values.

Table 1.3 summarizes the supervised algorithms which are used in machine learning.

A method of performance measurement for machine learning classification is a confusion matrix, which has been shown in Table 1.4 for a binary clarification problem, and Table 1.5 represents a confusion matrix for a three-class problem. It is immensely functional for evaluating Precision, Recall, Specificity, AUC-ROC Curve, and Accuracy.

Each entry of Tables 1.4 and1. 5 depicts the number of records from class I predicted to be of class j. For example, C_{10} is the number of records from class 1 incorrectly predicted as class 0. On the other hand, C_{00} represents the number of records from class 0 that were correctly predicted as class 0. From the confusion matrix we can find the total number of correct predictions made by the classification model as $(C_{11} + C_{00})$ and the total number of incorrect predictions as $(C_{10} + C_{01})$.

A good classification model is expected to have more records in cells C11 and C00 and fewer records in C01 and C10. The most popular performance metric for evaluating the merit of a classifier is the accuracy, defined by:

$$\text{Accuracy} = \frac{\text{Number of correct predictions}}{\text{Total number of predictions}}$$

$$= \frac{C_{11} + C_{00}}{C_{11} + C_{00} + C_{10} + C_{01}}$$

Similarly, to find the error rate of the classification model, we use the following equation:

$$\text{Error Rate} = \frac{C_{01} + C_{10}}{C_{11} + C_{00} + C_{10} + C_{01}}$$

TABLE 1.3

Supervised Algorithms

Algorithm	Type	Description
Linear regression	Regression	This technique correlates each feature to the output which helps to predict future values.
Logistic regression	Classification	This technique is an extension of linear regression, used for classification tasks, and takes its output variable as binary.
Decision tree	Regression/Classification	It is a model which is used for predicting the values by splitting the nodes into the children nodes by forming structure of a tree.
Support Vector Machine (SVM)	Regression	This algorithm is best used with a non-linear solver. It catches a hyper plane to distribute the classes optimally.
Naïve Bayes	Classification or Regression	Naïve Bayes classification technique finds the prior knowledge of an event in relation to the independent probability of each feature.
AdaBoost	Classification or Regression	It uses a mass of models to have a decision which weighs them based on the accuracy in prediction.
Random forest	Classification or Regression	Random forest uses the "majority vote" method on multiple decision trees to label the output.
Gradient-boosting	Classification or Regression	It focuses on the error generated by the preceding trees to update the results.

TABLE 1.4

Confusion Matrix for a Binary Classification Problem

	Predicted Class	
Actual Class	**1**	**0**
1	C_{11}	C_{10}
0	C_{01}	C_{00}

TABLE 1.5

Confusion Matrix for a Three-Class Problem

	Predicted Class		
Actual Class	**C1**	**C2**	**C3**
C1	C_{11}	C_{12}	C_{13}
C2	C_{21}	C_{22}	C_{23}
C3	C_{31}	C_{32}	C_{33}

The key objective of a classification model is to find the highest accuracy and lowest error rate.

1.5.1.1 Supervised Learning Use Cases

1. **Cortana:** this automated speech system is used for mobile applications. First it trains itself by using mobile phone voices and then it makes predictions based on this data.
2. **Weather Apps:** weather apps are used to predict future weather by exploring the conditions for a given time, based on previous data.
3. **Biometric Attendance:** the machines can be trained with inputs of biometric individuality which can be iris, thumb, or earlobe, etc. After training, the machine can easily identify the person.

1.5.2 Unsupervised Learning

No labeled data is provided in this type of learning. The algorithm finds the patterns within the dataset and acquires them. The algorithm clusters the data into various groups based on its concreteness. By this means, one can accomplish visualization of high dimensional data. In unsupervised learning we do not give goals to our model through training. The model needs to discover what direction it can realize without anyone else's input. Figure 1.5 shows the dataset which contains the data of clients that subscribe to an organization "abc." When buying in, they are given a participation card; thus the shopping center has total data about each client and all his/her purchases. Presently, by utilizing this information and solo learning strategies, shopping centers can undoubtedly amass customers, dependent on the parameters they are bolstering in.

Training data is:

- **Unstructured data**
- **Unlabeled data**

CustomerID	Genre	Age	Annual Income (k$)	Spending Score (1-100)
1	Male	19	15	39
2	Male	21	15	81
3	Female	20	16	6
4	Female	23	16	77
5	Female	31	17	40
6	Female	22	17	76
7	Female	35	18	6
8	Female	23	18	94

FIGURE 1.5
Data for unsupervised learning.

Data scientists prefer to choose unsupervised learning techniques over supervised learning. Some of the primary reasons for this are: i) this technique finds all kinds of unknown patterns in data; ii) it is easier to get unlabeled data than labeled data (hence the process of data collection is easier); iii) these methods help to find features which can be useful for categorization.

1.5.2.1 Types of Unsupervised Learning

- **Clustering:** comprehensively, this method is useful for grouping information dependent on various examples. For instance, if we are not given a response parameter as shown in Figure 1.6, then this system will be utilized to amass customers dependent on the information parameters given by available information.

- **Association:** this is a rule-based on a machine learning procedure which discovers some extremely valuable relationships between parameters of a huge informational index. Association rules permit us to generate associations in the midst of data objects inside enormous databases. This unsupervised technique is related to determining attention-grabbing relationships between variables in large databases. Generally, most of the machine learning algorithms work with numeric datasets and therefore tend to be mathematical. However, association rule mining is appropriate for non-numeric, categorical data, and needs impartial – more than simple – counting.

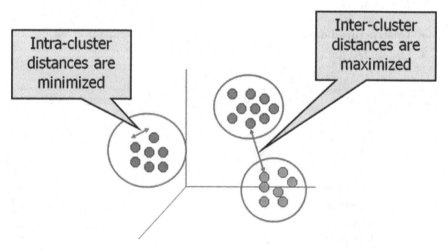

FIGURE 1.6
Clusters of data.

1.5.2.2 Clustering

Clustering is an unsupervised learning technique in which class labels are not provided in test samples. It is the process of grouping a set of objects into classes of similar objects. Collection of similar data objects is known as a cluster, as shown in Figure 1.6. Similar objects are grouped into one cluster. Clustering is also named data segmentation because it partitions large datasets into groups as per the similarity of records. Clustering-based processes are adaptable to changes and help to draw features that are used to distinguish the different groups. To determine the similarity between two data objects, a metric from the datasets (distance function) is used by the clustering technique. This distance function takes two objects as its input, and returns the distance between these two objects as its output in the form of a real number. A smaller value of this real number represents that two objects are more similar, as compared to a larger value. The goal of cluster analysis is to group data objects based on the information related to data which describes the objects and their relationships. In practice, various types of clustering techniques are used. A partial clustering technique divides sets of data objects into clusters in a manner that means each object belongs to a single cluster only, whereas in hierarchical clustering, nested clusters are organized as a tree. The root of the tree is the master cluster, which contains all the data objects, and each node in the tree represents the union of its children. In some situations, a point may be placed in more than one cluster. Such overlapping or non-exclusive clustering represents that an object simultaneously belongs to more than one cluster. For example, the person may be a patient as well as employee of the hospital at the same time. In fuzzy clustering, some membership weight is associated with every object that represents the probability of belonging to a cluster. Such clusters are treated as fuzzy sets. Another distinction between clustering techniques is complete and partial clustering, where each object is assigned to a cluster in complete clustering, whereas this does not happen in partial clustering. In clustering, the usefulness of a cluster is defined by the goals of its analysis. Therefore different kinds of clusters used are well separated into prototype-based, graph-based, density-based, and conceptual clusters. Based on this, various commonly used clustering techniques are the Partitioning Method, the Hierarchical Method, the Density-Based Method, and the Grid-Based Method.

The major applications of clustering include targeting similar people and deciding on things like the location for an activity (i.e., exam centers), the location for a business chain, or for planning a political strategy.

1.5.2.3 Association Rule

Association rule mining is also known as "market basket analysis". Association rule mining is a technique which aims to perceive frequently occurring patterns, correlations, or associations in datasets of various types of databases such as relational databases, transactional databases, and other forms of repositories. An association rule comprises of two parts – "if", in the form of the antecedent, and "and then", in the form of the consequent.

"If a customer buys shoes, he's 70% likely to buy socks."

In the above association rule, shoes are the antecedent and socks are the consequent. Figure 1.7 represents the process of association rule mining. In real life, the number of frequent item-sets is large, which results in a large number of association rules for a transactional database. The discovery of frequent item-sets with item constraints is therefore an important problem in association rule analysis.

Association rules are generated by meticulously evaluating data and looking for frequent if/then patterns. Based on the succeeding two parameters, these significant relationships are witnessed:

1. **Support:** indicates how often the if/then association appears in the database.
2. **Confidence:** expresses the number of times these relationships have been found to be true.

Some of the examples of association rules are:

1. **Market Basket Analysis:** this is the most classic example of association mining.
2. **Medical Diagnosis:** association rules in medical diagnosis can be useful for assisting physicians to cure patients. Diagnosis is not an

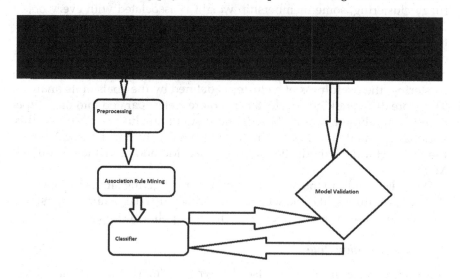

FIGURE 1.7
Process of association rule mining.

easy process and has a scope of errors which may result in unreliable end-results.

3. **Census Data:** this application of association rule mining has vast potential in associating sound public policy and carrying forth competent functioning of a democratic society.

4. **Protein Sequence:** proteins are sequences made up of 20 types of amino acids. The dependency of the protein functioning on its amino acid sequence has been a topic of prodigious research.

1.5.2.4 Unsupervised Learning Use Case

A companion welcomes "you" to his gathering where "you" meet total strangers. At that point, you will order them utilizing unsupervised learning (no earlier information) and this characterization can be based on age, dress, sexual orientation, instructive capability, or any other attribute you wish. Because you didn't have any earlier information about these individuals, you simply grouped them "on the go".

Table 1.6 illustrates the difference between supervised and unsupervised learning.

1.5.3 Reinforcement Learning (RL)

Reinforcement Learning (RL) is about identifying the proper action to exploit return in a certain situation, employed by numerous machines to find the best possible behavior they should take in a distinct state. It varies from supervised learning in such a way that in supervised learning the label key lies with the training data, so the model is trained with the correct answer itself, whereas in RL no label is provided but the reinforcement agent adapts to accomplish the particular task.

An example can be stated as follows:

There are an agent and a reward, with many hurdles stuck between. The role of the agent is to find the most promising path to get the reward. This can be seen more clearly in Figure 1.8 below.

TABLE 1.6

Supervised versus Unsupervised Machine Learning

Parameters	Supervised machine learning	Unsupervised machine learning
Input Data	Training of algorithms is through labeled data.	Unlabeled data is used directly by the algorithms.
Computational Complexity	Supervised learning is easy to understand and implement.	Computationally complex.
Accuracy	This is a more accurate and reliable method.	Comparatively not as accurate and trustworthy a method, but better for bigger data sets.

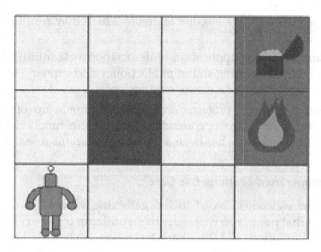

FIGURE 1.8
Reinforcement learning.

Figure 1.8 shows a diamond, a robot, and fire. The robot's job is to get the reward in the form of the diamond by avoiding the hurdle in the form of fire. The robot explores all possible paths, and then chooses the path with least hurdles based on its learning. Each right step will offer the robot a reward and each wrong step will subtract the reward. At last the total reward is calculated.

1.6 Conclusion

Machine learning is an innovative technology that is currently in a serious phase of several growing and established industries. Machine learning personalization algorithms are used to distribute recommendations to users and tempt them into an array of positive actions. Presently, many of such recommendations are erroneous and frustrating, which hampers users' familiarity – though in the future the personalization of algorithms is likely to be tweaked, leading to far more beneficial and successful experiences. Developers will be able to shape more fetching and discoverable applications that can commendably understand users' needs based on natural communication techniques. We presume that, shortly, robots will become extra intelligent and capable of finishing tasks. Drones, robots in manufacturing places, and other types of robots are likely to be increasingly used to make our lives easier (Figure 1.9).

Machine learning is one of the most disruptive technologies of the 21st century. Although this technology can still be considered as nascent, its

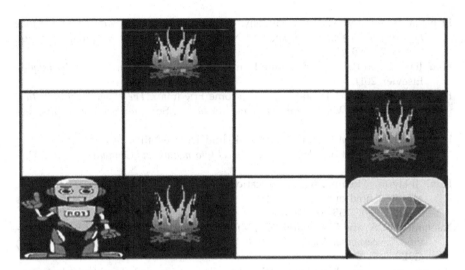

FIGURE 1.9
Reinforcement learning example.

future is bright. In the coming years, we are likely to see more advanced applications – one that stretch machine learning's capabilities to unimaginable levels.

References

Agrawal, Rashmi. 1–50. http://hdl.handle.net/10603/169657. https://shodhganga.inflibnet.ac.in/handle/10603/169657.

Agrawal, Rashmi. "Design and development of data classification methodology for uncertain data." *Indian Journal of Science and Technology* 9(3) (2016): 1–12.

Agrawal, Rashmi. "Integrated effect of nearest neighbors and distance measures in k-NN algorithm." In: *Big Data Analytics*, Aggarwal V., Bhatnagar V., Mishra D. (Eds). Springer, Singapore, 2018: 759–766.

Agrawal, Rashmi. "Integrated parallel K-nearest neighbor algorithm." In: *Smart Intelligent Computing and Applications*, Satapathy S., Bhateja V., Das S. (Eds). Springer, Singapore, 2019: 479–486.

Agrawal, Rashmi. "Technologies for handling big data." In: *Handbook of Research on Big Data Clustering and Machine Learning*, Fausto Pedro Garcia Marquez (Ed). IGI Global, 2020: 34–49.

Agrawal, Rashmi, and Babu Ram. "A modified K-nearest neighbor algorithm to handle uncertain data." *2015 5th International Conference on IT Convergence and Security (ICITCS)*. IEEE, Malaysia, 2015.

Batra, Mridula, and Rashmi Agrawal. "Comparative analysis of decision tree algorithms." In: *Nature Inspired Computing*, Panigrahi B., Hoda M., Sharma V., Goel S. (Eds). Springer, Singapore, 2018: 31–36.

El Naqa, Issam, and Martin J. Murphy. "What is machine learning?" In: *Machine Learning in Radiation Oncology*, El Naqa I., Li R., Murphy M. (Eds). Springer, Cham, 2015: 3–11.

Han, Jiawei, Jian Pei, and Micheline Kamber. *Data Mining: Concepts and Techniques.* Elsevier, 2011.

Hastie, Trevor, Robert Tibshirani, and Jerome Friedman. *The Elements of Statistical Learning: Data Mining, Inference, and Prediction.* Springer Science & Business Media, 2009.

Hawkins, Douglas M., Subhash C. Basak, and Denise Mills. "Assessing model fit by cross-validation." *Journal of Chemical Information and Computer Sciences* 43(2) (2003): 579–586.

Kim, Ji-Hyun. "Estimating classification error rate: Repeated cross-validation, repeated hold-out and bootstrap." *Computational Statistics and Data Analysis* 53(11) (2009): 3735–3745.

Neelamegam, S., and E. Ramaraj. "Classification algorithm in data mining: An overview." *International Journal of P2P Network Trends and Technology (IJPTT)* 4(8) (2013): 369–374.

Raschka, Sebastian. "Model evaluation, model selection, and algorithm selection in machine learning." *arXiv Preprint ArXiv:1811.12808* (2018).

Samuel, Arthur L. "Some studies in machine learning using the game of checkers." *IBM Journal of Research and Development* 3(3) (1959): 210–229.

Simeone, Osvaldo. "A brief introduction to machine learning for engineers." *Foundations and Trends® in Signal Processing® in Signal Processing* 12(3–4) (2018): 200–431.

Stamp, Mark. *Introduction to Machine Learning with Applications in Information Security.* Chapman and Hall/CRC, 2017.

Tarca, A. L., V. J. Carey, X. W. Chen, R. Romero, and S. Drăghici. "ML and its application in biology." *PLOS Computational Biology* 3(6) (2007): 116.

Witten, Ian H., and Eibe Frank. "Data mining: Practical machine learning tools and techniques with Java implementations." *Acm Sigmod Record* 31(1) (2002): 76–77.

Zheng, Alice. "Evaluating Machine Learning Models: A Beginner's Guide to Key Concepts and Pitfalls." (2015).

2

Medical Information Systems

Uday Sah, Abhushan Chataut, and Jyotir Moy Chatterjee

CONTENTS

2.1 Introduction 17
2.2 Types of Medical Information Systems 18
    2.2.1 General Medical Information Systems 18
    2.2.2 Specific Medical Information Systems 19
2.3 Types of General Medical Data 19
    2.3.1 Numerical Data 19
    2.3.2 Textual Data 20
    2.3.3 Categorical Data 20
    2.3.4 Imaging Data 20
2.4 History of Medical Information Systems 20
2.5 Collection of MIS Data through Various Platforms 21
    2.5.1 Traditional 22
    2.5.2 Electronic 22
2.6 Diagnosis and Treatment of Disease through MIS Data 22
2.7 Conclusion 23
References 23

2.1 Introduction

Medical information systems (MIS) are the universal purpose of computer-based data storage of disease diagnosis and related medical data that help investigate medical cures and other patient information (Johnson and Barnett 1977). The major purpose of MIS is to help the decision-maker (doctor or machine) find the most appropriate medicine and track patient health-related information. It could happen in real-time or could be from historical data. In the current era, millions of people are dying due to lack of a medical information system that can hold patient data and give insights form the data to make automation in healthcare industries possible. Medical information system stores various kinds of medical data like blood group, sugar level, and much more, to identify and easily recognized disease through symptoms.

MIS data are widely accepted for analytical use in artificial intelligence research to discover unique patterns of disease symptoms which may lead of the invention of a cure.

MIS data are stored in file orientation data structures that can easily be searched by doctors to find the major disease symptoms of a patient. This technology will rapidly grow in the future because the needs of scientific sampling and analysis for improved drug discoveries requires it. Medical information like this is important in terms of the clinical inspection and evaluation of disease. MIS can generate huge amounts of statistical data that require capable data management infrastructures for storage, retrieval, and management according to doctors' needs (Johnson and Barnett 1977).

For MIS information security is highly concern, because it moves patients' critical clinical information between different computers (Brook 2019). This information is sent through electronical channels. This method helps the many departments of hospital operational management to reduce their paper usage in prescriptions given by doctors as part of test information, as well as helping eliminate incorrect clinical information. MIS is integrative in nature for clinical data storage so it could be helpful in emergency situations when patients are unconscious and unable to perform the tests required by doctors. When this happens, the ability to retrieve their historical data can be important to safely treat or give an initial diagnosis of the patient. Most of the MIS and medical investigative research is based on unbiased data that are collected through various sensors and medical devices. In the current era, hospitals are more responsible when conducting medical research and collecting data in purist of making useful artificial intelligence applications that can save billions of people from deadly diseases. That kind of application interprets data in a such a way so as to predict deadly diseases in early stages.

2.2 Types of Medical Information Systems

There are several types of medical information systems that make it possible to manage huge amounts of health data for both general and specific purposes relating to the prevention and prediction of noxious diseases. Medical information systems can perhaps be defined according to two categories, but there are many other perspectives.

2.2.1 General Medical Information Systems

General medical information systems store basic information which relate to the disease or diagnoses of patients. Traditional electronic medical recording systems are a valuable tool for providing knowledge that can serve as a reference for quality decision-making in prescriptions (Ting et al. 2003). The systems contain basic monitoring, and up-to-date data collection from patients to track diagnoses and investigate disease. Examples include blood test information, sugar level information and related blood pressure, as well as urine information – all of which are very important in finding symptoms of underlying deadly diseases. They contain more data than found in specific medical information systems which helps to use the information resources to create and manage AI data resources. This kind of data demands high levels of cleaning and data accuracy for the future AI application of the medical information system. For example, patient data management and storage systems, etc.

2.2.2 Specific Medical Information Systems

Specific medical information systems are a special category of information system which store disease-specific data storage. This helps to accurately and properly diagnose and investigate stages of a disease. The systems contain various disease-specific data, for example, if a patient has brain cancer or a tumor the system used will contain only the data which is related to that disease. It also stores the symptoms and testing information needed for diagnosis by the doctors. It is a more disease-oriented medical information system, one that is precise and effective in finding symptoms and future treatment which relates to a particular disease. Examples include brain cancer medical information system, chest pain medical record system, and more.

2.3 Types of General Medical Data

There are various kinds of medical data generated by hospitals on a daily basis. That kinds of data required for diagnosis complex disease in scientific research and treatment of patient healthcare industries. The group of medical scientists have categorized and generalized the medical data in a four category. These are descripted below:

2.3.1 Numerical Data

Numerical data are the more common data in healthcare industries when making measurements of patient-generated data. For example, measurement of blood pressure, or sugar levels. It may be discrete or continuous in nature. If brain cancer has four stages, 0 is defined as the absence of brain cancer, 1 is defined as a low chance of brain cancer, 2 is defined as a medium chance of brain cancer, and 3 is defined as a high chance of brain cancer, and so on. That type of data is known as discreate numerical data. Another type is continuous data which cannot be counted and can only be described through range intervals (Rumsey 2016). For example, blood pressure in the range of 70–120 mmHg systolic and in diastolic 60–80 mmHg.

2.3.2 Textual Data

Textual data is one of the most popular and well-defined syntaxial word data for human understanding. It contains alphabetic data. For example, if the patient likely has heart disease then textual data will be more representative and effective in order to understand and provide a clear meaning for the reader to evaluate the words and sentences. Most of the medical data are textual data which provide clear meanings and disease descriptions relating to patients. This kind of information is useful when doctors diagnose and treat diseases. Textual medical data in machine learning can be used for such things as predicting heart disease in patients through doctors' prescribed medical report results.

2.3.3 Categorical Data

Categorical data refers to the type of textual data that can specify category and it is an effective way to divide and categorize when medical data are scattered. Categorical data are mostly used in categorial machine learning prediction, which is specifically the level of seriousness of disease – in other words, dividing patient seriousness into more comprehensible and visualized forms. Categorial data are represented by mathematical expressions which are not clear meaning but are useable during training and pre-process of AI application development. For example, blood group categized patient treatment or drug classification.

2.3.4 Imaging Data

In MIS, imaging data plays as important role in diagnosis and treatment of disease in hospitals. Imaging data are pixel-based multi-dimensional data which are most effective while developing image recognition and classification models to automatically recognize disease and investigate the seriousness of the disease. It also helps doctors to visualize anatomical and internal parts of the body's organs and, thus, identify infected areas. Some examples of imaging data include X-Ray data, ultrasound image data, Medical Resonance Imaging, and Computerized Tomography scan data. Each piece of data is stored in various MIS in unistructural databases like MongoDB. For some reason video data are stored in the form of frame imaging. In MRI data collection, information about visualized the location of water presence (Klein 2018).

2.4 History of Medical Information Systems

Doctors in the 1500s borrowed from bookkeeping practices and modeled themselves on Hippocrates when they recorded case histories on clay tablets.

Some kept account books written at the time of encounter, while others maintained journals or diaries which enabled them to study after a day of visiting patients. These all typically included date, patient's name, age, complaint, possible cause, a prescription, and proof of payment for recording the history of disease and cure. These were known as "casebooks" which were also the first age of information overload. This practice evolved from expensive parchment to more affordable paper technologies to modern-day computers.

From the early 1600s, the presentation of information in medical records led to the improvement of diagnosing and treating illness, which was through observation as well as actions in the treatment of patients. This became such a reputed method that it began to be used to teach other medical practitioners. Paper-based record keeping continued until the 1920s (NCBI 2015). In the 1960s, the development of computers led to disruption in healthcare and provided the opportunity to maintain records electronically. However, the cost of maintaining the mainframe computers and the storage of data led to only large organizations having full funded use of electronic technology. In the 1970s, as the size of computers became smaller, software began to be designed for day-to-day healthcare functions like patient registration, pharmacy use, and clinical laboratory ad billing but were still based by department. The multiple separate system integration was developed in the 1980s as "hospital information systems" (HIS) which were able to connect the financial and clinical systems, but the functions were very limited. Advancement in healthcare technology integration grew in the 1990s and gave access to computing systems that would share data and information across all the separate systems. In the 2000s, the importance of integrated electronic health records for better decision making grew. The electronic health record revolution began in 2004 leading to an increase in volume of data, accessibility to data, and management of health data relying on health informatics. From 2010 to present, the context of Health Information Technology focuses on value-based care over fee-based care and, thus, leads and improves patient outcomes by harnessing the growing volume, variety, veracity, and velocity of healthcare data to support clinical (as well as operational) decisions in healthcare. Many learning tools, such as machine learning, help improve patient outcomes by aiding healthcare professionals to improve care on both broader and larger scale.

2.5 Collection of MIS Data through Various Platforms

MIS data are collected by various platforms and sources that help data engineers to store the data in structural and unistructural databases. For example, MIS data are collected through heath record systems which are manually entered by hospital staff and employee. It can also be collected through human wearable devices. For now, we are going to divide medical data collection into two approaches. The first is Traditional and the second is Electronic. There are discussed in detail below.

2.5.1 Traditional

In the traditional method, patients' diagnoses details are stored in an MIS database after the hospitals; staff manually enter and store the data in an MIS system. Most hospitals are tradition-based thus they store test results by manually entering them into an MIS system. For example, hospital staff manually store patient details like name, gender, age, blood group, etc. The traditional method is one of the oldest methods of storing medical data, but it is a less accurate method for medical data collection and less useable for medical scientific research. In the traditional method most hospital work is still paper-based. Staff are busy and under too much time pressure which leads to patient data collection that is less accurate and beneficial for medical scientific research.

2.5.2 Electronic

Electronically collected data is a modern method of medical data collection. It is more accurate and up-to-date, real-time collected patient data that uses techniques which see data collected through various forms of electronic sensors. Nowadays, most countries have commercialized IoT devices for public use and this helps us save time in the collection of patient data by utilizing wearables. The latest wearable devices are well-equipped for collecting patient medical data and notifying both doctors and hospitals when a patient is in a critical situation. Electronic sensors are capable of sensing a patient's health status and directly sending doctors a portal to provide emergency help to the patient. Many current MIS are purely based on modern electronic sensor-based data collection for hospitals to recognize, diagnosis, and cure patients' diseases. Electronic-based medical data recording is widely acceptable for machine learning, and deep-learning activities for making better and more useful AI applications. Nowadays, big data are evolving so that data analytics can develop the innovative technology to support billions of patients receiving healthcare. This technology is capable of solving inaccurate medical data issues.

2.6 Diagnosis and Treatment of Disease through MIS Data

Diagnosis and treatment are essential roles of MIS data for curing deadly diseases in medical science. Medical big data are used in AI applications to make systems that can evaluate and that are self-able to provide medication appropriate to a patient's illness. In the current era, most medical data are alphanumeric or imaging data. THIS is helpful for doctors so they directly can diagnosis patient disease with the help of patient check-up reports. Diagnosis has important implications for medical science and patient care, for disease research, and for treatment which can all use checkup medical data. (Balogh et al. 2015).

To understand the diagnosis process, an example is outlined here: Once a patient suffers a health problem, the patient or his/her family gather any possible information about the health problem and collect the symptoms to easily extract data and explain what they are suffering from. Next, after contact with clinical hospitals for diagnosis and treatment about facing health problems, doctors see the types of symptoms and details to identify possible diseases and extract the data according to the information given by patients. Doctors are responsible for explaining to patients about why they facing health problems, and advising them on the best ways to overcome those health problems. Nowadays, a large amount of health activities and their symptoms can be collected through wearable devices which are easily connected to an MIS system. When doctors want to check an MIS, they can easily receive the data as well as information that can be used to provide clinical medication to the patient. When doctors communicate with patient, they gather information.

2.7 Conclusion

MIS offers many benefits over the executive systems that came before. They are a completely operational, online system, which permit incredible adaptability for information depiction and examination. They can be executed on a PC system of moderate expense. Permissible information types include numeric, categoric, content, and date. Each field may have one or many sections. It is easy to imagine a few arrangements of comparable information, including date-situated information, to be gathered for every person in the investigation.

References

Balogh, E. P., Bryan T. Miller, and John R. Ball. 2015. *Improving Diagnosis in Health Care*. Washington, DC: National Academies Press (US).

Brook, C., 2019. What Is a Health Information System? [Online]. Available at: https://digitalguardian.com/blog/what-health-information-system. [Accessed 6 January 2020].

Committee on Diagnostic Error in Health Care; Board on Health Care Services; Institute of Medicine; the National Academies of Sciences, Engineering, and Medicine, E. P. Balogh, B. T. Miller, J. R. Ball, editors. 2015. *Improving Diagnosis in Health Care*. Washington, DC: National Academies Press (US), December 29. 2, The Diagnostic Process. Available from: https://www.ncbi.nlm.nih.gov/books/NBK338593/.

Johnson, D. C., G. O. Barnett. 1977. Medinfo - A Medical Information System. *Medinfo - A Medical Information System*, pp. 191–201.

Klein, C., 2018. Intro to Analyzing Brain Imaging Data— Part I: fMRI Data Structure [Online]. Available at: https://medium.com/coinmonks/visualizing-brain-imaging-data-fmri-with-python-e1d0358d9dba [Accessed 27 Jan 2020].

Rumsey, D. J., 2016. Types of Statistical Data: Numerical, Categorical, and Ordinal [Online]. Available at: https://www.dummies.com/education/math/statistics/types-of-statistical-data-numerical-categorical-and-ordinal/. [Accessed 23 Jan 2020].

Ting, S. L., W. H. Ip, A. H, Tsang, G. T Ho. 2003. An Integrated Electronic Medical Record System (iEMRS) with Decision Support Capability in Medical Prescription. An Integrated Electronic Medical Record System (iEMRS) with Decision Support Capability In Medical Prescription, pp. 236–245.

3

The Role of Metaheuristic Algorithms in Healthcare

G. Uma Maheswari, R. Sujatha, V. Mareeswari, and E. P. Ephzibah

CONTENTS

3.1 Introduction 25
3.2 Machine Learning in Healthcare 26
3.3 Health Information System Framework 27
3.4 Privacy and Security of Data 28
3.5 Big Data Analytics in Disease Diagnosis 29
3.6 The Metaheuristic Algorithm for Healthcare 32
3.7 Conclusion 35
References 36

3.1 Introduction

The process of machine learning is known as the "training" of machines and the output generated is known as the "model". Machine learning is a data analytics tool which automates the building of analytical models. It is a system that gains knowledge from data, with minimal human intervention. Data is provided to the algorithm and it in turn creates new knowledge from what it has learned before. The classification model is meant to assess a category as "it's one thing or another". The model is educated during the categorization of the dataset. The clustering model is generated when a bunch of data is available but has not defined a result and simply wants to see distinctive trends in the data. The regression model is developed for value detection purposes. The algorithm will find a correlation between two variables, using data, and the result is predicted accordingly. Healthcare providers are able to provide better decisions about treatment options for patients, leading to overall changes in healthcare services with the help of machine learning. Machine learning algorithms are also useful in providing medical doctors with broad statistics of real-time data and advanced analyses about the condition of the patient, laboratory test outcomes, blood pressure, family history, clinical trial data, etc. The new aims of healthcare is preventative – to avoid illness at the early stages instead needing to go for assessment and diagnosis for treatment. Nevertheless, new technological developments like big data and machine learning provide more precise results that can be obtained for predicting disease. When machine learning models are exposed to raw data the iterative nature enables the model to change independently.

3.2 Machine Learning in Healthcare

Today, machine learning is helping to standardize hospital operating procedures. This also facilitates bacterial infection control and diagnosis, and also customizes medications. The rate of change in technology is improving drastically, which is reflected in healthcare sector as well. The fields of statistics, probability, and Artificial Intelligence comprise the fundamental machine learning subjects. In earlier medical treatments there were many manual documents and procedures which were very tedious. In technology, there are improvements for maintaining electronic medical records which are more efficient when compared to the manual records maintained earlier. In order to improve healthcare in the future, computational capacity and machine learning need to strengthen the electronic information given to doctors. By using this sophisticated kind of research, at the point of patient care, we can provide doctors with better information. Physicians need to be provided with more knowledge so they can act independently and make better decisions regarding patient diagnoses and choice of treatment, while recognizing the potential outcomes and costs for each. The importance of machine learning in healthcare lies in its ability to process large datasets beyond the scope of human capability, and then efficiently turn data analysis into clinical insights that help doctors to prepare and provide treatment, eventually leading to better outcomes, lower cost of care, and increased patient satisfaction. Machine learning can be used to train computers to see images, identify abnormalities, and point to areas that need attention – thus enhancing the accuracy of all of these processes. Long-term, machine learning may also support family practitioners. To improve further efficiency, reliability, and accuracy, machine learning may give objective opinions.

As has been mentioned, in healthcare the best method of machine learning is the doctor's brain. Doctors may be afraid that machine learning is the beginning of a phase that could make them redundant. This fear will be reduced by both machine learning and other future technologies in medicine. Machine learning is considered as a tool to be used by physicians to boost treatment. Different use cases must be identified in which machine learning technologies provide value from certain technology applications. This will be a step towards more incremental processing for more analytics, machine learning, and prediction algorithms to be incorporated into daily clinical practices. Medicine does have a system for researching and demonstrating safe and effective treatment. This is a prolonged trial process and is based on evidence to support the decision. When we consider machine learning, it needs to be ensured that that same process is in place to guarantee safety and effectiveness. We must consider the ethics of giving away some of the things we do to a machine. Many people may wonder if this is just a "fad" in technology, or if it does bring real value to healthcare. Health Catalyst believes that it is one of the most significant life-saving innovations ever developed and there will soon be the implementation and widespread use of machine learning in healthcare. We assume that prospects for clinical change and growth are not in fact limited to technology; reacceptance in machine learning is reduced in a guided, accurate, and patient-centric way. Doctors will receive daily advice on how to reaccept patients and reduce the risks. Through machine learning, a hospital system can recognize chronic diseases of patients who are undiagnosed. It also provides patients-centered preventive interventions to avoid the risk of developing chronic disease in patients.

3.3 Health Information System Framework

Deep learning is a promising end-to-end form of learning for accurate diagnosis of health status. There are two main components in an end-to-end system that emulate the healthcare cycle. The first is the deep recognition module focused on deep neural networks used to make health diagnoses. The second module is based on Bayesian inference graphs to determine the operation (Dai and Wang 2018). Cloud computing has taken on an important role in healthcare services too because of its ability to improve the efficiency of healthcare services. Optimum virtual machine selection achieves a significant performance enhancement by reducing the execution time of medical requests from stakeholders, and optimizing cloud resources utilization. For this, the virtual machine selection is optimized by a new model based on the cloud environment using a parallel Particle Swarm Optimization (Abdelaziz et al. 2018). Automatic machine learning – or auto AML – is a field that's been gaining a lot of popularity. Whenever we have a dataset and want to collect insights from it using machine learning there are a whole lot of steps that we have to complete, such as cleaning the data, selecting the most relevant features, and choosing the right model. This process can be both long and expensive because it requires a lot of guessing and checking to ensure we have the best possible results. The goal of auto AML is to automate as many of these steps as possible without compromising the accuracy of our results (Christopher 2019). Large volume of complex data has always entered the world of healthcare, flowing in at a very rapid pace. Across various sectors of the healthcare industry, a huge volume of data is generated by hospitals, the healthcare sector, medical devices, medical insurance, and research. Technological advancements enable the use of large volumes of data to improve the healthcare sector. By applying analytics, machine learning and big data allow trends and associations to be found and thus offer actionable insights to improve healthcare delivery (Dai and Wang 2018). In healthcare, a "database" refers to the health information system. Health management systems include the options to add, delete, modify, and access records of patients, as well as the operational management of a hospital system that supports policy decisions on healthcare (Hegde and Rokseth 2020).

3.4 Privacy and Security of Data

Every time a new patient is admitted to hospital, a new medical record is created. The medical record documents relevant information about the patient during their stay. It forms the legal record of care provided and is essential for clinical communication when the patient is discharged. The medical record is also sent to the hospital coders who take the information and convert it into code. These codes are then used to identify trends and patterns of disease, improve the quality of safety and care, and analyze the cost of providing quality care so that appropriate funding for healthcare services can be received. An incomplete or ambiguous medical record can lead to inaccurate coding. Due to strict coding rules, codas cannot make assumptions about diagnoses, procedures, medications, and complications. If a medical record is unclear, hospitals and their patients can miss out on the funding they are entitled to. If the details aren't clearly written down, it may as well not have happened. To avoid this, clinicians should ensure that clinical notes are complete, legible, and updated in a timely manner. They should clearly document the principal diagnosis as well as any additional diagnoses. The necessity of clinical records is to provide and compute clear information about symptoms and the medical treatment provided to patients and identify all diagnostic and therapeutic interventions. Researchers and planners use these clinical records, since clear and complete information about every patient improves outcomes and the overall healthcare system.

When we look at data analytics for medical research, we can break it up basic categories: genomics, imaging, clinical information, artificial intelligence, and deep learning type workflows. The problem is all of this data is typically not connected together, they are not able to be communicated. This requires more infrastructure, key provisions, storage, and then it is necessary to move and copy all of that data from different repositories into this file system. It is very time consuming and it wastes resources.

A better way is to create a data ocean, where all of that data is taken and put into one single place so that it's easier to access. It enables Watson, Docker, and Power and all these other frameworks that may well be used on a daily basis, or perhaps not. This framework allows the use of all your applications and even the new ones that will soon be released that we don't even know exist yet because they're being newly created by researchers daily. The next step is to stick this orchestration layer in between. This will allow you to use the entire infrastructure across all of your computer and all of your applications and workflows, allowing you to most efficiently use this entire infrastructure. Healthcare organizations are facing the problem of both patient data security and the need for productivity. As data vulnerabilities increase, the healthcare organizations are looking for more solutions in order to resolve these problems.

3.5 Big Data Analytics in Disease Diagnosis

Disease diagnosis is becoming a more challenging task as types of possible illnesses increase due to the lifestyle changes and modern work environments that pose great hurdles in the daily life of an individual. However, the medical field has also evolved a lot in last few decades with the intervention of Information Technology as a support to speed up the diagnosis process. Numeric data (generated from the various tests like blood test, urine tests, thyroid function tests) as well as image and text data (generated from CT scans, MRI scans, X-Rays, and more) are still used for the purpose of diagnosis. The recommendation system is built with the big data received from various sources and machine learning algorithms are deployed to get the greater insights. Big data is deployed in the cloud environment and utilized based on requirement. The advent of big data and usage of cloud computing greatly reduced the expense of infrastructure investment. Accuracy, execution time, and robustness metrics are used to gauge the performance of developed recommender systems that help in diagnosis along with treatment. The ontology constructed for each specialization aids in the clarity of the ongoing work. Medical ontology is evolving, certainly more than in any other field. Healthcare has begun to rely on the latest trend of deep learning, algorithm subset of machine learning, adding strength to the developing model that supports the various departments of healthcare. For any system to be reliable, a primary criterion is the intelligent creation of a database that supports the versatile data. Clinical data is required to be designed with proper analysis by experts. Huge amounts of work is required to provide stable data at the backend, and over that the rest of the work begins. Perfect features are required for the modeling of highly informative, human understandable system. Data preprocessing plays a vital role because the collected data is highly diverse. It may be doctors' notes, or laboratory reports in the form of numeric, text or, image. The flow of deploying machine learning begins with defining the clinical problem and requires proper justification, at the same. Extracting the data, selection, and refining the same for the scope point of view decides the structure of system. Analyzing the data, and constructing the model, along with its validation ensure it is working correctly. The human interaction machine will go through a number of trials before it's permitted to start its real work in the clinical environment. Neural networks are a form similar to the neuron structure of a human being and are part of evolutionary algorithms. This means that multiple layers, as hidden layers, define the principle of deep learning and enable it to work on huge versatile amounts of data cumulated from the healthcare system. Data preprocessing involves labeling, curating, and mapping with justification of each attributes used in system, such as storing proper indexing and hashing techniques for faster access based on the intention. These processes adds weightage for retrieving algorithms effective for study of the output or requirement of the system. This helps as the deciding factor is front end – proper designing – and training is vital in creating the best system (Chen et al. 2018; Makwakwa et al. 2014; Nilashi et al. 2017).

Machine learning is applied in the early detection of Parkinson's disease and plenty of work is being carried out to help needy patients at the earliest stage. Artificial Intelligence has begun entering the department of diagnosis and patient monitoring. Based on the gathered data points from the patient decision about readmission and attention requirement are tracked. Information and communication technology scholars across the world have started working with various disorders like autism, Parkinson's, the heart and thyroid, retinopathy, diabetics, and cancer alongside medical experts to help patients. Based on the data both supervised and unsupervised algorithms are used for the purpose of analysis. Classification and association rules are used in the categorical dataset. Clustering and regression are used often in the time series and historical datasets, to form clusters that provide insight about the nature of the data. Data attributes are the key factors that make the research or findings so interesting and informative in nature (Ngiam and Khor 2019; Nilashi et al. 2019; Astrom and Koker 2011).

Devices with various names based on the purpose of diagnosis, detection, and other healthcare-related terms have begun to emerge. A "point of care" diagnostic device is the name given to the devices that emerged in the clinical sector as a result of the digital era. Reaching the conventional laboratory for the preliminary diagnosis requires more time to reach particularly from very remote area. During an epidemic or acute disease times of high seriousness, patients require persistent monitoring that can be achieved with this point of care device. These devices are a result of an of the Internet of Things (IoT), along with handling voluminous, versatile data points with compact algorithms. The Internet of Things and its interconnection of various sensors and devices can remotely coordinate the patient alone with its expertise.

Various sensors are advancing the medical field, including for measuring temperature, checking blood pressure, and inner organ issues. The research in this field looks towards incorporating Artificial Intelligence that helps with diagnosis in non-invasive mode. Point of car diagnostic devices in the initial stage concentrated only on collection of data, but the mobility and scalability of the collected data required it to be provided at the correct location to convert it into treatment. Architecture and multiple layers were devised to substantiate its data flow and analysis (Nilashi et al. 2018; Amirian et al. 2017; Peeling 2015; Urdea et al. 2006).

Image analysis and video analysis is a research area in the medical arena that works towards disease diagnoses in the form of pictures in varied format. Pixel intensity provides the depth of severity. Preprocessing starts from acquiring the images, extracting, cleaning, and annotation paves the way for integration along with representation (Wong et al. 2019). Cancer is a common dreadful disease that threatens people across the globe. Oncology is supported by big data that helps in the analysis of various cancers like lung, breast, prostate, salivary gland, and melanoma. The prevalence of breast cancer is very high and earlier detection helps to save lives. Images of the breast help to identify the severity and stage of the cancer. Thermal cameras are used to capture the images and the intensity of the colors helps in a cancer diagnosis (or lack thereof) in a perfect manner. Acquired images are run in the various algorithms to get clarity on if the cells are benign or malignant (Thai et al. 2012; 38Willems et al. 2019; Rezk et al. 2017). Biomedical images within information and communication technology safeguards the lives of millions of people through early diagnosis and medication (De Ridder et al. 2015). Deep learning is used more nowadays to make use of neural network structures with many hidden layers to achieve a deep analysis of the cumulated data (Kouanou et al. 2018).

The big data analytics in the healthcare sector are being utilized to frame various architecture based on the input, process, and output. Extensive analytics are done by gathering works based on data types such as: clinical, patient, sentiment, administration, activity costs, pharmaceutical, R&D, and data from other databases. This is all in addition to big data techniques like modeling, machine learning, data mining, visualization, statistics, simulation, web mining, optimization methods, text mining, forecasting, and social network analysis. By using big data analytics, various values are derived and listed as personalized healthcare automated algorithms that can support professionals in decision making and novel business models. It also leads to products that provide services, healthcare information sharing, and coordination facilities, privacy protection practices, the ability to customize actions by grouping related populations, and the ability to identify problems at earlier stages. By matching the data type and big data to values, optimized decision making is feasible (Lee et al. 2017; Galetsi et al. 2020; Baro et al. 2015; Berger and Doban 2014). Extensive research work is being carried out on big data in healthcare to ease the burden on future generations and this is

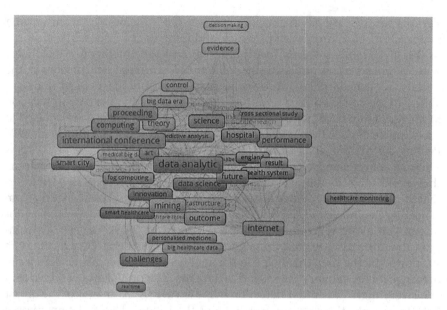

FIGURE 3.1
Terms of "Big data in the healthcare sector".

evident in the map that can be derived by mapping with the search word used in the Scopus repository. Figure 3.1 indicates the various related terms that illustrate the prevalence of big data in the healthcare sector (Liberatore and Nydick 2008).

Smart cities are a popular new phenomenon across the globe. Smart health is a component part of smart city projects and many federal governments are taking large steps to implement effective healthcare to all its citizens in extensive manner. Making decisions based on the collected big data, with the available methods, is a great boost for smart healthcare (vosviewer.com) (Hashem et al. 2016; Palanisamy and Thirunavukarasu 2019).

3.6 The Metaheuristic Algorithm for Healthcare

Metaheuristic algorithm research is a very innovative approach. It's suitable for solving large complex project involving large datasets. Optimal results are retrieved by proper analysis and application of the algorithm. The evolutionary algorithms developed rely on both the nature and characteristics of the nature. Based on genetic concepts the genetic programming established in 1989 by Goldberg. Many metaheuristics that are based on ant colony structure, honey bee structures, firefly, bat, cuckoo, grey wolf, whale, and so on, are evolving. Despite this biological and environmental background, some are generated based on mathematical applications like greedy approach, the traveling salesman problem, differential evolution, and so on. The latest research on metaheuristics is combining multiple concepts and naming them as hybrid metaheuristic algorithms. The idea and work are highly unpredictable in nature because the thought of integrating is very inspiring in nature and the ultimate aim is to get the optimal results (Wills 2014). Working on metaheuristic algorithms is getting to this phase by considering various nature-based phenomenon (everything from bees to cows). The truth behind this is evident when searching "metaheuristic algorithm" in Scopus with open source access, research articles, and English language journals in engineering and computer science have produced around 745 articles as the output. It's really in the beginning phase and definitely can be applied in various applications without any doubt. The secret is the correct mapping of the required data-based on the problem. The application of metaheuristic algorithms is widespread and its uses include: solving problems in production and planning, internet computing, transportation and logistics, the engineering and agriculture fields, the healthcare industry, and so on (Dokeroglu et al. 2019; Juan et al. 2015; Pelteret et al. 2018).

The elderly population is increasing across the globe and in this modern era lifetime longevity is higher due to a higher level of medical support both in diagnosis and treatment. The need to take care of elderly people and children is very challenging and more effort is required. Due to the advancement and interventions of various fields like data mining, machine learning, big data, the Internet of Things, data analytics, data science, soft computing, cloud computing, nature-inspired, and population-based metaheuristic algorithms in healthcare makes the way for researchers to make active contributions based on real-time applications (Shayanfar and Gharehchopogh 2018). Typical research issues begin with the way data needs to be cumulated and analyzed because of the varied type of data developed from text, image, video, and so on. Smart healthcare is a buzzword that circulates in both developed and developing countries. Optimizing the existing system is the aim of the developed countries. On the other hand, in developing countries the vision is to implement a smart healthcare system for their nation in an affordable manner with the support of the researchers. Metaheuristic algorithms possess a high potential to solve data mining problems like classification, clustering, and association rule. When compared with the neural network concept and exhaustive searching concepts, the processing time and solutions obtained in the metaheuristic approach are much faster and appreciable in nature. The availability of huge data in healthcare provides a great foundation for computer-based predictions and helps speed up the treatment process. Clinical prediction has been evolving at an exponential rate over the past few decades and it's mainly due to the extensive dataset in the researcher's hands – the computational intelligence used in the diagnosis of cardiac disease, cancer, and so on. The extensive work by utilizing the computation intelligence and metaheuristic algorithm is carried on for the prostate cancer prediction. This is gathered based on the collected dataset and is followed by preprocessing, feature selection, feature extraction, and providing the correct sample to apply the algorithm to get highly accurate results. Cross validation, along with a proper combination of training and testing, the dataset is the secret behind the performance of the constructed predictive model (Tsai et al. 2016).

Interesting work has been done on finding illicit pills within the shape concept. Image-based analyzing is very thought-provoking research in the medical field and includes x-ray interpretation, scan reports, pill analysis, and so on. The need for medications has increased and various socio-political and economic factors have begun to influence the medical field in the recent years. Inspection and checking are required and mandated to make the field safe and ensure the life of the people is not at stake. Through image processing the quality of pills is segregated (Cosma et al. 2017). Google trends show ample research work being carried out in metaheuristic algorithms over the past five years across the world. Figure 3.2 illustrates the trend of metaheuristic algorithms.

The most critical time for a patient is often addressed by the emergency department of hospitals. A higher level of coordination and commitment is the main requirement of the people serving in emergency departments. Part of the study of medicine insists practitioners attend to critical patients with higher care. Life is the timespan between the birth and death of the person. Caring for patients and providing satisfactory treatment is the duty of the healthcare centers. Shortening the waiting time is thus the most pressing requirement of any hospital because both caretaker and patient will be extremely anxious until they meet the practitioner and get support. Work is done by the genetic algorithm and simulated annealing to optimize the emergency department. It does this by helping make access to the practitioner for diagnosis purposes faster by scheduling the nurses on duty in the best way possible (Carneiro et al. 2019). Hospital stays tend to be mandatory in the case of critical illnesses. Proper treatment along with care both from hospital and

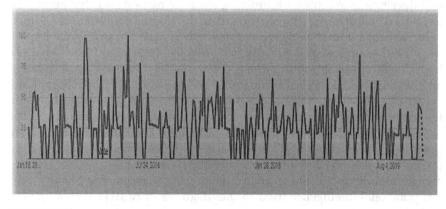

FIGURE 3.2
Trends of metaheuristic algorithms.

patient is key in creating an environment for a the sick person to get better. After a thorough study of a person's health, a patient may be discharged by hospital management after getting input from health experts. The ultimate aim of any doctor is to ensure the wellbeing of their patient. Longevity of life is in the interest of all the individuals. Research has addressed the problem of readmission of patients within a short time of discharge. Careful analysis of the key factors and health condition of the patient is required to understand this situation. Based on the analysis, they prepared a dataset with patient age, length of stay, admission acuity, comorbidity index score, gender, and few other parameters based on insurance factors. The ultimate aim of this task is to find the percentage of risk for readmission. Data mining and evolutionary algorithms are applied to make a thorough analysis (Zheng et al. 2015). Hospital admission, stay duration, and readmission all go together to encompass the complete healthcare of an individual. Various keywords that relate to metaheuristic algorithms in healthcare include: chemotherapy, processing, heuristic, admissions, analyze, compressing, environment, expectation, imaging, integration, mental, models, optimization, nature-inspired, local search, bio-inspired, and so on. The list is very exhaustive and provides an avenue for extensive research by way of the hybridization of various algorithms. Home healthcare is a great leap by the healthcare industry to provide immediate attention to a person in need. To provide the perfect healthcare in a timely manner, with the available resources, is achievable with the help of mathematical processes and metaheuristic s when fine-tuned as matheuristic (Yeh et al., Lin 2007; Moussavi et al. 2019).

Home healthcare systems require more planning and accuracy in order to meet the patient's requirements in a more personal environment. Need to work on with traversing from one place to another place both on the cost and time perspective are the main ingredients to consider. Various factors like planned distance, total distance, additional distance, and any sort of delay make up the matheuristic model. Transportation cost is the primary criteria for an organization to provide effective treatment. Along with this hybrid genetic algorithm, combining the perspective of time and fuzzy concept will enhance the system (Allaoua et al. 2013; Shi et al., 2017). It's very certain that metaheuristic algorithms will make the healthcare environment more affordable and user friendly with faster diagnoses and better. Discussions provided in this paper provide great support to the hybridization of metaheuristic algorithms and will glorify the research to a great extent.

3.7 Conclusion

Metaheuritics are the techniques directing the process of searching. Most of the procedures follow a random process and therefore the result is a collection of random variables. When compared with techniques like optimization and iteration methods, metaheuristics are able to provide satisfactory results with less computational effort. Therefore, metaheuristics are the best approach for task optimization. Much of the literature about metaheuristics is theoretical in nature, explaining empirical results based on algorithm-based computer experiments. But there are also some formal theoretical tests, frequently on convergence and the potential to find the global optimum. Several metaheuristic approaches have been published with statements of novelty and functional effectiveness. In recent decades, the healthcare industry is facing a higher level of uncertainty due to the appearance of new diseases and increases of casualty. Analyzing the stored historic datasets help in predicting the future seriousness with high levels of clarity. The evolution of metaheuristic algorithms is interesting and innovative in nature and it takes care to revolve around nature-inspired components. The healthcare industry along with Artificial Intelligence concepts will reach great heights and the scope of research is vast. Perfect analyzing of the attributes needing improvement will add a greater impact on performance metrics and early disease diagnosis.

References

Abdelaziz, Ahmed, Mohamed Elhoseny, Ahmed S. Salama, and A.M. Riad. "A machine learning model for improving healthcare services on cloud computing environment". *Measurement* 119 (2018): 117–128.

Allaoua, Hanane, Sylvie Borne, Lucas Létocart, and Roberto Wolfler Calvo. "A matheuristic approach for solving a home health care problem". *Electronic Notes in Discrete Mathematics* 41 (2013): 471–478.

Amirian, Pouria, Francois van Loggerenberg, Trudie Lang, Arthur Thomas, Rosanna Peeling, Anahid Basiri, and Steven N. Goodman. "Using big data analytics to extract disease surveillance information from point of care diagnostic machines". *Pervasive and Mobile Computing* 42 (2017): 470–486.

Åström, Freddie, and Rasit Koker. "A parallel neural network approach to prediction of Parkinson's disease". *Expert Systems with Applications* 38(10) (2011): 12470–12474.

Baro, Emilie, Samuel Degoul, Régis Beuscart, and Emmanuel Chazard. "Toward a literature-driven definition of big data in healthcare". *BioMed Research International* 2015 (2015) 1–9.

Berger, Marc L., and Vitalii Doban. "Big data, advanced analytics and the future of comparative effectiveness research". *Journal of Comparative Effectiveness Research* 3(2) (2014): 167–176.

Carneiro, Allan C., José G.F. Lopes, Marcelo M.S. Souza, Jeová F. Rocha Neto, Flávio H.D. Araújo, Romuere R.V. Silva, Fátima N.S. Medeiros, and Francisco N. Bezerra. "Parameter optimization of a multiscale descriptor for shape analysis on healthcare image datasets". *Pattern Recognition Letters* 125 (2019).

Chen, Jianguo, Kenli Li, Huigui Rong, Kashif Bilal, Nan Yang, and Keqin Li. "A disease diagnosis and treatment recommendation system based on big data mining and cloud computing". *Information Sciences* 435 (2018): 124–149.

Cosma, Georgina, David Brown, Matthew Archer, Masood Khan, and A. Graham Pockley. "A survey on computational intelligence approaches for predictive modeling in prostate cancer". *Expert Systems with Applications* 70 (2017): 1–19.

Dai, Y., and G. Wang. "A deep inference learning framework for healthcare". *Pattern Recognition Letters* 22(9) (2018): 1–9.

de Ridder, Mischa, Alfons J.M. Balm, Ludi E. Smeele, Michel W.J.M. Wouters, and Boukje A.C. van Dijk. "An epidemiological evaluation of salivary gland cancer in the Netherlands (1989–2010)". *Cancer Epidemiology* 39(1) (2015): 14–20.

Dokeroglu, Tansel, Ender Sevinc, Tayfun Kucukyilmaz, and Ahmet Cosar. "A survey on new generation metaheuristic algorithms". *Computers and Industrial Engineering* 137 (2019): 106040.

Galetsi, Panagiota, Korina Katsaliaki, and Sameer Kumar. "Big data analytics in health sector: Theoretical framework, techniques and prospects". *International Journal of Information Management* 50 (2020): 206–216.

Hashem, Ibrahim Abaker Targio, Victor Chang, Nor Badrul Anuar, Kayode Adewole, Ibrar Yaqoob, Abdullah Gani, Ejaz Ahmed, and Haruna Chiroma. "The role of big data in smart city". *International Journal of Information Management* 36(5) (2016): 748–758.

Hegde, J., and B. Rokseth. "Applications of machine learning methods for engineering risk assessment – A review". *Safety Science* 122 (2020): 104492.

https://www.vosviewer.com/ accessed January 13, 2020.

Juan, Angel A., Javier Faulin, Scott E. Grasman, Markus Rabe, and Gonçalo Figueira. "A review of simheuristics: Extending metaheuristics to deal with stochastic combinatorial optimization problems". *Operations Research Perspectives* 2 (2015): 62–72.

Kouanou, Aurelle Tchagna, Daniel Tchiotsop, Romanic Kengne, Djoufack Tansaa Zephirin, Ngo Mouelas Adele Armele, and René Tchinda. "An optimal big data workflow for biomedical image analysis". *Informatics in Medicine Unlocked* 11 (2018): 68–74.

Lee, June-Goo, Sanghoon Jun, Young-Won Cho, Hyunna Lee, Guk Bae Kim, Joon Beom Seo, and Namkug Kim. "Deep learning in medical imaging: General overview". *Korean Journal of Radiology* 18(4) (2017): 570–584.

Liberatore, Matthew J., and Robert L. Nydick. "The analytic hierarchy process in medical and health care decision making: A literature review". *European Journal of Operational Research* 189(1) (2008): 194–207.

Makwakwa, Lumbani, Mei-ling Sheu, Chen-Yuan Chiang, Shoei-Loong Lin, and Peter W. Chang. "Patient and health system delays in the diagnosis and treatment of new and retreatment pulmonary tuberculosis cases in Malawi". *BMC Infectious Diseases* 14(1) (2014): 132.

Moussavi, Seyed Esmaeil, M. Mahdjoub, and Olivier Grunder. "A matheuristic approach to the integration of worker assignment and vehicle routing problems: Application to home healthcare scheduling". *Expert Systems with Applications* 125 (2019): 317–332.

Ngiam, Kee Yuan, and Wei Khor. "Big data and machine learning algorithms for health-care delivery". *The Lancet Oncology* 20(5) (2019): e262–e273.

Nilashi, Mehrbakhsh, Othman Bin Ibrahim, Hossein Ahmadi, and Leila Shahmoradi. "An analytical method for diseases prediction using machine learning techniques". *Computers and Chemical Engineering* 106 (2017): 212–223.

Nilashi, Mehrbakhsh, Othman Bin Ibrahim, Abbas Mardani, Ali Ahani, and Ahmad Jusoh. "A soft computing approach for diabetes disease classification". *Health Informatics Journal* 24(4) (2018): 379–393.

Nilashi, Mehrbakhsh, Othman Ibrahim, Sarminah Samad, Hossein Ahmadi, Leila Shahmoradi, and Elnaz Akbari. "An analytical method for measuring the Parkinson's disease progression: A case on a Parkinson's telemonitoring dataset". *Measurement* 136 (2019): 545–557.

Palanisamy, Venketesh, and Ramkumar Thirunavukarasu. "Implications of big data analytics in developing healthcare frameworks – A review". *Journal of King Saud University-Computer and Information Sciences* 31(4) (2019): 415–425.

Peeling, Rosanna W. "Diagnostics in a digital age: An opportunity to strengthen health systems and improve health outcomes". *International Health* 7(6) (2015): 384–389.

Pelteret, Jean-Paul, Bastian Walter, and Paul Steinmann. "Application of metaheuristic algorithms to the identification of nonlinear magneto-viscoelastic constitutive parameters". *Journal of Magnetism and Magnetic Materials* 464 (2018): 116–131.

Rezk, Eman, Zainab Awan, Fahad Islam, Ali Jaoua, Somaya Al. Maadeed, Nan Zhang, Gautam Das, and Nasir Rajpoot. "Conceptual data sampling for breast cancer histology image classification". *Computers in Biology and Medicine* 89 (2017): 59–67.

Shayanfar, Human, and Farhad Soleimanian Gharehchopogh. "Farmland fertility: A new metaheuristic algorithm for solving continuous optimization problems". *Applied Soft Computing* 71 (2018): 728–746.

Shi, Yong, Toufik Boudouh, and Olivier Grunder. "A hybrid genetic algorithm for a home health care routing problem with time window and fuzzy demand". *Expert Systems with Applications* 72 (2017): 160–176.

Tack, Christopher. "Artificial intelligence and machine learning| Applications in musculoskeletal physiotherapy." *Musculoskeletal Science and Practice* 39 (2019): 164–169.

Thai, L.H., T.S. Hai, and Nguyen Thanh Thuy. "Image classification using support vector machine and artificial neural network". *International Journal of Information Technology and Computer Science (IJITCS)* 4(5) (2012): 32–38.

Tsai, Chun-Wei, Ming-Chao Chiang, Adlen Ksentini, and Min Chen. "Metaheuristic algorithms for healthcare: Open issues and challenges". *Computers and Electrical Engineering* 53 (2016): 421–434.

Urdea, Mickey, Laura A. Penny, Stuart S. Olmsted, Maria Y. Giovanni, Peter Kaspar, Andrew Shepherd, Penny Wilson et al. "Requirements for high impact diagnostics in the Developing World". *Nature* 444(1s) (2006): 73.

Willems, Stefan M., Sanne Abeln, K. Anton Feenstra, Remco de Bree, Egge F. van der Poel, Robert J. Baatenburg de Jong, Jaap Heringa, and Michiel W.M. van den Brekel. "The potential use of big data in oncology". *Oral Oncology* 98 (2019): 8–12.

Wills, Mary J. "Decisions through data: Analytics in healthcare". *Journal of Healthcare Management* 59(4) (2014): 254–262.

Wong, Zoie S.Y., Jiaqi Zhou, and Qingpeng Zhang. "Artificial intelligence for infectious disease big data analytics". *Infection, Disease and Health* 24(1) (2019): 44–48.

Yeh, Jinn-Yi, and Wen-Shan Lin. "Using simulation technique and genetic algorithm to improve the quality care of a hospital emergency department". *Expert Systems with Applications* 32(4) (2007): 1073–1083.

Zheng, Bichen, Jinghe Zhang, Sang Won Yoon, Sarah S. Lam, Mohammad Khasawneh, and Srikanth Poranki. "Predictive modeling of hospital readmissions using metaheuristics and data mining". *Expert Systems with Applications* 42(20) (2015): 7110–7120.

4

Decision Support System to Improve Patient Care

V. Diviya Prabha and R. Rathipriya

CONTENTS

4.1 Introduction..41
4.2 Related Work 42
4.3 Feature Selection...42
    4.3.1 Entropy Formula...44
4.4 Experimental Setup 47
4.5 Conclusion 47
References...51

4.1 Introduction

The amount of data is quickly increasing at a very fast pace in the healthcare sector. The extraction of relevant data from high volume data is a challenging task. The novel physiognomies of medical data are challenging for data mining. The wide variety and the huge volume of data is valuable only when a useful pattern is extracted. The required model is available in the raw data alongside data that is not useful. Obtaining such useful (Archenaa and Mary Anita 2016; Malykh and Rudetskiy 2018) knowledge with a pre-existing data mining approach that is crucial.

Similarly, forming decision-making tasks from raw data in various dimensions of other data are essential. Moreover, there are numerous reports available in hospitals based across cities (Liu et al. 2018) and villages. Forming the correct decision based on a patient's data helps both patients and doctors get a good result (Abraham 2016). High dimensional data with a large number of features show us the importance of feature selection.

Over the last few decades, feature selection with machine learning approaches an important area for research. The significance of choosing the best features helps the doctors and patients understand the medical (Sasikala et al. 2016) data in making the appropriate decision and diagnosis of infected patients as soon as possible. There are several method filters, and wrapper and embed methods for feature selection.

This chapter discusses the likelihood of patients being readmitted to the hospital after discharge, and how the knowledge of drugs taken by the patient and medical data can help in making these predictions. Several previous studies motivate us. An entropy-based measure is useful with the integration of machine learning techniques.

It is analyzing data using attribute selections for a predictive model by considering necessary attributes that support prediction and removing irrelevant attributes. Much of clinical data today consists of irrelevant attributes that weaken the prediction level. Thus, the proposed approach concentrates on decision entropy-based attribute selection. The subset of the attribute is selected based on entropy value and given as an input to the machine learning algorithms such as logistic regression (Prabha et al. 2019), support vector machines, decision trees, etc., for prediction of readmissions. This gives better accuracy than the existing model. It also suits for increasing data dynamically to handle new data for readmission prediction. This helps to reduce readmission risk and improves patient care.

The chapter is organized as follows: In section two, the basic concepts of entropy-based feature selection are explained. In section three, the algorithms and flow of PySpark-based algorithms are evaluated, and concentrations of features are reported. Section five concludes the paper.

4.2 Related Work

Frequent work has been carried out in the field of feature selection. The accurate prediction model needs to identify the relevant feature (Xing et al. 2001). The significant features represent the strengths and weaknesses of the features. For subset feature selection, a DFL algorithm (Maji 2010) is used to find the optimal features. Large datasets have more features, so it is important to categorize the relevant features. Differentiation entropy (Cassara et al. 2016) is used for feature subsets so that these important features can be selected. The neighborhood entropy works better for classical game theory process. It recommends that Shannon's entropy works well only for nominal data, and that it does not work well for other data values. A subset feature selection using entropy (Zheng and Chee 2011) for a huge amount of data is the most critical task here, and identifying the correct subset of feature is difficult in this approach (Ahmed and Kumar 2018; Masoudi-Sobhanzadeh et al. 2019).

4.3 Feature Selection

The basic filter and wrapper methods are performed in prevision papers, but that is not significant importance to feature selection. Feature selection for high dimensional datasets plays an important role in disease prediction

(Agrawal 2016; Li et al. 2016). In this paper, the main objective is to study the different types of entropy in large datasets. Entropy is used to identify the signs of attributes present in the dataset. The dataset is taken from the UCI repository. The first important step in data mining is data preprocessing. The main advantage is using Spark in Python is the PySpark. The first process is to import PySparkin to the PySpark context, and creating the PySpark context as SparkContext in the local environment.

The flowchart in Figure 4.1 represents the flow of the proposed method in the PySpark environment. The datasets are preprocessed as pipeline processes that combine multiple algorithms in the single process. Other processes are also carried out: StringIndexer for character variables, OnHotEncoder for the binary values and converting them to vectors as vector assembler. StringIndexer helps to convert the string values in the dataset into numeric form; for example, gender features consists of male and female. It converts this data into 0 for males and 1 for females. For OnHotEncoder, VectorAssembler is used for preprocessing. All these processes are simultaneous processes that reduce the computation time of the model.

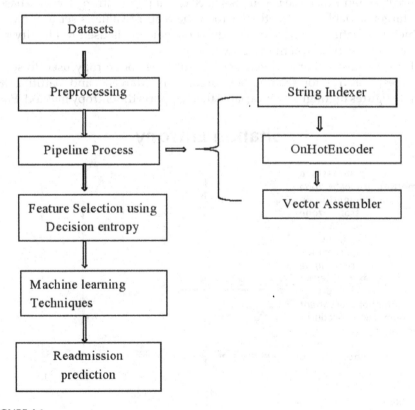

FIGURE 4.1
Steps for the proposed methodology.

4.3.1 Entropy Formula

Entropy is an essential approach used to identify the uncertainty of the predicted variables. Here, decision entropy performs the same based on the target value. The measurement of entropy is used to select the best variable for the target class. Different types of entropy are carried out to find the criteria for best feature selection. Following this, for each variable, the entropy formula is the following:

For each variable, the entropy is calculated as the following:

$$Entropy\_features = \sum_{i=1}^{n} -prob(f_i)\log_2(prob(f_i))$$

$$Decision\_Entropy = \begin{cases} 1 & H(Entropy\_features, target\_variable) >= 1 \\ 0 & H(Entropy\_features, target\_variable) < 1 \end{cases}$$

The entropy formula for decision entropy is formulated on the basis of if the entropy_features based on the target variable. If the entropy_features value is greater than 1 then the feature is selected, but if the entropy features based on target variable are less than 1 then the feature value is set to 0 means which the feature is rejected. The decision_entropy is used to identify relevant features based on the target variable.

Figures 4.2–4.5 characterize the different types of entropy used to select the best features for readmission prediction (Marcello and Battiti 2018). These figures highlight each variable that supports the entropy method. Each

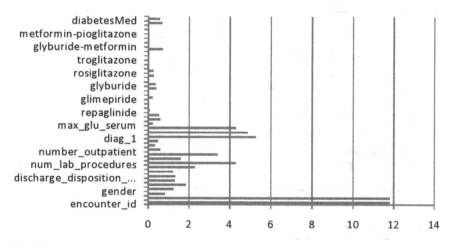

FIGURE 4.2
Shannon's entropy.

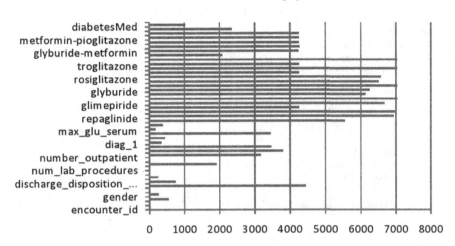

FIGURE 4.3
Relative entropy.

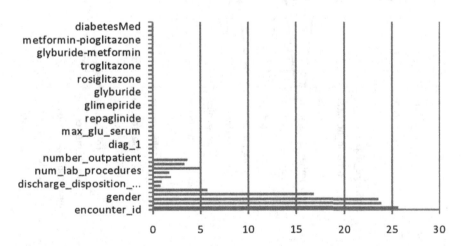

FIGURE 4.4
Boltzman's entropy.

selected attribute promptly changes from one entropy method to another. The cross-entropy method (Weiss and Dardick 2019) epitomizes the probability distribution of one method to other methods.

In the current work, different works based on entropy are obtained in the proposed work decision entropy is computed to improve the predictive accuracy. The entropy values are calculated based on the target value. If the values

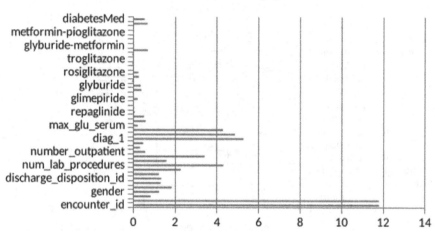

FIGURE 4.5
Cross-entropy.

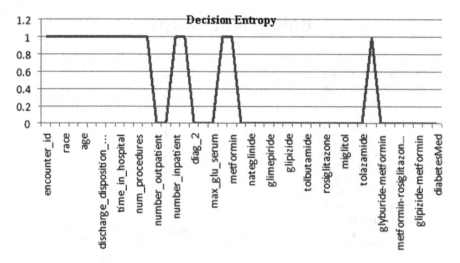

FIGURE 4.6
Decision entropy.

of the particular attribute are greater than 1 then that feature is selected for prediction, otherwise the feature is rejected. The feature values are similarly calculated. Figure 4.6 represents decision entropy, which provides a way to identify the optimal features and improves the best features. The best 11 features are selected for the prediction of readmission.

Table 4.1 represents readmission predictions for hospitals using different entropy methods. The proposed method of decision entropy is compared with the existing approach. The accuracy of the proposed approach is high when compared with the existing approach. Shannon's entropy, Boltzmann's entropy, and cross-entropy have a certain similar range of prediction. Additionally, relative entropy and decision entropy have similar ranges, of which overall performance accuracy of the proposed entropy performance is better than the existing approach which is at 92% accuracy.

4.4 Experimental Setup

The readmission prediction is of significant importance for both hospitals and patients. The goal of this chapter is to suggest a better prediction model for understanding whether the patient is likely to be readmitted or not. Table 4.2 indicates the different measures of the probability value of each variable. From Table 4.2, it can be observed that each step of the variable value consequently varies from one to another.

Table 4.3 represents the different measures signifying the importance of the variable. Biased represents the difference between the predicted values and target values. The bias value must be low for a good prediction model. Here, most of the values of the variables are low. Similarly, other measures such as co-variance, determination, t-tests, and p-values are calculated.

Figure 4.7 embodies the value of the density function used for each variable. The graph represents each variable with the density function to recommend the importance of the function. Figure 4.8 represents the graph plotting of the prediction of different entropy, which the proposed work performance better compared to other work.

4.5 Conclusion

In this chapter, a novel approach of decision entropy–based logistic regression (DELR) is put forward as an appropriate method for readmission

TABLE 4.1

Accuracy Prediction Using Entropy Methods

	Accuracy prediction (%)				
Entropy Methods	**LG**	**DT**	**RF**	**GBT**	**Average Value**
Shannon Entropy	66	67	63	67	65.75
Boltzmann Entropy	58	55	57	57	56.75
Cross Entropy	65	47	61	62	58.75
Relative Entropy	92	90	92	93	91.75
Decision Entropy	94	93	92	91	92.25

TABLE 4.2

Concentration Measures for Variables

Concentration	V1	V2	V3	V4	V5	V6	V7	V8	V9	V10	V11
Herfindahl	1.503	0.73	1.81	6.22	2.77	6.67	0.0	0.01	2.088	4.62	3.58
N- Herfindahl	8.44	0.80	3.96	4.80	1.35	5.27	9.54	0.01	6.68	3.20	2.61
Rosenbluth	1.63	0.88	1.96	6.10	2.77	6.69	0.01	0.01	2.23	3.24	3.86
Gini	0.133	0.88	0.27	0.767	0.48	0.78	0.87	0.91	0.36	0.57	0.63
Ricci-Schutz	0.95	0.88	0.19	0.767	0.48	0.78	0.87	0.88	0.26	0.47	0.50
Atkinson	0.17	0.88	0.06	0.753	0.48	0.78	0.87	0.89	0.10	0.28	0.49
Kolm	54.38	0.03	9.84	0.756	0.120	0.06	0.44	0.08	1.88	2.05	0.80
Co-efficient of variation	0.24	2.83	0.52	1.83	0.97	1.92	2.59	3.42	0.68	1.50	1.23
Squared Coefficient	0.05	8.02	0.27	3.38	0.95	3.71	6.72	11.63	0.47	2.25	1.52

TABLE 4.3

Measures for Variables

Title	V1	V2	V3	V4	V5	V6	V7	V8	V9	V10	V11
Biased Variance	2.6	0.09	6.6	0.24	0.24	0.1	0.36	0.3	8.64	2.3	3.07
Biased SD	15.97	0.31	8.28	0.49	0.49	0.3	0.60	0.60	2.93	5.22	1.75
Co variance	0.56	0.00	0.15	0.00	0.00	0	0.04	0.0	0.08	0.22	0.02
Correlation	0.07	0.00	0.03	0.03	0.03	0	0.14	0.1	0.06	0.08	0.02
Determination	0.005	7.25	0.00	0.00	0.00	0.0	0.02	0.0	0.03	7.98	0
T- test	19.09	2.26	10.2	9.76	9.13	2.6	38.8	38.8	16.3	2.37	6.52
p-value	4.27	0.02	1.60	1.57	6.81	0.0	0	0	4.71	0.01	6.72

Correction made in indicated in red text are correct and can be updated.

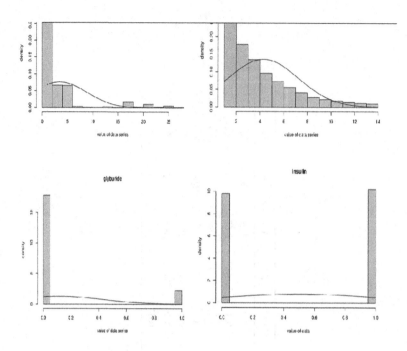

FIGURE 4.7
Value of data in the form of density.

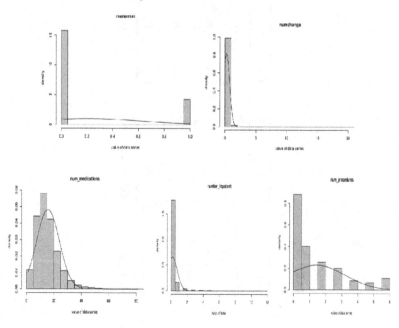

FIGURE 4.8
Accuracy Prediction.

prediction of patients. This method is compared with the existing method. The overall performances are better; as it is capable of rejecting irrelevant features and selecting only relevant features. The DELR method's performance has good accuracy of prediction at 92% effectiveness. Selecting better features improves the classification accuracy.

References

Agrawal, Rashmi. "A modified K-nearest neighbor algorithm using feature optimization". *International Journal of Engineering and Technology* 8(1) (2016): 28–37.

Archenaa, J., and E. A. Mary Anita. "Interactive big data management in healthcare using spark". In: *Proceedings of the 3rd International Symposium on Big Data and Cloud Computing Challenges (ISBCC–16')*. Springer, Cham, 2016.

Cassara, Pietro, Alessandro Rozza, and Mirco Nanni "A cross-entropy-based method to perform information-based feature selection." *arXiv Preprint ArXiv:1607.07186* (2016).

Frandsen, Abraham Jacob. "Machine learning for disease prediction". Theses and Dissertations, Brigham Young University, 5975 (2016).

Kauser Ahmed, P., and N. Senthil Kumar. "A comprehensive review of nature – inspired algorithm for feature selection". In: *Handbook of Research on Modeling, Analysis, and Application of Nature-Inspired Metaheuristic Algorithms*, Sujata Dash, B. K Tripathy (Eds). IGI Global, 2018.

Li, Falcao, Zan Zhang, and Chenxia Jin. "Feature selection with partition differentiation entropy for large-scale data sets". *Information Sciences* 329 (2016): 690–700.

Liu, Kanghuai, et al. "Big medical data decision-making intelligent system exploiting fuzzy inference logic for prostate cancer in developing countries". *IEEE Access* 7 (2018): 2348–2363.

Maji, Pradipta. "Mutual information-based supervised attribute clustering for microarray sample classification". *IEEE Transactions on Knowledge and Data Engineering* 24(1) (2010): 127–140.

Malykh, V. L., and S. V. Rudetskiy. "Approaches to medical decision-making based on big clinical data". *Journal of Healthcare Engineering* 2018 (2018): 6313–6322.

Marcello, Andrea, and Roberto Battiti. "Feature selection based on the neighborhood entropy". *IEEE Transactions on Neural Networks and Learning Systems* 29(12) (2018): 6313–6322.

Masoudi-Sobhanzadeh, Yosef, Habib Motieghader, and Ali Masoudi-Nejad. "FeatureSelect: A software for feature selection based on machine learning approaches". *BMC Bioinformatics* 20(1) (2019): 170.

Prabha, V., Diviya, and R. Rathipriya. "Readmission prediction using hybrid logistic regression". In: *International Conference on Innovative Data Communication Technologies and Application*. Springer, Cham, 2019.

Sasikala, S., S. Appavu Alias Balamurugan, and S. Geetha. "Multi Filtration Feature Selection (MFFS) to improve discriminatory ability in clinical data set". *Applied Computing and Informatics* 12(2) (2016): 117–127.

Weiss, Brandi A., and William Dardick. "An entropy-based measure for assessing fuzziness in logistic regression". *Educational and Psychological Measurement* 76(6) (2016): 986–1004.

Weiss, Brandi A., and William Dardick. "Separating the odds: Thresholds for entropy in logistic regression". *The Journal of Experimental Education* 76(6) (2019): 1–22.

Xing, E., M. Jordan, and R. Karp. "Feature selection for high-dimensional genomic microarray data". In: *Proceedings of the 18th International Conference on Machine Learning*. Morgan Kaufmann Publishers Inc., Williamstown, MA, 28 June – 1 July 2001, pp. 601–608.

Zheng, Yun, and Chee Keong Kwoh. "A feature subset selection method based on high-dimensional mutual information". *Entropy* 13(4) (2011): 860–901.

5

Effects of Cell Phone Usage on Human Health and Specifically on the Brain

Soobia Saeed, Afnizanfaizal Abdullah, N. Z. Jhanjhi,
Mehmood Naqvi and Shakeel Ahmed

CONTENTS

5.1 Introduction 53
5.2 Background 55
5.3 Radiation Produced by a Mobile Phone 56
5.4 MATLAB Tools 57
    5.4.1 Problem Statement 57
    5.4.2 Research Objective 57
5.5 State-of-the-Art Research and Technology 58
5.6 Discussion of Tools 59
5.7 Methodology 59
    5.7.1 Quantitative Approach 60
    5.7.2 Design Research 60
5.8 Method of Data Collection 60
    5.8.1 Sampling Technique 60
    5.8.2 Sample Size 60
    5.8.3 Instrument for Data Collection 60
    5.8.4 Research Model 60
5.9 K-Means Clustering 61
5.10 Result and Discussion 64
5.11 Conclusion 64
References 65

5.1 Introduction

Software engineering is about the theories, methods, procedures, processes, and tools used for the development of software. Software development as a method of software engineering goes hand-in-hand with research and development. Digital image handling is an inconceivable, broad, and limitless field which can utilize different applications which incorporate everything from the detection of fingerprint identification, to brain cancer detection (Norman et al. 2018; Das et al. 2017; Shree and Kumar 2018).

Malignancy is depicted as a startling tissue growth. Cerebral malignant growths are unusual masses of tissue where cells aggregate. What's more, they multiply in an unpredictable way – one that is obviously not under the control that ordinary cells are subjected to. The cell can be assessed as each organism's main basic unit. The human body contains about 100 billion cells and each has its own individual capabilities that relate to the body's ideal functioning, and these cells need to split in a measured way to form health new cells. In addition, each cell is highly fragmented and even terminated from time-to-time in order to create new cells. This process sometimes leads to the development a square of unnecessary cancer tissue. Cancer can happen anywhere in the body. Brain cancer for good and life can be assumed to be a true cancer. In terms of their starting lands and risks as cancers are shown (Lee et al. 2018; Klank et al. 2011).

The extent of radio-recurrence vitality relies on development of initial growth of cancer in terms of degree and type of utilization, of mobile phone, which is connected to PDA towers, from client to RF wave base station. Physicists have isolated each possible joint cause between versatile radiation and natural systems, for example., physical twists of proteins, inception of hailing pathways, and docking with receptors on cell layers. For each case, the discovered nature of portable radiation has been insignificant in affecting any dangerous change (Abdullah et al. 2013). A few examinations have looked into the effect of radio-recurrence fields on cerebral electrical work, psychological capacity, rest, pulse, circulatory strain, and more. This work was completed at the National Institute of Technology (NIT), Kerala, India. In this study, brain pain, dizziness, hip depth, and chest weight were assessed among the "constant" mobile phone users. An examination during the test details the increase of the heartbeat when holding a mobile phone near the chest and near the head. A huge difference was not found in the opposite conditions without a mobile phone. (Klank et al. 2011). Investigations into participant health history did not show any consistent evidence of adverse health effects from exposure to radio frequency fields, other than the effect of heating the tissues. In addition, researchers were unable to provide proof that links the final conditions and outcomes to electromagnetic field exposure and any declared side effects, for example, electromagnetic hypersensitivity among mobile users. (Kinaci et al. 2018).

Epidemiological research is looking at the risk of long-term exposure to radio frequencies. For the most part, it has sought to link brain tumors to the use of mobile phones. However, the same amount of cancer remains undetectable for many years after exposure to the cause of the tumor. Since mobile phones were not commonly used until the mid-1990s, epidemiological studies have been limited to cancers originating in recent times. The results of animal studies have shown that there is no risk of cancer due to long-term exposure to radio frequency fields (Lee et al. 2018). A few trials have attempted to find other possible long-term health effects of exposure to mobile radiation. In a test conducted in Amritsar, Punjab, India, the link between the use of mobile phones (exposure to RF radiation) and DNA chromosomes damage the lymphocytes of mobile phone customers. This risk may have long-term consequences for increasing tumor risk or other age-related changes. (Ferlay et al. 2015).

5.2 Background

Therapeutic images provide important information about the human heart. Mobile phones operate by transmitting signals and allowing the use of radio frequency waves by people from nearby base stations. This is actually an exposure of electromagnetic radiation, which can come from radio waves and microwaves and more. Exposure related to non-ionizing radiation can come from radio waves, microwaves, clear, soft, and warm waves, and RF waves. These types of radiation simply do not give off enough radiation to cause the development of a strong DNA lesion within the muscles. The strength of radio frequency waves differ in the strongest (ionizing) radiation-related forms (such as x-rays, gamma light, and bright radiation [UV]) that can dilute the binding substances in DNA. The real reason for this research is how microwaves work. Nevertheless, the amount of radiation released by mobile phones is much lower and inadequate to greatly alter body temperatures. Mobile phone use has increased dramatically (Kinaci et al. 2018; Ferlay et al. 2015; Gelb et al. 2018; Kant et al. 2018). The increasing use of this technology was a cause for concern in relation to wellbeing and safety. Earlier than expected in the 1990s, low-level exposure to an electromagnetic radio (RF) field has become of serious consequence on wellbeing. This was primarily examined by a group of specialists and an evaluation was conducted for possible aggressive effects on the wellbeing of multi-use communications. Radiation from every source is a critical secretion. X-rays are a perfect sample of radiation, but sunlight and heat in our bodies are always progressing strongly. There is a difference in radiation from "high-vital" high-energy radiation to "low-vital" low-energy radiation. This includes the proposed method, where electromagnetic radiation and gamma radiation are classified as being very vital and are programs with enough vitality that you can shed a good electron from your (ionized) molecule. This can easily damage DNA within cells, which can simply recognize progress. RF radiation is located at the lower end of impedance using the electromagnetic obtained, this a type of non-ionizing radiation (Abdullah et al. 2012; Miller 2016). Non-ionizing radiation provides enough basic elements to move or make vibrations of particles inside a molecule, yet they are insufficient for ionization (forcing particles to force them, for example, electrons). RF radiation has a higher centralization than is seen in the use of a noticeable degree of low-emission electromagnetic radiation. The basic elements are less than found in some impeccable types of non-ionizing radiation in the same cycle, because of a light that can be recognized alongside infrared radiation. Ionizing radiation generally has more energy. With the possibility of RF radiation being absorbed into a giant mammals' aggregate of substances containing mineral water, for example, reinforcements, fluids, and body tissues, then heat will be generated to create abnormality after burning the normal cells of the brain. This can easily provoke explosions along with tissue pain. Despite the fact that the radiation of the RF won't cause harm to the DNA in cells due to the manner in which ionizing radiation happens, there has been concern that the numerous ways of non-ionizing radiation may have more of a general impact that can cause disease in a couple of cases. The International Agency for Research on Cancer (IARC) renewed this cause authenticity, which was normal, which could be conceivable and outlines a general investigation of the connection between PDAS use notwithstanding the danger of mind (malignant) growth. Thereafter, the intervention became a general method of case-control studies that focus on the types of paradoxical carcinomas in tissues, which can be revealed by tons of centralized radio-frequencies caused by phones: brain carcinomas (glioma and meningioma), acoustic nerve (oral tumor), and parotid appendix. The aim was to understand whether the use of cells increases the risk of these cancers as well as whether the remote-controlled RF power will be cancerous (Jian et al. 2018; van der Kleij et al. 2018; Gamage and Ranathunga 2017).

5.3 Radiation Produced by a Mobile Phone

Unlike televisions, warning systems, PCs, and all other electrical contraptions, cell phones (also called mobile phones) are electronic devices that generate electromagnetic radiation using radio frequency (RF) imperatives. We work at low intensity (under 1 watt) by transmitting and tolerating electromagnetic radiation at the end of the range of the radiofrequency (RF). It is understood that radiation which is assigned to be "ionizing" can be devoured by isolated tissue and split molecules, such as gamma pillars and x-bars, and can cause growth. The tension is that the PDA and its array contraction (the radiation wellspring) are held close to the head. The damage to the DNA particles is accepted as the explanation. The radiation that a cell phone uses is part of the comparable electromagnetic range, and isn't ionizing. In this manner, the US FDA can control these contraptions to ensure that the radiation doesn't get to a level of threat to customers, but just once the nearness of a general prosperity danger has been developed. RF essentiality was incorrectly believed to equivalently cause development (Gupta and Pahuja 2017; Heinen et al. 2016).

5.4 MATLAB Tools

MATLAB is a multi-viewpoint numerical processing framework and type of prohibitive lingo programming made by Math Works. MATLAB awards coordinate controls, cutoff point plotting and information, use of computations, enhancement of UIs, and interfacing with activities written in different vernaculars, including: C, C++, C #, Java, Fortran, and Python (Lavanyadevi et al. 2017). Regardless of how normal MATLAB is for numerical processing, an optional device compartment uses the MuPAD significant motor, enabling access to the enrolling limits of the agent. An additional package for dynamic and embedded systems, Simulink, incorporates graphic multispace reenactment and model-based arrangement (Soobia et al. 2019a,b).

5.4.1 Problem Statement

Cancer is characterized as an unexpected tissue change. Brain cancer is an irregular mass of tissue in which cells begin dividing in an uncontrollable manner, evidently without the normal influences that govern normal cells. The cellular can be described as every organism's primary unit. The human body carries about a hundred billion cells, each with its own very precise skills in relation to the frame's most necessary functions, and those cells require fissures to cut up in a measured way to viably form new cells. In addition, each cell is highly fragmented and even terminated from time-to-time in order to create new cells. This process sometimes leads to the development a square of unnecessary cancer tissue.

The issue of mobile phone usage for more than 50 minutes, brain tissues on a single side of the head the mobile phone, radio wire processed more glucose when contrasted with the tissues about the backward side of the brain. In this research, the causes of brain cancer disease due and their links to the mobile phone – in relation to this expansion in glucose metabolism – are still unknown. The type of brain cancer rapidly created in the brain due to the usage of cellular phone is also unknown, and this is one of the major motives of our research area. The author is using a silicon-based neuron cell chip for the purpose of storing the damage cancer cells, which are created by cellular phones. It is being investigated how this relates to the growth of brain cancer. Further, authors have also used this chip to investigate the activity of cancerous cells and how we uncover the disadvantage of damaged cells of brain cancer.

5.4.2 Research Objective

- To find the brain cancer with the help of ROI algorithms.
- To evaluate the effectiveness of image testing in brain-imaging technologies that utilize MATLAB tools and data mining.

5.5 State-of-the-Art Research and Technology

There are several steps of cancer, which can occur by using a mobile phone from beginning stage to final stage of cancer due to extreme use of mobile phone in terms of RF waves. We also realize that the most common types in adults are meningiomas that are considered glioma called glioblastoma in several ways. Many types are extremely rare. Cancers of the brain may occur at any age. For example, vaccines are often more usual in adolescents with unit arthroplasty, and some are also necessary in adults. In general, age-related adult cancers are more common. Diffuse brain cancers and dangerous main brain cancers are unfortunately common than favorable (Li et al. 2015; Abdullah et al. 2013; Bishop and Favaro 2011). Early signs of brain cancer can include migraine sensations. This is due to the increase in intracranial mass. These indicators may come and go at the beginning of cancer growth, and in the morning they tend to be at their worst. Piracy can exacerbate pain during breathing and crouching. Additionally, epileptic seizures are often exacerbated or triggered. As the cancer progresses to a large mass, lethargy and "laziness" may occur. When the cancer grows, the surrounding brain tissue is likely to be affected (Saeed and Jafri 2015; Soobia et al. 2019). The separate parts of the cerebrum control the capacities of various parts of the body. From that point forward, depending on the impact on the part of the brain and the extent of that area's overall impact, the symptoms change on a case-to-case basis. For instance, symptoms often include: muscle shortening in the arm, leg, or part of the face or eyes, issues with removal, joint grouping, vision, hearing, voice, correspondence, or drinking. Further symptoms may include: loss of smell, unsteadiness, change in mood, disarray or shortcoming of memory, numbness in parts of the body, feelings of perplexity, changes in character, and indications of hormonal changes in pituitary disease (Usman and Rajpoot 2017; 21Lee et al. 2017; Oliveira et al. 2018). This is can be examined by monitoring of brain capabilities, neurological developments, reactions, vision, etc. MRI scans or CT scans are regular tests that are carried out to confirm or prevent brain cancer to examine more microscopic elements (Saeed and Jafri 2015; Soobia et al. 2019). If the cancer is distinguished, more scans and tests can be done. In some rare cases, to gather more data about cancer, a PET scan or angiography may be conducted. It may be assumed that a biopsy would confirm the type of cancer. A biopsy is a procedure where a tiny tissue sample is removed from a body part (Pim et al. 2012; Soobia et al. 2012; Liu et al. 2018). Under a microscope the sample is examine for odd cells. A small surgery, usually with sedatives, is required to obtain a brain biopsy. A small area of the skull is reduced to allow a fine needle to be inserted in order to withdraw a small tissue sample. By observing the acquired cells of a biopsy, a final diagnosis can be made about if there is a threat, and if so, an identification of the stage and type of cancer (Liu et al. 2016; Liang et al. 2018).

Information processing in the central nervous system interferes primarily with the interconnected relationship between the neurons. This relationship distinguishes how well large-scale social events of neurons can regulate, respect, and implement complex sensory boundaries, including learning and memory. The synaptic system between any particular groups of neurons isn't hard-wired; instead it is comprised of an abnormal state of flexibility, which constitutes the neuroplasticity in humans that gives us the ability to learn and memorize. While there is extensive research into the beginning of cellular and semi-nuclear commencement of synaptic versatility – at the level of junctions of neurons or smaller structures – the examination of larger neuronal groups has been demonstrated in reality tests. The ability to assess the activities of large neural frames at the same time and in a non-prominent way is a fundamental basis for understanding how neural frameworks work at the system level. Here, we present the leaps forward in the range of many bionic mixtures that have been properly linked to neural frames with silicon devices to detect the performance of synaptic-related neurons (Hazra et al. 2017).

5.6 Discussion of Tools

Generally, the tools discussed so far do not scale very well and there is no official standard of comparison available, thus, this is one of our objectives in this chapter. However, as per the literature studies regarding cancer investigation methods, where the MATLAB tools/code for the previously mentioned tools are concerned, there is very little information available on recommended resources. Tool comparison as used in different techniques is the most difficult task, because each investigation/detection technique has a different method. Apart from that, each tool has its own way of investigation/detection, so focusing on specific tasks is quite a difficult task.

5.7 Methodology

The research is conducted by first gathering the patient's cancer-related data. The data collected includes attributes like patient's gender, age, stage of cancer, and demography, etc. An initial bibliographic research approach can be implemented alongside the study of literature. In the previous stages, research methods and qualitative designs were used.

5.7.1 Quantitative Approach

For a quantitative approach I intend to use the following methodologies. Investigation or detection of damage cells of cancer:

1. Examine the brain cell through the usage of MATLAB software tools.
2. Propose a benchmark comparing the damaged and undamaged cancer cells with different tools.
3. Analyze the available data mining techniques used by available tools.

5.7.2 Design Research

Design research is sometimes called "enhancement research". It emphasizes problem solving. In our domain it is intended to create a detection or investigation process.

5.8 Method of Data Collection

This is secondary data that is taken from different medical organizations of Malaysia.

5.8.1 Sampling Technique

The sampling technique used to study sampling is random sampling and participants are randomly taken from various hospitals in Malaysia.

5.8.2 Sample Size

For data collection, the sample size is 150. The target population for selecting the sample was cancer patients and they were transferred to hospitals in various medical institutions and hospitals in Malaysia.

5.8.3 Instrument for Data Collection

The software SSPS Statistics is used as the instrument for the data collection.

5.8.4 Research Model

The assembly is used as a research model. Aggregation is a very powerful data mining technique that is used to define similarities between different groups. There are several aggregation algorithms in which the k-means algorithm is used to define hidden patterns of data. In my research, the k-mean algorithm explores invisible information by taking an attribute such as gender, age, cancer stage, demography, etc. This model identifies cancer at a very early stage.

5.9 K-Means Clustering

The K-Means aggregation algorithm was created in 1976 by MacQueen. It is an unsupervised collection that performs a certain number of separate groups and (non-dynamic) levels. The strategy is based on a clear and basic way to handle the request of a specific dataset through a specific number of groups (k-mean) previously created. K-mean estimates identify objects without k-objects, going to the initial meeting center. The accompanying step is to take each point that has a place within a specific set of data and move it to the closest center in perspective, near the article to the meeting center, using Euclidean division. After passing each item, it is necessary to recalculate the positions of the new group. The strategy is repeated until there is no match in the beam centers' k. This estimate reduces an objective limit known as the permissible limit for the square screw that was determined by the transition (Soobia et al. 2019).

$$J(v) = \sum_{i}^{c} \sum_{j=0}^{ci} \left(\left\| x_i - v_j \right\| \right)$$

Where,
'$\|xi - vj\|$' is the Euclidean distance between xi and vj,
here are the main steps for the K-Means algorithm:

1. Dataset distribution in Group K.
2. For each data point in the dataset:
   - Measure the distance from each group to the data point;
   - If the set is near the data point, and if you leave it, the data point will move to the nearest set.
3. Perform the previous step until any data point moves from one group to another. This stage shows that it is the end of the assembly process and that all groups are stable.
4. The choice of the primary section can greatly affect the resulting final groups, in the form of consistency and distances within the group and between groups as shown in Table 5.1:

TABLE 5.1

Statistical Data of Independent Sample

| | | Independent Samples Test | | | | | | | | |
| | | Levene's Test for Equality of Variances | | T-test for Equality of Means | | | | | 95% Confidence Interval of the Difference | |
		F	Sig.	t	Df	Sig. (2-tailed)	Mean Difference	Std. Error Difference	Lower	Upper
NART	Assumption of Eq. Variance	80.640	.000	7.483	42	.000	.727	.097	.531	.923
	without Assumption of Eq. Variance			7.483	21.000	.000	.727	.097	.525	.929
RAVLT	Assumption of Eq. Variance	13.644	.001	1.763	42	.085	.227	.129	−.033	.487
	without Assumption of Eq. Variance			1.763	37.978	.086	.227	.129	−.034	.488
Trail A	Assumption of Eq. Variance	40.000	.000	2.898	42	.006	.364	.125	.110	.617
	without Assumption of Eq. Variance			2.898	33.600	.007	.364	.125	.109	.619
Trail B	Assumption of Eq. Variance	40.000	.000	2.898	42	.006	.364	.125	.110	.617
	without Assumption of Eq. Variance			2.898	33.600	.007	.364	.125	.109	.619

(Continued)

TABLE 5.1 (CONTINUED)

Statistical Data of Independent Sample

		Independent Samples Test							
		Levene's Test for Equality of Variances		T-test for Equality of Means					95% Confidence Interval of the Difference	
		F	Sig.	t	Df	Sig. (2-tailed)	Mean Difference	Std. Error Difference	Lower	Upper
HPTR9	Assumption of Eq. Variance	23.579	.000	2.748	42	.009	.364	.132	.097	.631
	without Assumption of Eq. Variance			2.748	37.192	.009	.364	.132	.096	.632
HPTL9	Assumption of Eq. Variance	40.000	.000	2.898	42	.006	.364	.125	.110	.617
	without Assumption of Eq. Variance			2.898	33.600	.007	.364	.125	.109	.619
COWAT	Assumption of Eq. Variance	8.090	.007	1.600	42	.117	.227	.142	-.059	.514
	without Assumption of Eq. Variance			1.600	40.810	.117	.227	.142	-.060	.514
WDRT	Assumption of Eq. Variance	40.000	.000	2.898	42	.006	.364	.125	.110	.617
	without Assumption of Eq. Variance			2.898	33.600	.007	.364	.125	.109	.619
mwalk10	Assumption of Eq. Variance	22.120	.000	2.411	42	.020	.318	.132	.052	.584
	without Assumption of Eq. Variance			2.411	37.277	.021	.318	.132	.051	.585

5.10 Result and Discussion

Data mining has an unusual centralization of the scope of the drug, and addresses a comprehensive methodology that requires a deep understanding of the needs of restorative departments. The learning obtained through the use of data mining techniques can be used to determine productive decisions that improve compliance with human administration affiliation and patient prosperity. Data mining requires appropriate development and research techniques, as well as systems for reporting and viewing, after which results can be measured. Data mining, once started, handles an endless cycle of learning dissemination. As for affiliations, it offers one of the main things that make the business strategy not so bad. Today, there have been several attempts aimed at the applicable use of data mining in social protection of societies. The main ability of this framework lies in the possibility of examining a persuasive case in datasets in the social protection space. These illustrations can be used for clinical research. In any case, open and useful data is widely distributed; it is different and huge in nature. This data should be collected and stored in data warehouses in the formed structures, and it can be provided with a specific final goal for forming the specialist office information system. The progress of the data mining process is a procedure that the researcher organizes in an attempt to find new and hidden cases in the data, from which they can learn. This is a discovery that can help provide patients with restorative and distinctive healthcare organizations.

5.11 Conclusion

This type of study portrays cancer levels of serotonin using impression segmentation of brain cancer among MRI images, and illustrates the potential impacts of the proposed solution. In addition, taking up studies in view of security issues and substantial unique obstacles is an enormous task. The area of this study has always been the classification of brain cancer tactics from side-to-side. The MRI data from the Brain Web Database provides a valid example of the representation of brain cancer of the MRI. In this specific research work, we handle basic brain images that are thought of as cancers, choosing cancer section area that may relate to mobile phone use. These sorts of images are, on a very basic level, in correspondence with the sort and size of cancer enormous and should decide how progressive the cancer is by detecting or identifying cancer with the usage of the neuron silicon chip–based technology (using the neuron network). In this research, we have focused on how far reaching cancer is and we identify the range of tumor area from initial to final stage for particular dimensions of cancer cell. By utilizing a new technology such as neuron networks, we have tested multiple types of skulls to detect brain cancer location. In brain cancers, there are needed to include the main area regarding. Our research's accuracy is the most important measure of accomplishment. Thus, this study proports that MRI scans gather the best images and outcomes. In addition, it is important to store the sample or patches of brain cancer that identify how to control the brain cancer or reduce the dangers of cellular technology.

References

Abdullah, Afnizanfaizal, et al. "An improved swarm optimization for parameter estimation and biological model selection". *PLoS One* 8(4) (2013): 4.

Abdullah, Afnizanfaizal, et al. "Cerebrospinal fluid pulsatile segmentation-a review." In: *The 5th 2012 Biomedical Engineering International Conference.* IEEE, 2012.

Bishop, Tom E., and Paolo Favaro "The light field camera: Extended depth of field, aliasing, and superresolution". *IEEE Transactions on Pattern Analysis and Machine Intelligence* 34(5) (2011): 972–986.

Chaudhary, P., and R. Agrawal "A comparative study of linear and non-linear classifiers in sensory motor imagery based brain computer interface". *Journal of Computational and Theoretical Nanoscience* 16(12) (2019): 5134–5139.

Chaudhary, P., and R. Agrawal "Emerging threats to security and privacy in brain computer interface". *International Journal of Advanced Studies of Scientific Research* 3 (2018): 12.

Das, Suman, et al. "Detection and area calculation of brain tumour from MRI images using MATLAB". *International Journal* 4 (2017): 1.

Ferlay, Jacques, et al. "Cancer incidence and mortality worldwide: Sources, methods and major patterns in GLOBOCAN 2012". *International Journal of Cancer* 136(5) (2015): E359–E386.

Gamage, P.T., and Dr Lochandaka Ranathunga "Identification of brain tumor using image processing techniques". *Faculty of Information Technology, University of Moratuwa,* 2017. https://www. researchgate. net/publication/276133543.

Gelb, Sivan, et al. "Mechanisms of neuropsychiatric lupus: The relative roles of the blood-cerebrospinal fluid barrier versus blood-brain barrier". *Journal of Autoimmunity* 91 (2018): 34–44.

Gupta, Anjali, and Gunjan Pahuja. "Hybrid clustering and boundary value refinement for tumor segmentation using brain MRI". In: *IOP Conference Series: Materials Science and Engineering,* Vol. 225, No. 1. IOP Publishing, China, 2017.

Hazra, Animesh, et al. "Brain tumor detection based on segmentation using MATLAB." In: *2017 International Conference on Energy, Communication, Data Analytics and Soft Computing (ICECDS).* IEEE, India, 2017.

Heinen, Rutger, et al. "Robustness of automated methods for brain volume measurements across different MRI field strengths". *PLoS One* 11(10) (2016): 10.

Jian, Wen-xuan, et al. "Potential roles of brain barrier dysfunctions in the early stage of Alzheimer's disease". *Brain Research Bulletin* 142 (2018): 360–367.

Kant, Shawn, et al. "Choroid plexus genes for CSF production and brain homeostasis are altered in Alzheimer's disease". *Fluids and Barriers of the CNS* 15(1) (2018): 34.

Khan, A. Raouf, Noor Zaman, and Saira Muzafar "Health hazards linked to using mobile cellular phones". *Journal of Information and Communication Technology* 2(2) (2008): 101–108.

Khotanlou, Hassan, et al. "3D brain tumor segmentation in MRI using fuzzy classification, symmetry analysis and spatially constrained deformable models". *Fuzzy Sets and Systems* 160(10) (2009): 1457–1473.

Kinaci, Ahmet, et al. "Effectiveness of dural sealants in prevention of cerebrospinal fluid leakage after craniotomy: A systematic review". *World Neurosurgery* 118 (2018): 368–376.

Klank, R.L. et al. Migration in confinement: A micro-channel-based assay. In: Wells, C.M., M. Parsons, editors. *Cell Migration: Developmental Methods and Protocols.* Humana Press: Totowa, NJ, pp. 415–434, 2011.

Lavanyadevi, R., et al. "Brain tumor classification and segmentation in MRI images using PNN." In: *2017 IEEE International Conference on Electrical, Instrumentation and Communication Engineering (ICEICE).* IEEE, Yogyakarta, Indonesia 2017.

Lee, Chi-Hoon, et al. "Segmenting brain tumors with conditional random fields and support vector machines." In: *International Workshop on Computer Vision for Biomedical Image Applications.* Springer: Berlin, Heidelberg, China, 2005, 1–12.

Lee, Su Yeon, et al. "Regulation of tumor progression by programmed necrosis". *Oxidative Medicine and Cellular Longevity* 2018 (2018).

Li, Guodong, et al. "Automatic liver segmentation based on shape constraints and deformable graph cut in CT images". *IEEE Transactions on Image Processing: A Publication of the IEEE Signal Processing Society* 24(12) (2015): 5315–5329.

Liang, Fan, et al. "Abdominal, multi-organ, auto-contouring method for online adaptive magnetic resonance guided radiotherapy: An intelligent, multi-level fusion approach". *Artificial Intelligence in Medicine* 90 (2018): 34–41.

Liu, Jia, et al. "A cascaded deep convolutional neural network for joint segmentation and genotype prediction of brainstem gliomas". *IEEE Transactions on Bio-Medical Engineering* 65(9) (2018): 1943–1952.

Mendrik, Adriënne M., et al. "MRBrainS challenge: Online evaluation framework for brain image segmentation in 3T MRI scans". *Computational Intelligence and Neuroscience*, Japan, (2015): Japan, 1–12.

Miller, Kimberly. *Cancer Treatment & Survivorship Facts & Figures.* American Cancer Society Estimated Numbers of Cancer Survivors Report, (2016): 1–44.

Moeskops, Pim, et al. "Automatic segmentation of MR brain images with a convolutional neural network". *IEEE Transactions on Medical Imaging* 35(5) (2016): 1252–1261.

Oliveira, Gustavo Casagrande, Renato Varoto, and Alberto Cliquet Jr. "Brain tumor segmentation in magnetic resonance images using genetic algorithm clustering and adaboost classifier". *BIOIMAGING.* 2018.

Saeed, Soobia, and Afnizanfaizal Abdullah "Recognition of brain cancer and cerebrospinal fluid due to the usage of different MRI image by utilizing support vector machine". *Bulletin of Electrical Engineering and Informatics* 9(2) (2020): 619–625.

Saeed, Soobia, Afnizanfaizal Abdullah, and N.Z. Jhanjhi "Analysis of the lung cancer patient's for data mining tool". *IJCSNS* 19(7) (2019a): 90.

Saeed, Soobia, and Afnizanfaizal Bin Abdullah "Investigation of a brain cancer with interfacing of 3-dimensional image processing." In: *2019 International Conference on Information Science and Communication Technology (ICISCT)*. IEEE, Pakistan, 2019.

Saeed, Soobia, Afnizanfaizal Abdullah, and N.Z. Jhanjhi "Implementation of Fourier transformation with brain cancer and CSF images". *Indian Journal of Science and Technology* 12(37) (2019b): 37.

Saeed, Soobia, and Raza Jafri "Estimation of brain tumor using latest technology of mobile phone". *Journal of Information and Communication Technology (JICT)* 9(1) (2015): 32–09.

Saunders, Norman R., et al. "Physiology and molecular biology of barrier mechanisms in the fetal and neonatal brain". *The Journal of Physiology* 596(23) (2018): 5723–5756.

Sharma, Geeta, et al. "A detailed study of EEG based brain computer interface." In: *Proceedings of the First International Conference on Information Technology and Knowledge Management*, New Dehli, India, Vol. 14, Dehli, India, 2017.

Shree, N. Varuna, and T.N.R. Kumar "Identification and classification of brain tumor MRI images with feature extraction using DWT and probabilistic neural network". *Brain Informatics* 5(1) (2018): 23–30.

Usman, Khalid, and Kashif Rajpoot "Brain tumor classification from multi-modality MRI using wavelets and machine learning". *Pattern Analysis and Applications* 20(3) (2017): 871–881.

van der Kleij, Lisa A., et al. "Fast CSF MRI for brain segmentation; Cross-validation by comparison with 3D T1-based brain segmentation methods". *PLoS One* 13(4) (2018): 4.

6

Feature Extraction and Bio Signals

A. Mary Judith, S Baghavathi Priya, N. Kanya, and Jyotir Moy Chatterjee

CONTENTS

6.1   Introduction 69
6.2   Feature Extraction 71
    6.2.1   Common Spatial Patterns 72
    6.2.2   Adaptive Common Spatial Patterns 72
    6.2.3   Adaptive CSP Patches 72
    6.2.4   Canonical Correlation Analysis 73
    6.2.5   Band Power Features 73
    6.2.6   Adaptive Band Power Features 74
    6.2.7   Time Point Features 74
    6.2.8   Time Points with Adaptive XDAWN 74
6.3   Feature Selection and its Approaches 75
    6.3.1   Filter Approach 76
    6.3.2   Wrapper Approach 76
6.4   Conclusion 78
References 78

6.1 Introduction

To use a Brain-Computer Interface (BCI), two stages required are: 1) an offline preparing stage organization during which the arrangement is balanced and 2) an online stage where the structure sees brain development examples and makes an understanding of them for the activity of the PC. The practical online BCI structure begins with the patient conveying a specific example, which is followed by evaluating the EEG signals. EEG signals are routinely pre-taken care of using diverse, and spatial channels (Blankertz et al. 2008), alongside the component expulsion from the signs. Before making an interpretation of the sign in order to provide an input on whether a particular mental action has been performed or not, the EEG signal features are first arranged (Lotte et al. 2007) by a classifier.

Spatial channels are occasionally used for preprocessing the signal features so as to find a change to make a lot of bogus channels by direct mix of the underlying channels. These channels improve the sign to clamor proportion (SNR) and decrease the data dimensionality. Spatial channels depend upon subject-unequivocal information, with the objective that different strategies were made to achieve a particular degree of client freedom. The ghastly information depicts how the force changes and is used in some specific recurrence groups. The transient records depict how the important EEG signals differ with time. This demonstrates the signal utilization at selective time factors or in particular time frames

The essential step which includes extraction targets depicts the sign through several relevant qualities. Such features should lead to the information being embedded in the sign, which is imperative when depicting the mental exercises to recognize, rejecting the antiques, and other non-critical information. Features expelled are usually distributed into a component vector. Features can likewise be tuned by distinguishing the most noteworthy channels or recurrence groups to indicate unmistakable cerebrum movement.

A learning calculation is stood up to with the goal of picking the capabilities and to concentrate on the component determination issue. The regulated learning calculations have a standard plan to improve the classification of exactness on example test information. Rather than trying to achieve exactness, we prioritized finding the capabilities that are most relevant and used them for learning. In administered machine learning, an enlistment calculation is normally provided with fixed preparing of an informational index, in which each datum is depicted by the vector esteems and the features' class name. For example, in clinical visualization issues, the capabilities would potentially comprise of the stature, weight, and so forth, and the class mark may demonstrate whether the healthcare professional diagnosed the disorder of the individual.

As it is understandable to acquire better accuracy for different features, the component subsets need not be one of a kind. For an ideal element subset created by a list of capabilities, choice calculation delivers the most advanced conceivable precision. Alongside the most effective capacity, the pertinence of highlight is likewise a crucial imperative. A component is exceptionally applicable if its disposal brings about execution disintegration. Additionally, an element has less importance in the event that it isn't relevant in every case and in the presence of capabilities which are worse than the general execution. On the off chance that the element is firmly important, it can't be expelled without exactness misfortune. Powerless pertinence infers that the trademark can infrequently add to forecasting exactness.

Different exceptional BCI classifiers (Nicolas-Alonso and Gomez-Gil 2012) exist and are being used. Numerous methodologies often utilize the linear discriminant analysis (LDA) as a classifier. The creators (Shenoy et al. 2006; McFarland et al. 2011) demonstrated that the LDA classifier is retrained on unmistakable informational indexes which deliver a result with a decent classification execution. Another avenue is to utilize a lot of covariance networks as clarified in Vidaurre et al. (2011a and b). The support vector machine (SVM) (Li et al. 2008) and other probabilistic neural classifiers (Millan and Mouriño 2003) are intermittently used to for updates. There are other classification calculations, for example, clump calculations are used to hold the whole dataset and in the event that new records are brought to the preparation dataset, at that point the classification model is recomputed. Additionally, an online classifier intends to explicitly refresh the classification model as new records are received.

Noticeably, in order to improve spatial channels, which have become a key section of classifications, these readings are joined in order to demonstrate these estimations, to report how they were used for BCIs and identify the outcomes. This section is aware of their points of interest and disadvantages and it aims to give examples of how and when to use a specific classification procedure as well as highlighting some of the challenges that must be overcome to enable further advancement in the sign classification. Tripathy et al. (2019) endeavored to progress over explores concerning machine learning for enormous data informative and different techniques with respect to introduce day figuring circumstances for various social applications. Chatterjee (2018a) gave a short review of how machine learning can be utilized in bioinformatics. Chatterjee (2018a) endeavored to give a reasonable and thorough understanding of the IoT in BD structure, examining its different issues and challenges, and concentrating on giving potential recommendations of machine learning procedures.

This section is composed as follows: segment two introduces the ordinarily utilized EEG highlight extraction and its strategies, segment three briefs on the determination systems, and, finally, the procedure is outlined.

6.2 Feature Extraction

In BCI pattern recognition and machine learning systems utilize a classifier, but the additionally incorporate extraction and determination procedures to show the signs in a smaller and more appropriate manner. In particular, the EEG signals are consistently isolated under time region (band-pass channel) and spatial area (spatial channel) before the capabilities are expelled from the consequent signs. The element choice calculation perceives and chooses the best capabilities which, at that point, prepares the classifier. This features different techniques for highlighting extraction strategies to pick the most material features and ways to evaluate the resulting pattern recognition. Despite the fact that there are various component extraction strategies available, the two most regular types of features that could work well are time point features. Additionally, frequency band power features could be an option.

6.2.1 Common Spatial Patterns

Common spatial patterns (CSP) are utilized (Ramoser et al. 2000) to separate features from EEG pointers. The features obtained are absolutely based at a definitive part. Partition resources of CSP are generally attractive for separating two populaces of EEG. The CSP and spatial channels learn the preparation realities rapidly and don't perform appropriately with an enormous amount of heterogeneous measurements (Congedo 2013). A more prominent and pertinent approach is to promptly regularize the CSP trademark and not the covariance grids (Lotte and Guan 2011). Traditional unaided procedures which understand PCA or managed systems that are understanding of CSP can consequently be utilized. Dornhege et al. (2004) have proposed an invariant CSP (iCSP), that regularizes the basic spatial patterns' objective component and decreases the impact of old rarities. The regularization approach is currently proving to be progressive and successful.

6.2.2 Adaptive Common Spatial Patterns

Adaptive common spatial patterns are compelling for patients with hearing difficulty and for crippled patients. An adaptive CSP (ACSP) system was used to manage the intra and bury changeability issues in the bio signal. In order to improve the segregation power, the adaptive CSP makes an analysis of the objective subject and simultaneously overhauls the spatial channels. It additionally supports in characterizing the single preliminary EEG records under testing conditions while preparing data as accessible from one subject and with no preparation records from the objective subjects. The ordinary CSP and its multisubject expansions assess the spatial channels and are additionally arranged for classification (Devlaminck et al. 2011). During classification, in order to improve the multisubject by large execution of CSP, the ACSP approach joins the objective subjects' data with the CSP learning on preliminary premise.

6.2.3 Adaptive CSP Patches

Adaptive CSP patches refer to the capability of the CSP analysis to make small arrangements of channels (patches) and the blending of features. The theory is that applying CSP examination on just two or three channels, the threat of overfitting is diminished with basic CSP, which is then resolved on every single open channel. This is in light of the fact that the number of parameters to fit for each fix isn't as much as that for CSP. The patches can join a substitute number of encompassing channels. Moreover, the focal points of the patches can be picked dependent on the number of channels open and in the assignment. For each fix, different channels identical to the number of included channels are a delayed consequence of the CSP assessment. From those channels, one for each class is picked – for instance, two channels for each fix are achieved. From the ensuing gathering of channels, of the six most helpful ones, three for each class are chosen. Vidaurre et al. (2011) also examined the co-adaptive preparing (both machine and user are continually learning) by using adaptive features and an adaptive LDA classifier. This enabled a couple of users, who were previously unfit to control the BCI, to become able to do so. Co-adaptive preparing that utilizes adaptive CSP patches has been show to be extensively and progressively beneficial (Sannelli et al. 2011). In particular, CSP patches can be seen as a CSP regularize without the need of assessing hyper parameters. It uses covariance grids of lower estimation, improving the gauge of the parameters and thus, basically improving the customer's introduction using the preparation data. It might be assumed that the CSP approach is useful with very few channels or with multi-channel accounts but it is astoundingly proficient, as the amount of alteration data required is thoroughly diminished – interestingly with the bleeding edge.

6.2.4 Canonical Correlation Analysis

Also known as CCA, canonical correction analysis is used for a spatial channel. The goal of CCA is to identify direct changes which builds an understanding of the association between crude EEG signal and the perfect waveform to get a successful spatial channel. The standard CCA is summarized to tensor CCA and multiset CCA which are adequately used to amass the SSVEP flags in BCI (Zhang et al. 2017). Tensor canonical correlation analysis (TCCA), and its successor multiset-standard canonical correlation analysis (MsetCCA), is one of the profitable systems utilized for recurrence recognition in signals. The MsetCCA procedure displays various linear changes which complete the spatial sifting to extend the correlation among canonical variates. This isolates the SSVEP essential capabilities from different arrangements of EEG data gained at a similar boost recurrence. What's more, the improved reference signals are molded by the mix of regular features and furthermore depend absolutely on those features. Expansive test analysis with signals indicate that the tensor CCA and MsetCCA system improves the precision of SSVEP recurrence recognition in correlation with the standard canonical technique, especially with few channels and little available time. The pervasive results exhibited by the tensor CCA and MsetCCA strategy are a promising chance for precision in SSVEP repeat recognition (Zhang et al. 2014).

6.2.5 Band Power Features

Band power features refers to the signs power for a particular repeat band in a given channel, which is clear up at the midpoint or over a specific timeframe. These features can be prepared in various ways and are extensively used for BCIs' oscillatory development, for instance changes in EEG signal amplitudes. With such a limit, the band power features are the best quality level fof eatures for BCI subjects' mental imagery, where some BCI focuses on mental states by disentangling the mental job that need to be done using developments or emotions, or for steady-state visually evoked potential (SSVEP) signals. Various ways to deal with producing band power features from EEG signals are clarified in Brodu et al. (2011). Regardless, at first the EEG signals are band-pass separated from a particular channel to a recurrence band which then squares the ensuing sign to process the signal force lastly midpoints over some stretch of time (for example 1s).

6.2.6 Adaptive Band Power Features

Adaptive band power features highlight and hold up a non-control state, taking up the least amount of time, requiring no BCI ace, and having online capacities subject to only two terminals. The classifiers work commendably in the independently directed globally. The structure performs preliminary based exception rejection and readies a linear discriminant assessment classifier subject to an auto-picked logarithmic band-power. The BCI at first isolated a total of six logarithmic band-powers included in the gatherings from 9 to 13 and 16 to 26 Hz (Faller et al. 2012) from bipolar acceptances at C3 (FC3 – CP3), Cz (FCz – CPz), and C4 (FC4 – CP4). The system proceeded to pick the most extraordinary discriminability as shown by the Fisher model.

6.2.7 Time Point Features

Time point features are a connection of EEG tests from all channels. Ordinarily, these capabilities are expelled after the pre-arrangement, prominently down-testing and band-pass or low-pass filtration. These features mastermind the Event Related Potential that changes the EEG signals amplitude time at an occasion (Lotte 2014). P300 spellers utilizes these features most as often as possible.

6.2.8 Time Points with Adaptive XDAWN

The purpose of xDAWN is to find a change that updates the isolation among signals and antiquities and licenses to diminish the data. The channels could be found by extending the signal-to-noise notwithstanding noise proportion (SSNR) as talked about by the summarized Rayleigh technique. In the standard xDAWN figuring (Rivet et al. 2009), this procedure is tended to by uniting the QR matrix decomposition (QRD) and the singular value decomposition (SVD). The event-related potentials are regularly found by the xDAWN model. The following are recognized as its downsides.

Right off the bat, counts are done in bunch model that stores all data in memory. Furthermore, if the signal fluctuates or additional data should be joined to ad lib the channel, the channels must be recomputed. This is normally not common sense in light of the essential computational effort it requires. Regardless, the solidification of additional information is indispensable for adjustment. As opposed to using the QRD and SVD to find the perfect channels, a consistent methodology that relies upon the recursive least squares (RLS) technique (Rao and Principe 2001) can be used. This strategy has the going with focal points conversely with the customary method: as required for modification, it grants to combine new data into the channel estimation framework and also, it consolidates the refreshed coefficients that changes with the advancing states. The gradual estimation lessens the amount of required memory needed for the computation of the ideal channels.

The adaptive xDAWN (axDAWN) widens the xDAWN spatial channel using a recursive least square approach and is viewed as a novel spatial channel. This upgrade has huge points of interest where it allows the slow estimation of the channel coefficients which are profitable for the memory and computational exertion, and empowers the solidification of new data to alter the present channel to the swaying conditions or another subject.

6.3 Feature Selection and its Approaches

This section displays the ordinarily used component determination systems, as these features are normally the commitment to classifiers. The element choice advances are applied after the extraction to pick the capabilities with various advantages.

1. At first, among the various features that can be isolated from EEG signals, few may be excessive or distinctive to the mental states highlighted by the BCI.

2. Additionally, the number of parameters that will be improved by the classifier is identified with the number of features. Lessening the number of features prompts the classifier to propel the least parameters. Thus, this declines possible overtraining effects and therefore improves the execution – especially there are fewer planning tests.

3. Thirdly, from a data extraction point of view, if only a few features are picked and situated, it is less difficult to identify which highlight has high relevance to the objective cerebrum state.

4. Fourthly, a model with fewer features and less parameters conveys brisk distinguishing proof for another example, as it should be compelling by calculation.

5. Finally, amassing and memory of data will be decreased.

6.3.1 Filter Approach

Channel strategies rely upon proportions of association between the capabilities and the objective independent of the classifier used. The confirmation coefficient, which is processed by squaring the Pearson correlation coefficient, is used as an element situating rule (Hastie et al. 2001). The coefficient of confirmation could likely be used for a two-class issue, stamping −1 or +1 as two distinct classes. The linear conditions among features and target classes are perceived by the correlation coefficient. The clear non-linear preprocessing technique could be applied to misuse non-linear associations. In a similar manner, situating criteria subject to information speculation can be used, for instance on the normal information between each component and the objective (Peng et al. 2005). Many channels highlight choice strategies and request estimation of likelihood densities and the joint thickness of the element and class name of the data. The main course of action is to speak to the features and target class names. The additional aim is to inexact their densities with a nonparametric technique, for instance, Parzen windows. If the densities are evaluated by an ordinary appropriation and the result is achieved through common information, it would look like being obtained by the coefficient of correlation. Channel approaches have linear and multifaceted natures concerning the amount of capabilities. Regardless, this would provoke a decision on repetitive capabilities.

The essential inconvenience of this methodology is the place it completely neglects the effects of the chosen highlight sets of the acceptance calculations' execution. Strategies that fall under the channel approach are: 1) The FOCUS estimation, initially described for without noise, are Boolean spaces which completely see all arrangements of features, picking the most immaterial list of capabilities which are satisfactory to distinguish the mark of value on all the preparation set; and 2) The relief estimation, which apportions a pertinence weight to each list of capabilities that are expected to demonstrate the centrality of the component to the objective information. This technique follows a randomized figuring. It plays out an irregular test on the preparation set and the pertinence value is refreshed. refreshes the significance, regards subject to the difference between the picked event, and the two nearest instances of the proportionate and converse class. On the off chance that the greatest features are relevant to the idea, it would choose most of them − notwithstanding the reality where just a few are needed for basic idea clarification.

6.3.2 Wrapper Approach

Wrapper approaches unravel to the detriment of a progressively drawn out estimation time. A classifier is used this way to deal with recover include sets. The wrapper system chooses a lot of features, moves them to the classifier for preparation, and checks the consequent exhibition. Finally, it drops the pursuit or proposes another subset if the standard isn't satisfied.

An enlistment calculation of the wrapper approach exists within the element choice calculation. This calculation looks through the element subset using the acceptance calculation to break down and evaluate the capabilities. The wrapper strategy is a direct methodology where the enlistment estimation is taken as a black box. To complete a preparation with different courses of action of features ousted from the data, the acceptance count is performed on the information. The element subset with the most significant evaluation is picked as the end and puts forward which acceptance count will be performed. The consequent classifier is additionally evaluated on an unused autonomous test set.

This methodology prompts a hunt of the potential contentions which require a space express, a hidden express, an end state, and a web searcher (Kohavi and John 1997). The chosen hunt space affiliation makes each state indicate a list of capabilities. All of the listed capabilities in a state determine if the component is accessible (1) or missing (0). The accessibility of a state would be either resolve, incorporate, or eradicate a list of capabilities from the state consequently clinging to the most frequently used hunt space in measurements. The target of this hunt is to find the state with the most raised appraisal, using a heuristic way to deal with it directly. The exactness estimation is utilized as both the heuristic and the appraisal work, as the actuated classifiers' real precision isn't known.

The heuristic capacity makes the classification exactness cross-approve the smaller datasets as often as possible, and more often than the big datasets. Since smaller datasets take less effort to prepare, the time taken to assess the exactness (the consequence of the acceptance count time and the cross-endorsement span) doesn't turn out to be exorbitantly fast. This heuristic technique has a disadvantage where smaller datasets experience cross-approval to overcome the greatest distinction producing the least information. For greater datasets, the wrapper approach can be utilized to save significant extra time. Likewise, the embedded method fuses the component choice and the appraisal in a particular system.

The univariate includes determination estimation and surveys the particular force of each element autonomously. By then, the best individual element is chosen. Univariate methodologies are uncommonly speedy and computationally compelling, yet they are simultaneously risky. Since only individual element proficiency is considered, the potential redundancies or complementarities among the features are ignored. The multivariate computations evaluate the various classes of features and hold the supreme features. This calculation utilizes proportions of classification on the preparation set or multivariate shared information measures for the count of the subset of features. This exhibition measure engages to truly consider the impact of redundancies or complementarities among features. Evaluating the value of subsets of features prompts incredibly high computational necessities. Multivariate methodologies normally rely upon heuristics or game plans to diminish the number of subsets to evaluate. They are currently hazardous, yet generally speaking garner a lot of ideal exhibitions over univariate strategies. In any case, the multivariate methodologies may be too deferred for use when the number of features is high.

6.4 Conclusion

Filtering sought after by band force and time focuses include extraction are the most notable extractions used in the EEG-dependent on bio signal handling in comparison to the other segment types that have been examined and used. The most generally utilized extraction is network features. This element type gauges the association and synchronization among signals across different sensors and recurrence bands, which could be assessed using stage lock values and direct exchange capacities. It has been distinguished that a blend of various features, for example, time focuses and band force, or band force and network features, and so on, bring about the most accurate classification in correlation of utilization to a solitary component type. Merging different element types extends dimensionality; consequently, it requires the assurance of the most significant features to keep away from dimensionality issues. Systems to diminish the dimensionality issues are additionally delineated right now. Choice of features have given huge upgrades to BCI, as clarified in section three. For example, the LDA for BCI of P300 framework and recurrence assurance following the sifting strategies. This section likewise discusses the element choice strategies which will be done following the element extraction process. Among all the determination systems examined, the wrapper methodologies (for example, the channel choice dependent on SVM, extraction by linear regressor highlight choice by hereditary calculations and P300, or highlight choice by developmental calculations under multiresolution analysis) are the generally utilized strategies. Unmistakably, metaheuristic strategies are becoming progressively more likely to be conceivably used for highlight assurance to keep up a vital good way from the curse-of-dimensionality.

References

B. Blankertz, R. Tomioka, S. Lemm, M. Kawanabe, and K.-R. Muller. Optimizing spatial filters for robust EEG single-trial analysis. *IEEE Signal Processing Magazine*, 25(1), 41–56, 2008.

N. Brodu, F. Lotte, and A. Lécuyer. Comparative study of band-power extraction techniques for motor imagery classification. In: *Computational Intelligence, Cognitive Algorithms, Mind, and Brain (CCMB) IEEE Symposium on*, 1–6. IEEE, Paris, France, 2011.

J. Chatterjee. IoT with big data framework using machine learning approach. *International Journal of Machine Learning and Networked Collaborative Engineering*, 2(02), 75–85, 2018a.

J. M. Chatterjee. Bioinformatics using machine learning. *Global Journal of Internet Interventions and IT Fusion*, 1(1), 28–35 2018b. [ISSN: 2582-1385 (online)].

M. Congedo. *EEG Source Analysis. Habilitation `a Diriger des Recherches (HDR)*. Univ. Grenoble Alpes, Grenoble, France, TEL, 2013.

D. Devlaminck, B. Wyns, M. Grosse-Wentrup, G. Otte, and P. Santens. Multisubject learning for common spatial patterns in motor-imagery BCI. *Computational Intelliegnce and Neuroscience*, 2011(217987), 1–9, 2011.

G. Dornhege, B. Blankertz, G. Curio, and K. R. Muller. Boosting bit rates in noninvasive EEG single-trial classifications by feature combination and multi-class paradigms. *IEEE Transactions on Bio-Medial Engineering*, 51(6), 993–1002, 2004.

J. Faller, C. Vidaurre, T. Solis-Escalante, C. Neuper, and R. Scherer. Autocalibration and recurrent adaptation: Towards a plug and play online ERD-BCI. *IEEE Transactions on Neural Systems and Rehabilitation Engineering* 20(3), 313–319, 2012.

T. Hastie, R. Tibshirani, and J. Friedman. *The Elements of Statistical Learning*. Springer, New York, New York, 2001.

R. Kohavi and G. H. John. Wrappers for feature subset selection. *Artificial Intelligence*, 97(1), 273–324, 1997. Relevance.

Y. Li, C. Guan, H. Li, and Z. Chin. A self-training semi-supervised SVM algorithm and its application in an EEG-based brain computer interface speller system. *Pattern Recognition Letters*, 29(9), 1285–1294, 2008.

F. Lotte. A tutorial on EEG signal-processing techniques for mental-state recognition in brain– computer interfaces. In: *Guide to Brain-Computer Music Interfacing*, 133–161. Springer, 2014.

F. Lotte, M. Congedo, A. Lécuyer, F. Lamarche, and B. Arnaldi. A review of classification algorithms for EEG-based brain-computer interfaces. *Journal of Neural Engineering*, 4(2), R1–R13, 2007.

F. Lotte and C. Guan. Regularizing common spatial patterns to improve BCI designs: Unified theory and new algorithms. *IEEE Transactions on Bio-Medical Engineering*, 58(2), 355–362, 2011.

D. J. McFarland, W. A. Sarnacki, and J. R. Wolpaw. Should the parameters of a BCI translation algorithm be continually adapted? *Journal of Neuroscience Methods*, 199(1), 2011.

J. R., Millan and J. Mouriño. Asynchronous BCI and local neural classifiers: An overview of the adaptive brain interface project. *IEEE Transactions on Neural Systems and Rehabilitation Engineering*, 11(2), 159–161, 2003.

L. F. Nicolas-Alonso and J. Gomez-Gil. Brain computer interfaces, a review. *Sensors*, 12(2), 1211–1279, 2012.

H. Ramoser, J. Muller-Gerking, and G. Pfurtscheller. Optimal spatial filtering of single trial EEG during imagined hand movement. *IEEE Transactions on Rehabilitation Engineering*, 8(4), 441–446, 2000.

Y. Rao and J. Principe. An RLS type algorithm for generalized eigen- decomposition in neural networks for signal processing XI, 2001. In: *Proceedings of the 2001 IEEE Signal Processing Society Workshop*, North Falmouth, MA, 263–272, 2001.

B. Rivet, A. Souloumiac, V. Attina, and G. Gibert. xDAWN algorithm to enhance evoked potentials: Application to brain computer interface. *Biomedical Engineering, IEEE Transactions On*, 56(8), 2035–2043, 2009.

H. Peng, F. Long, and C. Ding. Feature selection based on mutual information: Criteria of max- dependency, max-relevance, and min-redundancy. *IEEE Transactions on Pattern Analysis and Machine Intelligence*, 27(8), 1226–1238, 2005.

C. Sannelli, C. Vidaurre, K.-R. Mu üller, and B. Blankertz. CSP patches: An ensemble of optimized spatial filters. an evaluation studies. *Journal of Neural Engineering*, 8, 2011.

P. Shenoy, M.Krauledat, B.Blankertz, R. P.Rao, and K. Müller To-wards adaptive classification for BCI. *Journal of Neural Engineering*, 3(1), 2006.

H. K. Tripathy, B. R. Acharya, R. Kumar, and J. M. Chatterjee. Machine learning on big data: A developmental approach on societal applications. In: *Big Data Processing Using Spark in Cloud*, 143–165. Springer, Singapore, 2019.

C. Vidaurre, M. Kawanabe, P. von Bünau, B. Blankertz, K. R. Müller. Toward unsupervised adaptation of LDA for brain computer interfaces. *Biomedical Engineering, IEEE Transactions On*, 58(3), 587–597, 2011a.

C. Vidaurre, C. Sannelli, K.-R. Müller, and B. Blankertz. Co-adaptive calibration to improve BCI efficiency. *Journal of Neural Engineering*, 8(2), 025009, 2011b.

Y. Zhang, G. Zhou, J. Jin, X. Wang, and A. Cichocki. Frequency recognition in SSVEP-based BCI using multiset canonical correlation analysis. *International Journal of Neural Systems*, 24(04):1450013, 2014.

Y. Zhang, G. Zhou, J. Jin, Y. Zhang, X. Wang, and A. Cichocki. Sparse Bayesian multiway canonical correlation analysis for EEG pattern recognition. *Neurocomputing*, 225, 103–110, 2017.

7

Comparison Analysis of Multidimensional Segmentation Using Medical Health-Care Information

Soobia Saeed, Afnizanfaizal Abdullah, N. Z. Jhanjhi,
Memood Naqvi, and Azeem Khan

CONTENTS

7.1 Introduction 81
7.2 Literature Review 83
    7.2.1 Static Structure of Literature Review with Another
        Research Comparison 84
7.3 Methodology 84
    7.3.1 Original Result of Image Testing in Binary Transformation 86
    7.3.2 High Dimension Structured Graphs 87
        7.3.2.1 Grab-Cut 87
7.4 Algorithm 87
7.5 Result Comparison and Discussion 88
7.6 Conclusion 89
Acknowledgments 91
References 91

7.1 Introduction

Graph cutting option in Image Segmented program, graph cut is a semi-automatic segmentation technology that can be used by a researcher to separate an image into front and back components. We can draw lines in the image, called scribbles, to determine what is placed in the foreground and what is placed in the background. The segmented image automatically divides based on the scribble and displays the split image. The researcher can improve segmentation by drawing more scribbles on the image until they are satisfied with the result.

Graph cut technology applies graphics theory to image processing to achieve rapid segmentation. The technique creates a graphic for the image where each pixel is a loop connected to a weighted edge. The more tightly the pixel is bound the more weight. The algorithm cuts the weak edges, splitting the objects in the image. The split image uses a specific set of the graph cut algorithm called "slow adjust". The information for graphics segmentation on segmentation technology, such as graphics segmentation "grab-cut", is an image selected area.

The integrated graphics clipping algorithms have been successfully applied to a wide range of vision and graphics problems. This article focuses on the simplest graphic cutting app: segmenting an object in image data. In addition to its simplicity, this application embodies the best features of harmonic graphics cutting methods of vision: the optimum global level, practical efficiency, and numerical durability, the ability to integrate a wide range of signals, optical restrictions, untied topological character sectors, and the applicability of ND problems. It has also been proven that the graphics-based methods used to extract objects have exciting links with previous hash methods, such as snakes, active geodesic systems, and level groups. Improved division energies with realistic fragments consolidate limit association and locale-based properties similarly as Mumford-Shah's utilitarian style. We give the motivation and a point-by-point specialized portrayal of the fundamental consonant advancement system for picture division by cutting s/t illustrations.

Figure 7.1 shows the process of graph cutting and also the selected region of cutting area as we can use this tool for selecting the specific area for detecting the disease.

The high-dimensional segmentation process is used to cut graphics and find image quality. All images use the same process but the quality is different across four dimensions. After implementing the images, we can find

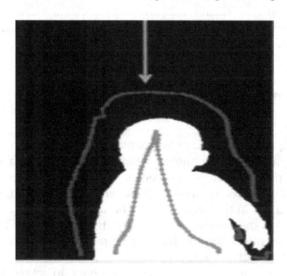

FIGURE 7.1
Graph cutting using MATLAB.

something unique to choose the pictures Or, the quality of all the images improved compared to the 3D images, but if we use the color images in 4D segmentation, the result is more better then black and white images especially The quality of the images varies in colon versus white and black, as mentioned in the experimental results.

7.2 Literature Review

Segmentation is one of the most significant assignments in the field of PC vision and has been studied for a long time. One of the best-known image splitting techniques is grab-cut (Saeed et al.), which is a moderate way to split the foreground and background of 2D images. This is already implemented in many photo editing software applications. Grab-cut depends on graphic cutting algorithms (Boykov and Jolly 2001; Boykov and Kolmogorov 2004; Boykov, Veksler, and Zabih 2001). Graphics cuts can be applied to dimensional information, including pictures, video successions, and 3D structures (Gamage and Ranathunga 2017), and can likewise be stretched out to different ticks (Mendrik et al. 2015). In graph cut methods, data is treated as a header and edging layout structure. The head is the top of each pixel, and adjacent pixels are tied with a balanced edge based on their similarity. In cases involving segmentation of multiple poster images, each poster also has a special summit called a station. Pixel heads are associated with all stations, where mark weights determine the likelihood of classification. The way to find pieces in a graph at the lowest cost is to get hash with the least amount of energy available, and the minimum flow algorithm will solve this problem. (Cho, Kim, and Tai 2014; Fiss, Curless, and Szeliski 2015; Ferlay, Soerjomataram, Dikshit et al. 2015; Chen, Lin, Yu, Kang, and Yu 2014; Ferlay, Soerjomataram, Dikshit et al. 2015). The top of the growth is attached to one end after cutting, which means placing the opposite poster on the other side. Our method also uses the scheme-splitting process. These segmentation techniques are known as moderate strategies since they are proof requiring client intercession. While some realistic section strategies (Abdullah et al. 2012; Abdullah et al. 2013; Saeed et al. 2019a; Saeed and Jafri 2015) can deal with information from any separation, they are not always perfect for high-dimensional information, for example, video clips. Video information has a conflicting structure along the time hub, in contrast to 3D storage data. Therefore, fragmentation methods can be strengthened by taking into account the dysfunctional neighborhood relationships (Jarabo et al. 2014; D. Horn and Chen 2007). Video segmentation quality can be improved by identifying live neighborhood relationships that correspond to neighborhood frame pixels. A problem with clear 4D field data that is similar to video data is that repetition is evident in the complex field (Bishop, Tom E., and Paolo Favaro, 2007).

Our research method is the first method that uses a graphic cut method to focus on segmenting a 4D light field. Meanwhile, some unsupervised approaches may be used for wide-angle or 4D focus images. Kolmogorov and Zabih (2002) suggested dividing the 4D light fields based on a levelling method (Kolmogorov and Zabih 2002; Kowdle et al. 2012; Levoy and Hanrahan 1996) that applies an active contour method to a large 4D portion. The researchers Lin, Chen, Kang, and Yu (2015), suggest a method for deep marking of multiple-width images based on the fact that foreground objects cannot be excluded by deeper objects. Additionally, Saeed, Abdullah, Jhanjhi, and Abdullah (2019b), Maeno et al. (2013), and Marx et al. (2009) suggest a method to automatically extract objects from images of different lengths using the contrast signal. The technique uses contrast and appearance signals in multiple images to determine the probability of foreground objects. Shaw et al. define areas of transparent species as bright areas, and an uncensored approach is suggested. This method uses the light field distortion function (Ng et al. 2005; Osher and Sethian 1988; Lin et al. 2015, which represents the possibility that pixels belong to a transparent object area, as well as the method for segmenting divided binary graphics. Despite the success of these methods, the uncensored methods are not suitable for clearly selecting the region for its liberation because the areas of interest differ from one user to another, (Saeed and Abdullah 2019; Platt 1999; Rother, Kolmogorov, and Blake 2004). This suggests a segmentation method for images using a 4D light field that uses presence and contrast signals similar to (Wanner and Goldluecke 2012; Wanner, Meister, and Goldluecke 2013) with respect to supervised methods. They train a randomly chosen forest workbook to combine appearance and inequality in order to deal with different types of information in nature and obtain a specific probability for each brand. Despite its success, the only way that segmentation results occur is in the two-dimensional central image (Wanner, Straehle, and Goldluecke 2013; Xu, Nagahara, Shimada, and Taniguchi 2015).

7.2.1 Static Structure of Literature Review with Another Research Comparison

Table 7.1 shows the complete details of other research relating to the current work of graph cutting as mention in previous section and introduction.

7.3 Methodology

The proposed research aims to collect data relating to the detection of brain cancer (due to the creation of CSF leaks) with a high MRI interface. The

TABLE 7.1

Comparison of Previous Research

Name	Author's Affiliation	Techniques	Responses/Results
Brain Tumor (Cancer)	Miller 2016	To Provide the information of Cancer, Brain cancer, spin and spinal cord	High Response time
Brain tumor with MRI	Giorgio 2013	To Provide the details of Deep Neural Network	High Response time, High Accuracy
Cerebrospinal Fluid-CSF	Altaf et al. 2016	To Provide the detail of CSF	High Response time
Cerebrospinal Fluid leakage	Green et al. 2017	To Provide the experimental results of CSF leakage	High Response time
4D light field segmentation method	Mihara et al. 2018	To provide the Results of light field editing tools	High Response time, High Accuracy
Light Field Toolbox	Mihara et al. 2018	To provide the Results of light field editing tools and Photoshop R	High Response time, High Accuracy

researcher discusses damaged brain cells caused by cell abnormalities. It is a qualitative research study, therefore; it includes extensive primary and secondary sources, including comparative research studies from contemporary publications. The main goal of our work is to build a framework that can recognize the field of tumors or isolate between malignant tumors and benign tumors. Initially, the MRI image is outfitted with a specific final image fix target for the rest of the procedures with the help of the high-dimensional clear field toolbox and its graphical representation.

The sampling groups used for the study are medical brain images of humans. The researcher will practically implement and simulate experiments (3D and 4D image segmentation process) for tests on humans and their random brain tissue (a sample from the human brain) from Malaysia. The main goal of our proposed model is to detect the leakage point using graph cutting that can detect cerebrospinal fluid loss in the brain and tumor area, or that can differentiate between the patients who are with and without tumors. The data is collected through various sources, which apply the necessary research tools. The graph cutting tool is one of the main tools which will be highlighted in the main point, and which will be used to help identify the disease. In this research, graph cutting algorithms explore the missing information by taking the attribute such as stage of cancer and CSF leakage. This model identifies cancer at a very early stage.

Figure 7.2 shows the structure of the methodological work as we follow the direction of this method step by step and proposed the algorithm

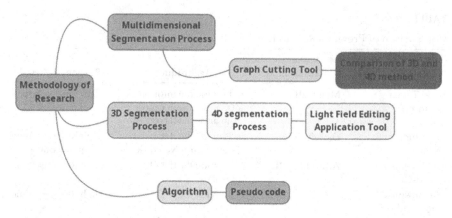

FIGURE 7.2
Conceptual framework of methodology.

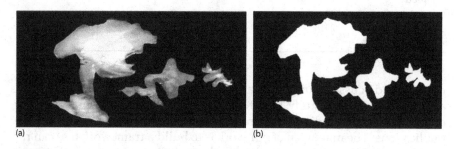

FIGURE.7.3
(a) Binary transformation graph cutting tool in MATLAB.

7.3.1 Original Result of Image Testing in Binary Transformation

The binary transformation form of graph cutting is given below:

Figure 7.3 (a) shows the selected area of region in a skull and implements the filter tool using the graph cutting tool in this image after the binary transformation to refine the image.

Figure 7.3 (a) and (b) show the end stage of cancer (tumor) as this stage is not recovered as it is clearly visible in the images. In this figure shows that image is the last stage of cancer (tumor) with few forms of CSF leakage as this is totally converted to the hard shell of the tumor as well as cancer which is deposited in the upper side of the brain. After implementation of the graph cutting method, it clearly displays the size of the tumor in 3D format. Grabcut is a graphic form of clip art. The algorithm estimates the black and white distribution of the target object and the greyscale in the background using the Gaussian model and starting with turning a user-defined chart in the object into a clip. This is used to create a random Markov field in pixel tags using the control function.

7.3.2 High Dimension Structured Graphs

The explanation of high dimension graph structured is given below:

7.3.2.1 Grab-Cut

Grab-cut is a graphic form of clip art. The calculation assesses the shading dissemination of the objective article and the foundation shading utilizing the Gaussian mixture model and starts with turning a client characterized pattern in the item into an area. This is utilized to make an arbitrary Markov field in pixel labels by utilizing the control work. The incline is towards a similar blurb in the associated zones and improves the graph to gather their qualities. This gauge might be more exact than the first taken from the limit outline. This methodology is rehashed in two stages until combination happens. Clients of mistakenly grouped and improved areas can likewise address gauges. The technique likewise amends the outcomes to protect the edges.

7.4 Algorithm

The relevant algorithms are given below:

Algorithm.1: For Detection of CSF Spot in Image (One Input and One Output-2D)

```
1. % Convert RGB DICOM into L*a*b* BW space.
2. X = rgb2lab (BW);
3. % Create vacant mask.
4. BW = false (size(X,1),size(X,2));
5. m = size(BW, 1);
6. n = size(BW, 2);
7. added Area = poly2mask(xPos, yPos, m, n);
8. BW = BW | added Area;
9. % Create concealedDICOM.
10.ConcealedDICOM (repmat(~BW,[1 1 3])) = 0;
11.End;
```

Algorithm.2: For Texture Feature Image Include (One Input and One Output)

```
1.% Convert RGB DICOM into L*a*b* BW space.
2.X = rgb2lab(BW);
3.% Create vacantconcealment.
4.BW = false (size(X, 1), size(X, 2));
```

```
5. m = size(BW, 1);
6. n = size(BW, 2);
7. Added Area = poly2mask (xPos, yPos, m, n);
8. % Create concealed DICOM.
9. Concealed DICOM = BW
10.Concealed DICOM (repmat(~BW,[1 1 3])) = 0;
11.End;
```

**Algorithm.3: For Detection of CSF Spot in Image
(Two Outputs and One Input)**

```
12.% Convert RGB DICOM into L*a*b* color space.
13.X = rgb2lab (RGB);
14.% Create vacantconcealment.
15.BW = false (size(X,1),size(X,2));
16.% Draw Freehand
17.m = size(BW, 1);
18.n = size(BW, 2);
19.Added Area = poly2mask (xPos, yPos, m, n);
20.BW = BW | added Area;
21.% Create concealed DICOM.
22.Concealed DICOM = RGB;
23.Concealed DICOM (repmat(~BW,[1 1 3])) = 0;
24.End;
```

7.5 Result Comparison and Discussion

These comparisons are based on semi-supervised machine learning as we work on the comparison between 3D and segmentation of the dimensional images. The findings of the tests are conducted by a dataset called "Malignant Brain Cancer with CSF Leakage" by compiling previous and current images using graph-cutting algorithms. Using the training dataset, we trained several supervised machine-learning models. In this article, the researcher reveals a brain cancer as we analyse both dimensions MRI images and interfacing image field segmentation. Initially, the MRI handled the prepared image method with the ultimate goal of adjusting the image for the rest of the procedure. According to this study, brain cancer and CSF were detected due to the interface of the 4D image segmentation process.

Therefore, the research study consists of primary and secondary sources, followed by a cutting technique for the software using graph-cutting tool that uses images of original medical samples to measure the extent of damaged cells in the brain and applies the method of cutting graphics using MATLAB tools and algorithms. In this study, the researcher proposes a 4D modulation method that monitors the light field that can be used to emit light with changing colour and binary. By creating a 4D hierarchy, 4D light fields can be divided to reduce the graphics algorithm generated by the 4D scheme. The researcher uses this technique to release damaged brain samples from the brain's skull. These results demonstrate the effectiveness of our approach to light editing applications. Light field methods can be useful in improving the quality of photo editing applications and compound lighting field tubes, as they reduce the effects of artistic edges.

We aim to overcome the value of lost data in the computational experiments of the proposed new method. To do this, we used a structured algorithm of graphs with correlation and multiple types of data in time series. We explained that improving the calculated data to determine the variables of the verification method is related to the delay of the test time and the training vector resulting from the time delay. The graph cut method demonstrates the accuracy of images with results, and maintains color change and binary change, as well as producing outputs and inputs.

Table.7.2 shows the comparison between the 3D and 4D (Figure 7.4.a, Figure 7.4.b) dimension image segmentation processes, as we can see the huge difference between the results and accuracy of the images. In the 4D image, the researcher used a light field image segmentation process. In light field segmentation process shows the two inputs and generates the output in binary transformation after the implementation of the graph cutting tool with a filter on the edge cutting image but in 4D only one input generates the binary transformation in output form.

7.6 Conclusion

In this article, the researcher suggests that there is a supervised 4D field for structured 4D graphics, and that 4D light field images can be divided using a graphic clipping algorithm. Experimental results show that our method achieves greater accuracy than previous methods using general lighting field data sets from the American Cancer Society Center and CSF. In addition, the researcher applied the proposed method to the original images and showed the result in changing the color and duo with one and two directors. These results demonstrate the efficiency of our clear field image editing process using the graphics algorithm. The problem is calculation time duration. Because the use of the graphic cut algorithm requires a large amount of calculation time when there are many peaks; the obvious future goal is to solve this problem.

TABLE.7.2

Comparison of Previous and High Dimension Image

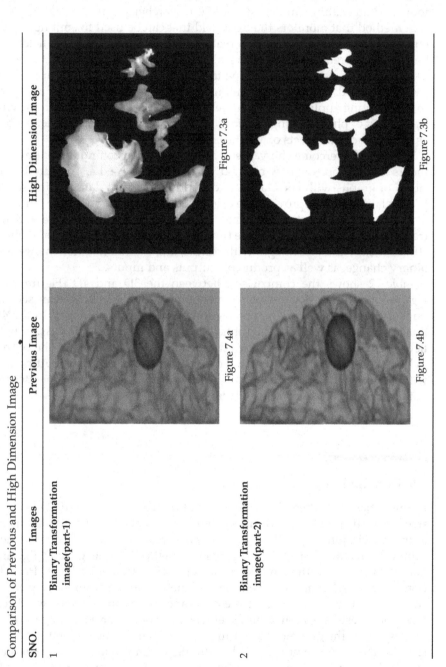

SNO.	Images	Previous Image	High Dimension Image
1	Binary Transformation image(part-1)	Figure 7.4a	Figure 7.3a
2	Binary Transformation image(part-2)	Figure 7.4b	Figure 7.3b

Acknowledgments

The authors are grateful to the Department of Software Engineering, and the faculty of computing, at Universiti Teknologi Malaysia-UTM, Malaysia for the financial support needed to carry out this work.

References

Abdullah, Afnizanfaizal, et al. "An improved swarm optimization for parameter estimation and biological model selection". *PLoS One* 8(4) (2013): 4.

Abdullah, Afnizanfaizal, et al. "Cerebrospinal fluid pulsatile segmentation-a review". *The 5th 2012 Biomedical Engineering International Conference*, IEEE, Thailand 2012.

Adelson, Edward H., and James R. Bergen. *The Plenoptic Function and the Elements of Early Vision*, Vol. 2. Vision and Modeling Group, Media Laboratory, Massachusetts Institute of Technology, Cambridge, MA: MIT Press, 1991.

Altaf I, Vohra AH and Shams S. "Management of cerebrospinal fluid leak following posterior cranial fossa surgery". *Pak. J. Med. Sci.* 2 (2016): 1439–1443.

Berent, Jesse, and Pier Luigi Dragotti "Unsupervised extraction of coherent regions for image based rendering". Proceedings of the British Machine Vision Conference 2007, University of Warwick, BMVC, United kingdom, (2007).

Bishop, Tom E., and Paolo Favaro. "The light field camera: Extended depth of field, aliasing, and superresolution". *IEEE Transactions on Pattern Analysis and Machine Intelligence* 34(5) (2011): 972–986.

Boykov, Yuri Y., and M.-P. Jolly. "Interactive graph cuts for optimal boundary & region segmentation of objects in ND images". *Proceedings of the Eighth IEEE International Conference on Computer Vision. ICCV 2001*, Vol. 1. IEEE, Vancouver, BC, Canada, 2001.

Boykov, Yuri, and Vladimir Kolmogorov. "An experimental comparison of min-cut/max-flow algorithms for energy minimization in vision". *IEEE Transactions on Pattern Analysis and Machine Intelligence* 26(9) (2004): 1124–1137.

Boykov, Yuri, Olga Veksler, and Ramin Zabih. "Fast approximate energy minimization via graph cuts". *IEEE Transactions on Pattern Analysis and Machine Intelligence* 23(11) (2001): 1222–1239.

Chen, Can, et al. "Light field stereo matching using bilateral statistics of surface cameras". *Proceedings of the IEEE Conference on Computer Vision and Pattern Recognition*, San Juan, Puerto Rico, USA, 2014.

Cho, Donghyeon, Sunyeong Kim, and Yu-Wing Tai. "Consistent matting for light field images". *European Conference on Computer Vision*, Springer, Cham, 2014.

Ferlay, Jacques, et al. "Cancer incidence and mortality worldwide: Sources, methods and major patterns in GLOBOCAN 2012." *International Journal of Cancer* 136(5) (2015): E359–E386.

Fiss, Juliet, Brian Curless, and Rick Szeliski. "Light field layer matting". *Proceedings of the IEEE Conference on Computer Vision and Pattern Recognition*, San Juan, Puerto Rico, USA, 2015.

Gamage, P. T., and Dr Lochandaka Ranathunga. "Identification of brain tumor using image processing techniques". *Faculty of Information Technology, University of Moratuwa,* 2017. https://www. researchgate. net/publication/276133543.

Giorgio A, De Stefano N. "Clinical use of brain volumetry". *J Magn Reson Imaging* 37(1) (2013): 1–55.

Green AL, et al. "A multicentre, prospective, randomized, controlled study to evaluate the use of a fibrin sealant as an adjunct to sutured dural repair". *Br. J. Neurosurg.* 2(2) (2014): 1–7.

Greig, Dorothy M., Bruce T. Porteous, and Allan H. Seheult. "Exact maximum a posteriori estimation for binary images". *Journal of the Royal Statistical Society: Series B (Methodological)* 51(2) (1989): 271–279.

Hajime Mihara et al. "4D Light Field Segmentation with Spatial and Angular Consistencies". *MEXT* Japan, 2 (2018): 1–8.

Horn, Daniel Reiter, and Billy Chen. "Light shop: Interactive light field manipulation and rendering". *Proceedings of the 2007 Symposium on Interactive 3D Graphics and Games,* New York, 2007.

Jarabo, Adrian, et al. "How do people edit light fields?" *ACM Transactions on Graphics (Proc. SIGGRAPH)* 33(4): 1–12, (2014).

Kimberly Miller. "Cancer treatment & survivorship facts & figures", *American Cancer Society* 2(1) (2016): 1–44.

Kolmogorov, Vladimir, and Ramin Zabih. "Multi-camera scene reconstruction via graph cuts". *European Conference on Computer Vision.* Springer, Berlin, Heidelberg, 2002.

Kowdle, Adarsh, Sudipta N. Sinha, and Richard Szeliski. "Multiple view object cosegmentation using appearance and stereo cues." *European Conference on Computer Vision.* Springer, Berlin, Heidelberg, 2012.

Levoy, Marc, and Pat Hanrahan. "Light field rendering". *Proceedings of the 23rd Annual Conference on Computer Graphics and Interactive Techniques,* New York, 1996.

Lin, Haiting, et al. "Depth recovery from light field using focal stack symmetry". *Proceedings of the IEEE International Conference on Computer Vision,* France, 2015.

Marx, K., Andrew Lumsdaine, and Todor Georgiev. "The focused plenoptic camera". *IEEE International Conference on Computational Photography (ICCP).* IEEE, 2009.

Maeno, Kazuki, et al. "Light field distortion feature for transparent object recognition". *Proceedings of the IEEE Conference on Computer Vision and Pattern Recognition,* San Juan, Puerto Rico, 2013.

Mendrik, Adriënne M., et al. "MRBrainS challenge: Online evaluation framework for brain image segmentation in 3T MRI scans". *Computational Intelligence and Neuroscience* 2015, 1–12, (2015).

Nagahashi, Tomoyuki, Hironobu Fujiyoshi, and Takeo Kanade. "Video segmentation using iterated graph cuts based on spatio-temporal volumes". *Asian Conference on Computer Vision.* Springer, Berlin, Heidelberg, 2009.

Ng, Ren, et al. "Light field photography with a hand-held plenoptic camera". *Computer Science Technical Report CSTR* 2(11) (2005): 1–11.

Osher, Stanley, and James A. Sethian. "Fronts propagating with curvature-dependent speed: Algorithms based on Hamilton-Jacobi formulations". *Journal of Computational Physics* 79(1) (1988): 12–49.

Platt, John. "Probabilistic outputs for support vector machines and comparisons to regularized likelihood methods". *Advances in Large MARGIN Classifiers* 10(3) (1999): 61–74.

Rother, Carsten, Vladimir Kolmogorov, and Andrew Blake. "'GrabCut' interactive foreground extraction using iterated graph cuts." *ACM Transactions on Graphics (TOG)* 23(3) (2004): 309–314.

Saeed, Soobia, Afnizanfaizal Abdullah, and N. Z. Jhanjhi. "Analysis of the lung cancer patient's for data mining tool". *IJCSNS* 19(7) (2019a): 90.

Saeed, Soobia, Afnizanfaizal Abdullah, and N. Z. Jhanjhi. "Implementation of Fourier transformation with brain cancer and CSF images". *Indian Journal of Science and Technology* 12(37) (2019b): 37.

Saeed, Soobia, and Afnizanfaizal Abdullah. "Recognition of brain cancer and cerebrospinal fluid due to the usage of different MRI image by utilizing support vector machine". *Bulletin of Electrical Engineering and Informatics* 9(2) (2020): 619–625.

Saeed, Soobia, and Afnizanfaizal Bin Abdullah. "Investigation of a brain cancer with interfacing of 3-dimensional image processing". *2019 International Conference on Information Science and Communication Technology (ICISCT)*. IEEE, Pakistan, 2019.

Saeed, Soobia, and Raza Jafri. "Estimation of brain tumor using latest technology of mobile phone". *Journal of Information and Communication Technology (JICT)* 9(1) (2015): 32–09.

Wanner, Sven, and Bastian Goldluecke. "Globally consistent depth labeling of 4D light fields". *2012 IEEE Conference on Computer Vision and Pattern Recognition*. IEEE, Rhode Island, 2012.

Wanner, Sven, Stephan Meister, and Bastian Goldluecke "Datasets and benchmarks for densely sampled 4D light fields"1–9. *VMV* 13 (2013).

Wanner, Sven, Christoph Straehle, and Bastian Goldluecke. "Globally consistent multi-label assignment on the ray space of 4d light fields". *Proceedings of the IEEE Conference on Computer Vision and Pattern Recognition*, Washington, D.C., 2013.

Xu, Yichao, et al. "Transcut: Transparent object segmentation from a light-field image". *Proceedings of the IEEE International Conference on Computer Vision*, France, 2015.

8

Deep Convolutional Network Based Approach for Detection of Liver Cancer and Predictive Analytics on Cloud

Pramod H. B. and Goutham M.

CONTENTS

8.1 Introduction 95
    8.1.1 Types of Liver Diseases 98
8.2 Medical Images and Deep Learning 100
    8.2.1 Micro-Service Architecture 101
    8.2.2 Integration of NVDIA GPU for Deep Learning on Cloud 101
    8.2.3 Presenting the Sockets and Slots for Processors 102
    8.2.4 Clock Details of Deep Learning Server 102
    8.2.5 Threads for Deep Learning–Based Computations 103
    8.2.6 Available Hard Disk for Use 103
    8.2.7 Memory 103
    8.2.8 Overall Details of Used Computing Environment with Deep Convolutional Networks 103
8.3 Deep Learning for Liver Diagnosis with the Projected Model 103
8.4 Proposed Model and Outcomes 104
8.5 Conclusion 107
References 109

8.1 Introduction

Health is one of the most important things for human beings and thus it needs to be maintained with the utmost care. Since the advent of human life, the wish to live better and for longer has been of great interest to researchers. A number of techniques and approaches in the medical sciences exist whereby the enormous paradigms and theories relate to the understanding of human life (Ferlay et al. 2010; Lu et al. 2006; Moghbel et al. 2018; Prasoon et al. 2013).

This chapter focuses on the advanced implementation of deep learning based on convolutional networks for medical diagnosis, and it places a specific focus on diseases of the liver as the liver is one of the key components and organs within the human body (Ronneberger et al. 2015; Stollenga et al. 2015; Roth et al. 2015; Wang et al. 2015).

Nowadays, the world faces an enormous number of diseases of which many are life-threatening. Some organs are considered as particularly sensitive as far as dangerous diseases are concerned, and these are:

1. Liver

2. Heart

3. Kidney

4. Lungs

If even a small segment of a hazardous disease touches these organs, it will be quite dangerous for the person's life.

Life-threatening diseases are chronic, often incurable diseases, which have the effect of considerably limiting a person's life expectancy (Li et al. 2016; Çiçek et al. 2016; Havaei et al. 2017; Chen et al. 2017). These include cancer, diabetes, neurological conditions, coronary heart disease, and HIV/Aids. Others include:

1. Dengue

2. Ebola

3. Plague

4. Enterovirus

5. Cholera

6. MRSA

7. Cerebrovascular

8. Chagas

9. Meningococcal

10. Necrotizing

Liver disease occurs as a result of infections in different ways as mentioned here:

1. Hepatitis A: Fatigue, Diarrhea, Fever, Nausea

2. Hepatitis B: Weakness, Pain, Yellowing

3. Hepatitis C: Muscle Aches, Yellow Tinge, Bowel Movements

The common symptoms of the liver disease are:

1. Dark urine

2. Yellow skin and eyes, known as jaundice

3. Vomiting

4. Pale, bloody, or black stool

5. Nausea

6. Swollen ankles, legs, or abdomen

7. Itchy skin

8. Easy bruising

9. Decreased appetite

10. Ongoing fatigue

11. Jaundice

12. Diarrhea

13. Confusion

14. Fatigue and weakness

15. Nausea

The following are the key risk factors associated with liver issues:

1. Getting a tattoo or body piercing with non-sterile needles

2. Sharing needles

3. Having a job where you're exposed to blood and other bodily fluids

4. Unsafe sex

5. Diabetes

6. High cholesterol

7. Having a family history of liver disease

8. Being overweight

9. Exposure to toxins or pesticides

10. Taking certain supplements or herbs, especially in large amounts

11. Ascites

12. Accumulation of fluid in the abdomen

13. Endoscopy

14. Nonsurgical procedure

15. Jaundice

16. Yellowing of the skin and the whites of the eyes

17. Tumors

18. Abnormal growth of cells

19. Varices

20. Shunts

Various issues that affect the human liver can be identified in a CT Scan or through deep images of the liver, with medical imaging and dynamic libraries used for getting the images.

These issues include:

1. Lesions
2. Injuries
3. Bleeding
4. Infections
5. Abscesses
6. Infections
7. Obstructions

In terms of the cumulative health of the human liver, fatty liver cells with less than 5% are considered to be healthy. If these values move beyond 5%, it is considered as a fatty liver which is one of the key diseases throughout the world nowadays.

Statista is one of the key portals for research and statistical analytics whereby the enormous research surveys and development are discussed with a high degree of accuracy and presentation. In the following research analytics, liver transplants are presented. There have been huge related elevations conducted in the United States in 2018, and it must be taken into consideration by the researchers as liver disease is being research using deep learning (Wolpert 1992; Soler et al. 2001; Moltz et al. 2008; Wong et al. 2008).

The statistical analytics present the major locations of key countries that are suffering from health issues and liver problems, as shown in graphical outcomes in terms of ethnicity.

Figure 8.1 highlights the assorted stages of liver issues which need to be evaluated and understood while presenting a predictive analytics on liver disease.

8.1.1 Types of Liver Diseases

1. Laennec's cirrhosis
2. Hepatic encephalopathy
3. Non-cirrhotic portal fibrosis
4. Hy's law
5. Peliosis hepatis
6. Liver failure
7. Wilson's disease
8. Liver abscesses
9. Epithelial-mesenchymal transition
10. Bland embolization
11. Alcoholic liver disease

Health Liver ➡ <5% Fatty Liver Cells

Steatosis (Fatty Liver) ➡ >5% Fatty Liver Cells

Nash Without Fibrosis ➡ Steatosis + Inflammation + Ballooning

Nash With Fibrosis ➡ Steatosis + Inflammation + Ballooning + Fibrosis (1 to 3)

Cirrhosis Or Cancer ➡ Advanced Fibrosis

Or Other Outcomes

FIGURE 8.1
Stages of liver issues.

12. Cirrhosis
13. Hepatosplenomegaly
14. Chronic liver disease
15. Zahn infarct
16. Fibrolamellar hepatocellular carcinoma
17. Alpha-1 antitrypsin deficiency
18. North American Indian childhood cirrhosis
19. Hepatopulmonary syndrome
20. Gastric antral vascular ectasia
21. Focal fatty liver
22. Congenital hepatic fibrosis
23. Acute liver failure
24. Congenital hypofibrinogenemia
25. Fatty liver disease
26. Primary biliary cholangitis
27. Pediatric end-stage liver disease
28. Hepatolithiasis
29. Hepato-biliary diseases
30. Viral hepatitis
31. Hepatotoxicity

32. Mucinous cystic neoplasm
33. Acute fatty liver of pregnancy
34. Alveolar hydatid disease
35. Congestive hepatopathy
36. Steatohepatitis
37. Polycystic liver disease
38. Indian childhood cirrhosis
39. Bacillary peliosis
40. Liver cancer
41. Progressive familial intrahepatic cholestasis
42. Non-alcoholic fatty liver disease
43. Zieve's syndrome

All of these illnesses and diseases need to be analyzed with effective algorithms.

8.2 Medical Images and Deep Learning

There is a very close relationship between Artificial Intelligence (AI), machine learning, deep learning, convolutional networks, and deep learning–based convolutional networks. These paradigms are widely used for solving the high-performance computations associated with medical imaging and many other related challenges (Jimenez-Carretero et al. 2011; Huang et al. 2014; Vorontsov et al. 2014; Le et al. 2016; Kuo et al. 2017). Figure 8.2 presents the close association between the terms AI, machine learning, and deep learning which are widely integrated for data analytics in the medical domain.

All these research streams are closely associated and when used together from the highest degree of performance and computational intelligence. The usage patterns of these approaches can be extracted from the enormous implementation patterns which are used in assorted research domains and even in cloud-based platforms and research environments (33Conze et al. 2017; Hoogi et al. 2017; Chaieb et al. 2017; Christ et al. 2017; Han 2017; Vorontsov et al. 2017).

The following are the tools and technologies used for the implementation of deep learning–based algorithms in cloud-based environments so that there is no need to purchase the dedicated infrastructure (Table 8.1).

The key features embedded in the suites include: (Chlebus et al. 2017; Zhou et al. 2017a; Farag et al. 2017; Zhou et al. 2017; Roth et al. 2017).

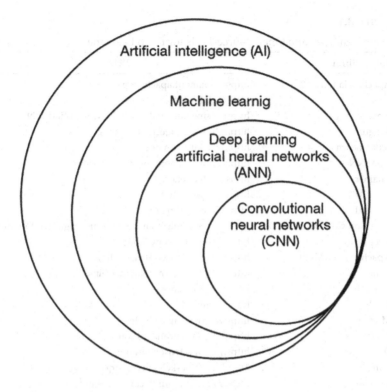

FIGURE 8.2
Association in assorted segments of Artificial Intelligence.

8.2.1 Micro-Service Architecture

1. APIs for Java, Python, and Scala
2. Massive amounts of data processed using clusters
3. Scalability on Hadoop for big data
4. Parallel computing and training
5. Distributed architecture with multi-threading
6. Support for GPU for scalability on Amazon Web Services (AWS) cloud
7. Support to CPU and GPU (Table 8.2)

8.2.2 Integration of NVDIA GPU for Deep Learning on Cloud

!nvidia-smi
!nvidia-smi -L
!lscpu | grep "Model"

TABLE 8.1

Prominent Free and Open Source Tools for Deep Learning

Tool / Library	URL
Apache Mahout	https://mahout.apache.org/
DLib	http://dlib.net/
Apache Singa	https://singa.incubator.apache.org/en/index.html
Shogun	http://www.shogun-toolbox.org/
Scikit-Learn	http://scikit-learn.org/
OpenNN	http://www.opennn.net/
Chainer	https://chainer.org/
OpenAI	https://openai.com/
Edward	http://edwardlib.org/
Microsoft Cognitive Toolkit	https://www.microsoft.com/en-us/cognitive-toolkit/
DeepLearning4j	https://deeplearning4j.org/
Apache Spark MLib	https://spark.apache.org/mllib/
Lime	https://github.com/marcotcr/lime
PyTorch	http://pytorch.org/
Torch	http://torch.ch/
MXNet	https://mxnet.apache.org/
Neon	http://neon.nervanasys.com
TensorFlow	https://www.tensorflow.org/
Caffe	http://caffe.berkeleyvision.org/
Gensim	https://radimrehurek.com/gensim/
Oryx 2	http://oryx.io/
MLDB	https://mldb.ai/
Keras	https://keras.io/

TABLE 8.2

Cloud-Based Deep Learning Services for High Performance Computations

Cloud Service	URL
Google Colaboratory	http://colab.research.google.com
PaperSpace	https://www.paperspace.com
Neptune	https://www.neptune.ml
Nvidia GPU Cloud	https://www.nvidia.com/en-us/gpu-cloud
BigML	https://www.bigml.com
GPU Eater	https://www.gpueater.com

8.2.3 Presenting the Sockets and Slots for Processors

!lscpu | grep "Details of Socket"

!lscpu | grep "Number of Cores / Socket:"

8.2.4 Clock Details of Deep Learning Server

!lscpu | grep "MHz"

8.2.5 Threads for Deep Learning–Based Computations

!lscpu | grep "L3 Cache"

!lscpu | grep "Thread(s) per Core"

8.2.6 Available Hard Disk for Use

!df –hT /

8.2.7 Memory

!cat /proc/meminfo | grep "MemAvailable"

8.2.8 Overall Details of Used Computing Environment with Deep Convolutional Networks

1. CPU
   - Xeon Processors
   - 45MB Cache
   - 1 Single core Hyper Threaded (1 Core, 2 Threads)
   - 3Ghz (No Turbo Boost)
2. GPU
   - 2496 CUDA cores
   - Compute 3.7
   - 1xTesla K80
   - 12GB GDDR5 VRAM
   - Server Idle Time: 90 minutes
   - RAM: More than 12 GB on Cloud
   - Disk: More than 30 GB on Cloud

8.3 Deep Learning for Liver Diagnosis with the Projected Model

Images of the liver are taken by medical imaging and automation libraries. The predicted mask has the association and knowledge of the key points and features which are required for predictive analytics. The images are captured by medical images and other IT-based tools. The neural network is formed and thereby the dynamic network is formed as can be seen in Figure 8.3.

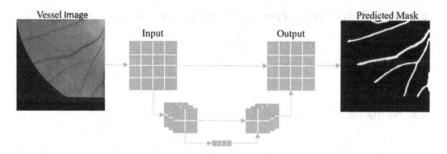

FIGURE 8.3
Prediction of mask from the vessel image.

The key segments and phases in the projected approach include the following:

1. Initial convolutional layers
2. Inception-resnet-A block
3. Reduction
4. Inception-reset-B block
5. Reduction
6. Inception-resnet-C block
7. Average Pooling
8. Towards the neural features

The models mentioned herein refer to the pre-trained models which are prominently used for the deep learning–based environment. These models are quite effectual in achieving higher performance accuracy as they have the key features in the repository with pre-trained models and the learning environment for the predictive analytics as presented in Figure 8.4.

The training data has the image dataset with the contouring data. In addition, the reinforcement learning is used so that the error factors can be reduced in integration of the convolutional and recurrent neural networks as depicted in Figure 8.5. The automatic contouring results are obtained with the focus on the higher degree of performance.

The training datasets and the testing datasets are the key components in the deep learning based–environment, as these are required for the effectual predictive analytics as presented in Figure 8.6.

8.4 Proposed Model and Outcomes

The proposed model includes the training of the datasets of the Cancer genome that makes up the benchmark dataset and is under research by

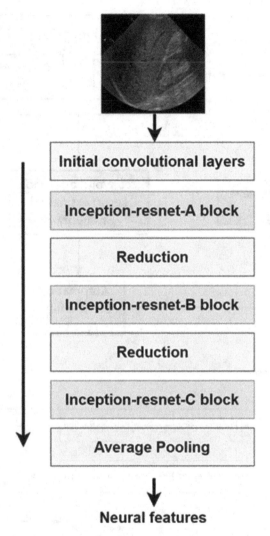

FIGURE 8.4
Flow of the network formation and further analytics.

enormous numbers of research groups. The assorted research groups are making use of the dataset for the training and testing and validation of the datasets, including for the approaches of machine learning, deep learning and many others high performance integrations and presented in Figure 8.7.

epoch train_loss valid_loss accuracy

1   0.834818   1.048996   0.616667 (20:21)

CPU times: user 3min 21s, sys: 46.6 s, total: 4min 8s

Wall time: 20min 34s

Total time: 32:52

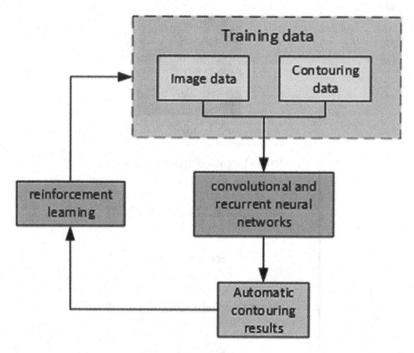

FIGURE 8.5
Key points and phases.

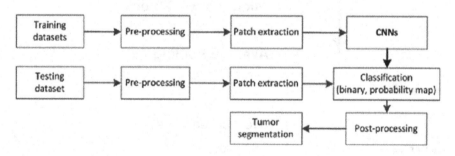

FIGURE 8.6
Training and testing datasets with deep learning aspects.

epoch train_loss valid_loss accuracy

1	0.189783	0.225980	0.918750 (10:32)
2	0.162783	0.235727	0.912500 (11:26)
3	0.139040	0.232577	0.918750 (10:53)

Figure 8.8 depicts the flow of projected work for the above research approach and thereby can be used to gather analytical outcomes (Table 8.3).

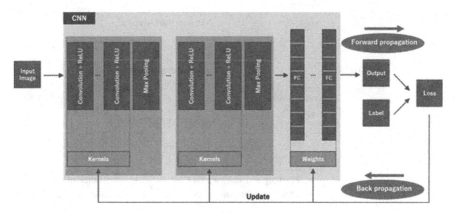

FIGURE 8.7
Training and testing datasets with the related aspects of deep learning.

The results obtained as in Figure 8.9, from the deep learning–based convolutional neural network–based results, presents that the effectiveness in the outcomes can be achieved with a higher degree of performance and effectiveness.

8.5 Conclusion

Medical diagnosis is very important process in which there is a need to integrate high performance algorithms. Liver or Hepatic Cancer is one of the riskiest disorders in which the continuance problem arises. In this chapter, the dataset of liver cancer from the appraisal bit of Cancer Imaging Archive is set up in the model of significant getting the hang of having multilayered neural frameworks so the model can be set up with the dataset. The presented scenario has the tweaking and trade work with the source work and the affirmed layers of the neural framework so the monstrous evaluation of the key concentrations and features of dangerous development can be removed. The work is having the parameters for the appraisal of results in different centers including precision, execution time, cost factors, and the multifaceted nature with the objective that the total execution of the proposed system should be conceivable. The work has joint significant learning with the convolutional frameworks concerning the grounds that there are minute and exact zone extractions from the photos of liver infection for dealing with and the vivacious mining. With the tremendous evaluation of the features and related key impressions from the liver peril pictures, the test data or beginning late passed on liver pictures can be empowered and further accuracy segments can be found on the probabilities of thought of

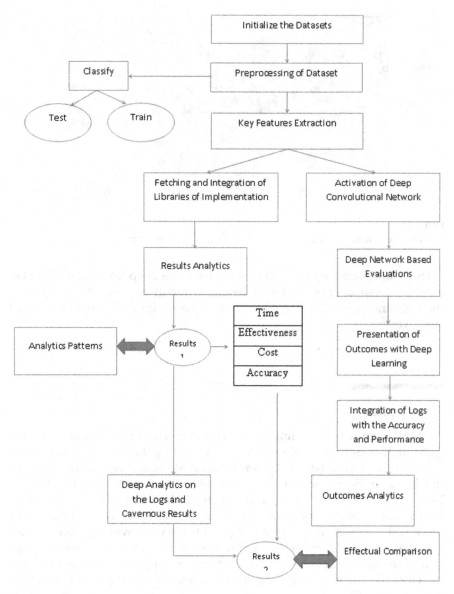

FIGURE 8.8
Flow of proposed work.

infection. The proposed approach is depended upon with the promise to the prosperity sciences and regardless of for the space of telemedicine in which the remote ID and treatment of the challenging issue is required. The significant neural framework–based system is executed using the open source suites of TensorFlow and Keras, so the status and testing should be conceivable with a more raised degree of accuracy on the benchmark datasets of

TABLE 8.3

Analytics of Accuracy Levels

Scenario	Accuracy: Traditional Aspects	Accuracy: Projected Approach
1	71	97
2	70	94
3	71	93
4	73	93
5	71	93
6	79	91

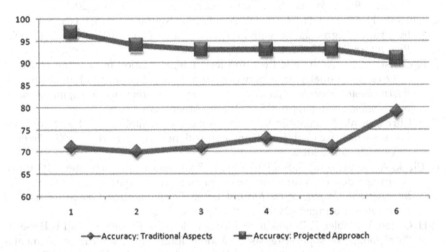

FIGURE 8.9
Analytics of the outcomes.

liver cancer. Notwithstanding the convolutional neural framework, the additional layers with the tweaking factors are used so the general precision of the check is raised with reliably raised degree of need and least destruction up or botch rate and more significant levels of accuracy. The chapter presents the accuracy levels associated with the cumulative performance for liver disease diagnosis using deep convolutional networks.

References

Rashmi Agrawal, "Predictive analysis of breast cancer using machine learning techniques". *Ingeniería Solidaria*, 15(29), pp. 1–23, 2019.

I. Ben-Cohen, E. Diamant, M. Klang, Amitai, and H. Greenspan, "Fully convolutional network for liver segmentation and lesions detection". In: *International Workshop on Large-Scale Annotation of Biomedical Data and Expert Label Synthesis*, Springer, pp. 77–85, 2016. Athens, Greece.

J. Cai, L. Lu, Y. Xie, F. Xing, and L. Yang, "Improving deep pancreas segmentation in ct and mri images via recurrent neural contextual learning and direct loss function". *arXiv Preprint ArXiv:1707.04912*, 2017.

F. Chaieb, T. B. Said, S. Mabrouk, and F. Ghorbel, "Accelerated liver tumor segmentation in four-phase computed tomography images". *Journal of Real-Time Image Processing*, 13(1), pp. 121–133, 2017.

H. Chen, Q. Dou, L. Yu, J. Qin, and P.-A. Heng, "Voxresnet: Deep voxelwise residual networks for brain segmentation from 3D MR images". *NeuroImage*, 2017. 170, 446–455.

H. Chen, D. Ni, J. Qin, S. Li, X. Yang, T. Wang, and P. A. Heng, "Standard plane localization in fetal ultrasound via domain transferred deep neural networks". *IEEE Journal of Biomedical and Health Informatics*, 19(5), pp. 1627–1636, 2015.

G. Chlebus, H. Meine, J. H. Moltz, and A. Schenk, "Neural network-based automatic liver tumor segmentation with random forest-based candidate filtering." *arXiv Preprint ArXiv:1706.00842*, 2017.

P. F. Christ, et al., "Automatic liver and lesion segmentation in ct using cascaded fully convolutional neural networks and 3d conditional random fields". In: *International Conference on Medical Image Computing and Computer-Assisted Intervention*, Springer, pp. 415–423, 2016. Athens, Greece.

P. F. Christ, et al., "Automatic liver and tumor segmentation of ct and mri volumes using cascaded fully convolutional neural networks". *arXiv Preprint ArXiv:1702.05970*, 2017.

Ö. Çiçek, A. Abdulkadir, S. S. Lienkamp, T. Brox, and O. Ronneberger, "3D u-net: Learning dense volumetric segmentation from sparse annotation". In: *International Conference on Medical Image Computing and Computer- Assisted Intervention*, Springer, 424–432, 2016. Athens, Greece.

P.-H. Conze, V. Noblet, F. Rousseau, F. Heitz, V. de Blasi, R. Memeo, and P. Pessaux, "Scale-adaptive supervoxelbased random forests for liver tumor segmentation in dynamic contrast-enhanced ct scans". *International Journal of Computer Assisted Radiology and Surgery*, 12(2), 223–233, 2017.

Q. Dou, H. Chen, Y. Jin, L. Yu, J. Qin, and P.-A. Heng, "3d deeply supervised network for automatic liver segmentation from ct volumes". In: *International Conference on Medical Image Computing and Computer-Assisted Intervention*, Springer, 149–157, 2016. Athens, Greece.

L. Farag, H. R. Roth Lu, J. Liu, E. Turkbey, R. M. Summers, R. M. Summers, "A bottom-up approach for pancreas segmentation using cascaded superpixels and (deep) image patch labeling". *IEEE Transactions on Image Processing: A Publication of the IEEE Signal Processing Society*, 26(1), 386–399, 2017.

Jacques Ferlay, H. R. Shin, F. Bray, D. Forman, C. Mathers, D. M. Parkin, "Estimates of worldwide burden of cancer in 2008: GLOBOCAN 2008". *International Journal of Cancer*, 127(12), 2893–2917, 2010.

X. Han, "Automatic liver lesion segmentation using a deep convolutional neural network method". *arXiv Preprint ArXiv:1704.07239*, 2017.

M. Havaei, A. Davy, D. Warde-Farley, A. Biard, A. Courville, Y. Bengio, C. Pal, P.-M. Jodoin, and H. Larochelle, "Brain tumor segmentation with deep neural networks". *Medical Image Analysis*, 35, 18–31, 2017.

C. F. Hoogi, G. M. Beaulieu, E. Heba Cunha, C. B. Sirlin, S. Napel, D. L. Rubin, D. L. Rubin, "Adaptive local window for level set segmentation of CT and MRI liver lesions". *Medical Image Analysis*, 37, 46–55, 2017.

G. Huang, Z. Liu, L. van der Maaten, and K. Q. Weinberger, "Densely connected convolutional networks". In: *Proceedings of the IEEE Conference on Computer Vision and Pattern Recognition, 2017.* Athens, Greece.

W. Huang, Y. Yang, Z. Lin, G.-B. Huang, J. Zhou, Y. Duan, and W. Xiong, "Random feature subspace ensemble based extreme learning machine for liver tumor detection and segmentation". In: *Engineering in Medicine and Biology Society (EMBC), 2014 36th Annual International Conference of the IEEE,* IEEE, 4675–4678, 2014. Chicago, Illinois.

D. Jimenez-Carretero, L. Fernandez-de Manuel, J. Pascau, J. M. Tellado, E. Ramon, M. Desco, A. Santos, and M. J. Ledesma-Carbayo, "Optimal multiresolution 3d level-set method for liver segmentation incorporating local curvature constraints". In: *Engineering in Medicine and Biology Society, EMBC, 2011 Annual International Conference of the IEEE,* IEEE, pp. 3419–3422, 2011 Boston, Massachusetts.

C.-L. Kuo, S.-C. Cheng, C.-L. Lin, K.-F. Hsiao, and S.- H. Lee, "Texture-based treatment prediction by automatic liver tumor segmentation on computed tomography". In: *Computer, Information and Telecommunication Systems (CITS), 2017 International Conference on. IEEE,* pp. 128–132, 2017. Paris, France.

T.-N. Le, et al., "Liver tumor segmentation from mr images using 3D fast marching algorithm and single hidden layer feedforward neural network". *BioMed Research International,* 2016, 1–8.

X. Li, Q. Dou, H. Chen, C.-W. Fu, and P.-A. Heng, "Multi-scale and modality dropout learning for intervertebral disc localization and segmentation". In: *International Workshop on Computational Methods and Clinical Applications for Spine Imaging,* Springer, pp. 85–91, 2016. Athens, Greece.

X. Li, Q. Dou, H. Chen, C.-W. Fu, X. Qi, D. L. Belav`y, G. Armbrecht, D. Felsenberg, G. Zheng, and P.- A. Heng, "3d multi-scale fcn with random modality voxel dropout learning for intervertebral disc localization and segmentation from multi-modality mr images". *Medical Image Analysis,* 2018, 3419–3422.

Rui Lu, Pina Marziliano, and Choon Hua Thng, "Liver tumor volume estimation by semi-automatic segmentation method". In: *IEEE Engineering in Medicine and Biology 27th Annual Conference,* IEEE, p. 2006, 2005.

F. Lu, F. Wu, P. Hu, Z. Peng, and D. Kong, "Automatic 3d liver location and segmentation via convolutional neural network and graph cut". *International Journal of Computer Assisted Radiology and Surgery,* 12(2), pp. 171–182, 2017.

Mehrdad Moghbel, S. Mashohor, R. Mahmud, M. I. B. Saripan, "Review of liver segmentation and computer assisted detection/diagnosis methods in computed tomography". *Artificial Intelligence Review,* 50(4), pp. 497–537, 2018.

J. H. Moltz, L. Bornemann, V. Dicken, and H. Peitgen, "Segmentation of liver metastases in ct scans by adaptive thresholding and morphological processing". In: *MICCAI Workshop,* 41(43) 195, 2008.

Adhish Prasoon, et al., "Deep feature learning for knee cartilage segmentation using a triplanar convolutional neural network". In: *International Conference on Medical Image Computing and Computer-Assisted Intervention,* Springer, Berlin, Heidelberg, 2013.

Olaf Ronneberger, Philipp Fischer, and Thomas Brox, "U-net: Convolutional networks for biomedical image segmentation". In: *International Conference on Medical image Computing and Computer-Assisted Intervention.* Springer, Cham, 2015.

Holger R. Roth, et al., "Deeporgan: Multi-level deep convolutional networks for auto-mated pancreas segmentation". In: *International Conference on Medical Image Computing and Computer-Assisted Intervention,* Springer, Cham, 2015.

H. R. Roth, L. Lu, N. Lay, A. P. Harrison, A. Farag, A. Sohn, and R. M. Summers, "Spatial aggregation of holistically-nested convolutional neural networks for automated pancreas localization and segmentation". *arXiv Preprint ArXiv:1702.00045,* 2017.

K. Simonyan and A. Zisserman, "Very deep convolutional networks for large-scale image recognition". *arXiv Preprint ArXiv:1409.1556,* 2014.

L. Soler, H. Delingette, G. Malandain, J. Montagnat, N. Ayache, C. Koehl, O. Dourthe, B. Malassagne, M. Smith, D. Mutter, J. Marescaux, "Fully automatic anatomical, pathological, and functional segmentation from ct scans for hepatic surgery". *Computer Aided Surgery: Official Journal of the International Society for Computer Aided Surgery,* 6(3), 131–142, 2001.

Marijn F. Stollenga, et al., "Parallel multi-dimensional lstm, with application to fast biomedical volumetric image segmentation". *Advances in Neural Information Processing Systems,* 2015. 2998–3006.

C. Sun, S. Guo, H. Zhang, J. Li, M. Chen, S. Ma, L. Jin, X. Liu, X. Li, and X. Qian, "Automatic segmentation of liver tumors from multiphase contrast-enhanced CT images based on fcns". *Artificial Intelligence in Medicine,* 2017. 83, 58–66.

N. Tajbakhsh, J. Y. Shin, S. R. Gurudu, R. T. Hurst, C. B. Kendall, M. B. Gotway, and J. Liang, "Convolutional neural networks for medical image analysis: Full training or fine tuning?" *IEEE Transactions on Medical Imaging,* 35(5), 1299–1312, 2016.

K.-L. Tseng, Y.-L. Lin, W. Hsu, and C.-Y. Huang, "Joint sequence learning and cross-modality convolution for 3d biomedical segmentation". *arXiv Preprint ArXiv:1704.07754,* 2017.

Z. Tu, "Auto-context and its application to high-level vision tasks". In: *Computer Vision and Pattern Recognition, 2008. CVPR 2008. IEEE Conference on. IEEE,* 1–8, 2008.

E. Vorontsov, N. Abi-Jaoudeh, and S. Kadoury, "Metastatic liver tumor segmentation using texture-based omni-directional deformable surface models". In: *International MICCAI Workshop on Computational and Clinical Challenges in Abdominal Imaging,* Springer, 74–83, 2014. Paris, France.

E. Vorontsov, G. Chartrand, A. Tang, C. Pal, and S. Kadoury, "Liver lesion segmentation informed by joint liver segmentation". *arXiv Preprint ArXiv:1707.07734,* 2017.

J. Wang, J. D. MacKenzie, R. Ramachandran, and D. Z. Chen, "Detection of glands and villi by collaboration of domain knowledge and deep learning". In: *International Conference on Medical Image Computing and Computer- Assisted Intervention,* Springer, 20–27, 2015.

X. Wang, Y. Zheng, L. Gan, X. Wang, X. Sang, X. Kong, and J. Zhao, "Liver segmentation from CT images using a sparse priori statistical shape model (sp-ssm)". *PLoS One,* 12(10), p. e0185249, 2017.

D. H. Wolpert, "Stacked generalization". *Neural netIEEE Transactions on Medical Imaging 12 Works,* 5(2), 241–259, 1992.

D. Wong, J. Liu, Y. Fengshou, Q. Tian, W. Xiong, J. Zhou, Y. Qi, T. Han, S. Venkatesh, and S.-c. Wang, "A semi-automated method for liver tumor segmentation based on 2d region growing with knowledge-based constraints". In: *MICCAI Workshop,* 41(43), 159, 2008.

Y. Zhou, L. Xie, E. K. Fishman, and A. L. Yuille, "Deep supervision for pancreatic cyst segmentation in abdominal CT scans". In: *International Conference on Medical Image Computing and Computer-Assisted Intervention*, Springer, 222–230, 2017a.

Y. Zhou, L. Xie, W. Shen, Y. Wang, E. K. Fishman, and A. L. Yuille, "A fixed-point model for pancreas segmentation in abdominal CT scans". In: *International Conference on Medical Image Computing and Computer- Assisted Intervention*, Springer, 693–701, 2017b. Quebec City, Canada.

9

Performance Analysis of Machine Learning Algorithm for Healthcare Tools with High Dimension Segmentation

Soobia Saeed, Afnizanfaizal Abdullah, N. Z. Jhanjhi,
Memood Naqvi and Mamoona Humayun

CONTENTS

9.1 Introduction.. 115
9.2 Literature Review... 117
9.3 Methodology 118
    9.3.1 Proposed Framework 118
    9.3.2 Light Field Toolbox for MATLAB... 119
    9.3.3 High Dimensional Light Field Segmentation Method............. 119
    9.3.4 High Dimensional Structured Graphs 119
9.4 High Dimension Structured Graphs... 119
    9.4.1 Grab-Cut.. 119
    9.4.2 Image Testing Value 120
    9.4.3 Image Testing Result... 120
    9.4.4 Graph Cut Value for B/W Image 121
    9.4.5 Image Testing Value 121
    9.4.6 Image Testing Result 121
9.5 Algorithm.. 123
9.6 Result and Discussion... 124
9.7 Conclusion 125
9.8 Future Work.. 125
Acknowledgment.. 125
References.. 126

9.1 Introduction

Graph cutting option in Image Segmented Image cutting program, Graph Cut is a semi-automatic segmentation technology that can be used by a researcher to separate an image into front and back components. We can draw lines in the image, called scribbles, to determine what you want in the foreground and what you want in the background. The split image automatically divides the image based on its scribble and displays the split image. The researcher can improve fragmentation by drawing more scrawls on the image to be satisfied with the result.

Graph Cut technology applies graphics theory to image processing to achieve rapid fragmentation. The technique creates a graphic for the image where each pixel is a knot connected to a weighted edge. The more likely the pixel is bound the more weight. The algorithm cuts the weak edges, splitting the objects in the image. The split image uses a specific set of the Graph Cut algorithm called Slow Adjust. The information about graphics segmentation on segmentation technology, such as local graphics segmentation "grab-cut" is an image clip.

The integrated graphics clipping algorithms have been successfully applied to a wide range of vision and graphics problems. This article focuses on the simplest graphic cutting app: segmenting an object in image data. In addition to its simplicity, this application embodies the best features of harmonic graphics cutting methods of vision: the optimum global level, practical efficiency, numerical durability, the ability to integrate a wide range of signals, optical restrictions, untied topological character sectors and the applicability of ND problems (Boykov et al. 2015, Adelson and Bergen 1991, Berent and Dragotti 2007, Bishop and Favaro 2011, Boykov and Jolly 2001).

Figure 9.1 shows that introducing a general concept for the first time to use binary graphic cutting algorithms to split and verify objects using MATLAB programming software, this idea was extensively studied in drawing and computer vision societies. We provide links to an extensive variety of recognized additions based on iterative reassessment, parameter getting to know, multi-domain procedures, hierarchy, slender tiers, and different technologies that require medical, imaging, and video packages (Abdullah et al. 2013: Cho et al. 2014: Fiss et al. 2015; Abdullah et al. 2012; Gortler et al. 1996; Greig et al. 1989).

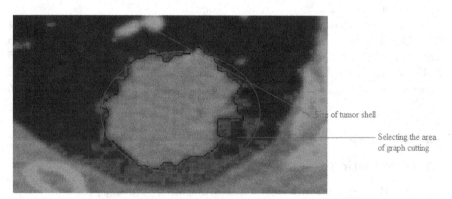

Size of tumor shell

Selecting the area
of graph cutting

FIGURE 9.1
Binary graphic cutting value of brain cancer.

9.2 Literature Review

Segmentation is one of the most significant assignments in the field of PC vision and has been studied for a long time. One of the best-known image splitting techniques is grab-cut (Mendrik et al. 2015; Gustavo et al. 2018; Gupta and Pahuja 2017), a directed frontal area/foundation division technique for 2D pictures that has just been executed in many picture altering programming applications. Grab-cut depends on realistic cutting calculations (Saeed and Abdullah 2019; Saeed and Jafri 2015; Horn and Chen 2007). Illustration slices can be applied to dimensional information, including pictures, video groupings, and 3D structures (Jarabo et al. 2014), and can likewise be reached out to numerous segmentation labels (Kolmogorov and Zabih 2002). This recommends a division strategy for pictures utilizing a 4D light field that utilizations nearness and difference signals (Kowdle et al. 2012), as used for regulated strategies. They train an arbitrary woods classifier to fuse appearance and disparity so as to manage these various sorts of data in nature and get a particular likelihood for each brand. Notwithstanding its prosperity, the main way that division results happen is the information is viewed as a schematic structure with vertices and edges in methods for cutting the guide. The head is at the highest point of every pixel, and, in light of its comparability, the contiguous pixels are associated with a reasonable perspective. This mark likewise has an uncommon peak called a terminal in cases including division of various blurb images. Pixel heads are joined to all stations, where the brand's edge loads decide the probability of order. The best approach to discover pieces in the diagram at the most minimal expense is to get hash with minimal measure of accessible vitality and this issue will be tackled utilizing the base greatest stream calculation (Levoy and Hanrahan 1996; Lin et al. 2015; Saeed et al. 2018), two-dimensional segmentation picture. Growing vertex is attached to one end after cutting, which means the opposite poster is set to the opposite side. Our approach also uses the process of splitting the scheme. Such methods of segmentation are known as moderated methods because in the form of guides they require user input. While some methods of graphics clipping (Saeed et al. 2019a, Maeno et al. 2013, and Marx 2009) can handle data from any distance, they are not always ideal for high-dimensional data like video clips. Video data has an inconsistent structure along the time axis, unlike 3D storage data. Therefore, methods of segmentation can be strengthened by taking proper account of dysfunctional neighborhood relationships (Nagahashi et al. 2009). Enhance the best of video segmentation by way of defining temporary neighborhood relationships similar to neighborhood frames pixels. One trouble with clean 4D field data that is much like video facts is that iteration is obvious in a complex field. Our working approach is the primary technique that makes use of the image cut technique to concentrate on segmenting a 4D light field. In the meantime, certain unsupervised processes can be used to segment multi-huge pictures or 4D spotlights. The author (Adelson and Bergen 1991) Suggested a 4D light field segmentation primarily based on a level setting technique (Ng et al. 2005), which applies an active contour technique to a massive 4D volume phase. The author (Osher and Sethian 1988), suggest a method for depth tagging multiple-width images based on the fact that foreground objects cannot be excluded by deeper objects. The researcher suggested a method to automatically extract objects from multi-width images using the contrast signal. The researcher's technique uses contrast and appearance signals in multiple display images to determine the probability of foreground objects (Platt 1999).To identify areas of transparent species as a bright zone, an uncensored approach is proposed. The method makes use of the light field distortion feature (Rother et al. 2004), which represents the likelihood of a pixel belonging to an obvious object area, in addition to a segmented binary photographs segmentation method. While those techniques are a success, uncensored methods aren't suitable for truly selecting the for field editing due to the fact the regions of interest vary from user to person (Wanner and Goldluecke 2012).

This proposes a division technique for pictures utilizing a 4D light field that utilizations nearness and differentiation signals like (S. Wanner, Meister, and Goldluecke 2013), as for regulated strategies. They train an irregular backwoods classifier to fuse appearance and imbalance so as to manage these various kinds of data in nature and acquire a particular likelihood for each brand. In spite of its prosperity, the main way that division results happen is the two-dimensional central images (Wanner, Straehle, and Goldluecke; Xu et al. 2015; Saeed et al. 2019b).

9.3 Methodology

The basis of this study is the detection of brain cancer due to the interaction of MRI-4D images with LFT segmentation. The researcher discusses the cellular damage of brain cells or tissues due to brain cell abnormalities. The main goal of our work is to build a framework that can recognize or isolate the CSF spill field between tumors and not silent tumors. Initially, an MRI image is equipped with a specific final target to shape the image for the rest of the procedures.

9.3.1 Proposed Framework

The examination for the most part, comprises of two parts, which include:
Light Field Toolbox, high dimensional light field segmentation method, high dimensional structured graphs

9.3.2 Light Field Toolbox for MATLAB

The purpose of using a set of tools to work with luminous images (also known as plenoptic images) in MATLAB is to decode, calibrate correct, correct, color, filter basic images, and display luminous images.

9.3.3 High Dimensional Light Field Segmentation Method

The purpose of choosing a light field is basically a three-dimensional structure as the sounds of each pixel corresponding to the rays. The two dimensions determine the location of those rays, while the other two determine their direction. In the case of images measured by a camera based on the viewfinder such as Lytro, the two dimensions choose a lens image. The other two choose pixels within the image of this lens to maintain fractionation accuracy.

9.3.4 High Dimensional Structured Graphs

The purpose of choosing a high dimensional pattern structure is to implement the pattern cutting algorithm to reduce energy function. The solution provides the optimum mark for every beam. It has been observed that the solution becomes almost perfect for dividing multiple classifications.

9.4 High Dimension Structured Graphs

Grab-Cut is representing the improved method of light field image segmentation process which is given below:

9.4.1 Grab-Cut

Grab-Cut is a graphic form of clip art. The algorithm estimates the color distribution of the target object and the background color using the Gaussian Mix model and begins with a user-defined schema in the object into a section. This is used to create a random Markov field in pixel tags using the control function. The same poster is preferred in continuous areas and the improvement of the graph whose values can be inferred because this estimate may be more accurate than the original taken from the bounding frame. This system is repeated in two steps until convergence takes place. Incorrectly classified and optimized place users also can accurately estimates. The process additionally corrects the effects to keep the edges.

Figure 9.2 shows the remaining area after the cutting of the whole image as we can see that the above area is more clear and visible with colored form.

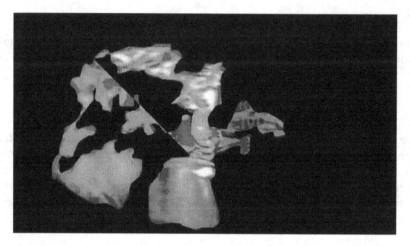

FIGURE 9.2
Selecting the region of the whole image.

FIGURE 9.3
Identify the binary image of selecting region of image.

9.4.2 Image Testing Value

Figure 9.3 shows the remaining area after the cutting of the whole image as we can see that the above area is more clear and visible after the binary transformation of image segmentation process which converts into black and white form that will create more visible to detect diseases.

9.4.3 Image Testing Result

Figure 9.2 shows the more visible area after the filtering tool implementation that can appear clearer and more useful in identifying the diseases as well.

Figure 9.3 shows the more visible area after the filtering tool implementation that can appear more clear and useful to identify the diseases as well with binary transformation as the above context shows that the result generates after the input of the second time. However, it is also is in the form of black and white but we use BW filter for reefing the image more.

9.4.4 Graph Cut Value for B/W Image

Figure 9.4 shows the selected region of CSF matter inside the skull as the researcher easily detects the selected damaged area of cancer. The above figure shows the selection area of input 1 for the segmentation process with different pixel quality.

Figure 9.5 shows that the yellow color for cutting the edge of the area that can easily and cut the specific area and transform into the next step of the segmentation process. The above figure shows the selection area of input 2 for the segmentation process with a different resolution of the picture.

9.4.5 Image Testing Value

Figure 9.6 shows the more visible area after the filtering tool implementation that can appear clearer and more useful in identifying the diseases as well but the quality is less compare to color figures.

9.4.6 Image Testing Result

Figure 9.7 shows the more visible area after the filtering tool implementation that can appear more clear and useful to identify the diseases as well with binary transformation as the above context shows that the result generates after the input of the second time.

As we can see the huge difference of both image type and after evaluation, it is clear that the light field segmentation is better for color imaging

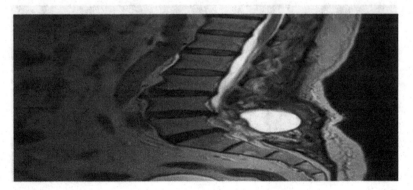

FIGURE 9.4
Graph cut value of original image.

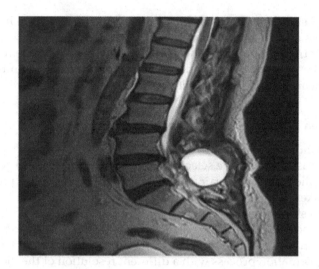

FIGURE 9.5
Graph cut value of input 1.

FIGURE 9.6
Graph cut value of input 2.

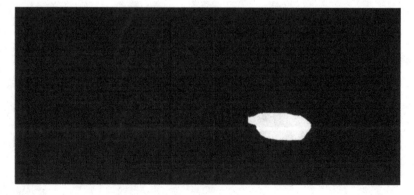

FIGURE 9.7
Original colors of image testing result for binary image.

transformation to compare to black and white image because after the implementation the quality of the image is more visible that can we prefer to use color images in segmentation form.

9.5 Algorithm

The 4-dimesion algorithm is given below:

Algorithm.1: *For Detection of CSF Spot in Image (Two Outputs and One Input):*

```
1.% Translate RGB image into L*a*b* color space.
2.X = rgb2lab(RGB);
3.% Create empty mask.
4.   BW = untruthful(size(X,1),size(X,2));
5.   % Draw Freehand
6.   m = size(BW, 1);
7.   n = size(BW, 2);
8. addedArea = poly2mask(xPos, yPos, m, n);
9. BW = BW | addedRegion;
10.  % Create masked image.
11.  CoveredImage = RGB;
12.  CoveredImage(repmat(~BW,[1 1 3])) = 0;
13.End;
```

Algorithm.2: *Detection of CSF Image 1 with Binary Gary Scale and Original Image Detection:*

```
1.Variables have been created in the base workstation.
2.Whos:
3.   BW1    →    670x1269   →     850230 logical
4.   BW2    →    583x480    →     279840 logical
5.   Covered →    Image1    →    670x1269x3      2550690 uint8
6.   Covered →    Image2    →    583x480x3       839520 uint8
7.Figure, imshow(BW1)
8.Figure, imshow(maskedImage1)
```

Algorithm.3: *For Texture Feature Image Include (One Input Two Output)*

```
1. % Translate RGB image into L*a*b* color space.
2. X = rgb2lab(RGB);
3. % Produce empty front-size.
4. BW = untruthful(size(X,1),size(X,2));
```

```
5. % Draw Freehand
6.    m = size(BW, 1);
7.    n = size(BW, 2);
8. AddedArea = poly2mask(xPos, yPos, m, n);
9. BW = BW | addedArea;
10.% GenerateCovered image.
11.  CoveredImage = RGB;
12.  Covered Image(repmat(~BW,[1 1 3])) = 0;
13.End;
```

Algorithm.4: *For size of images*

1.Variables have been shaped in the base workspace.
2.Whose

For Name, Size, Bytes Class and Attributes

```
3.BW1    →     670x1269;
4.BW2    →     670x1269;
5.maskedImage1   →   670x1269x3;
6.Covered Image2   →   670x1269x3;
7.Figure, imshow(BW2);
8.Figure, imshow(Covered Image2);
```

9.6 Result and Discussion

In this research article, the researcher reveals brain cancer researchers because of the interface of MRI-4D images. Through the use of 4D image field segmentation. Initially, MRI handled the pre-prepared image method with the ultimate goal of adjusting the image for the rest of the procedure. Based on this study, brain cancer and CSF were detected due to the interface of the 4D image segmentation process. Therefore, it consists of a research study after primary and secondary sources, followed by a cutting technique from the MATLAB drawing tool using images from original medical samples to measure the extent of damaged cells in the brain within the LCR. To implement the method of cutting graphics using MATLAB tools and algorithms; in this study, the researcher proposes a 4D modulation method that monitors the light field that can be used to emit light with color shift and binary. By building a structured 4D diagram, the 4D light fields can be divided to reduce the graphics algorithm generated by the 4D diagram. The researcher uses this technique to free the damaged brain samples from the brain skull. These results demonstrate the effectiveness of our approach to light editing applications. Lighting field methods can be useful in improving the quality of photo editing application and compound lighting field tubes, as they reduce border artistic effects.

The researcher evaluates ways to overcome the value of lost data in the computational experiments of the proposed new method. We use a structured graphics break algorithm with correlation and multiple types of data loss in time series data. The researcher explained that improving the calculated data to determine the variables of the validation method is related to the time delay of the test and the training vector resulting from the time delay. The graphics cut method demonstrates the accuracy of the images with the results and maintains the color shift with the color shift and binary and produces one output and one input.

9.7 Conclusion

In this article, the researcher indicates a supervised 4D area for dependent 4D graphics, 4D light field pictures may be segmented with the aid of a picture clipping algorithm of rules. Experimental outcomes display that our method achieves extra accuracy than previous methods using general lighting field data sets from the UK's Brain Cancer Research Centre and CSF. In addition, the researcher applied the proposed method to the original images and showed the result in a color and binary shift with one and two outputs. These results show the efficiency of our process of light field photo editing using the algorithm of graphics. The problem is calculation time, as using a graphic cutting algorithm requires large quantities of calculation time when there are many peaks; the obvious future goal is to solve this issue.

9.8 Future Work

The features of the tumor are detected and will be useful for therapeutic use. The researcher analyzes all results in the 2D and 3D sense, and also generates the novelty of MRI tools and Future work also includes segmenting and identifying further images with more functionality helping to identify multiple types of tumors.

Acknowledgment

Authors are grateful to the Department of Software Engineering, faculty of computing, Universiti Teknologi Malaysia-UTM, Malaysia for financial support to carry out this work.

References

Abdullah, Afnizanfaizal, et al. "Cerebrospinal fluid pulsatile segmentation-a review." In: *The 5th 2012 Biomedical Engineering International Conference*, IEEE, 2012.

Abdullah, Afnizanfaizal, et al. "An improved swarm optimization for parameter estimation and biological model selection." *PLoS One* 8(4) (2013): 4.

Adelson, Edward H., and James R. Bergen. *The Plenoptic Function and the Elements of Early Vision*. Vol. 2, Vision and Modeling Group, Media Laboratory, Massachusetts Institute of Technology, 1–12,1991.

Berent, Jesse, and Pier Luigi Dragotti. "Unsupervised extraction of coherent regions for image based rendering." *BMVC*, 1–10,(2007).

Bishop, Tom E., and Paolo Favaro. "The light field camera: Extended depth of field, aliasing, and superresolution." *IEEE Transactions on Pattern Analysis and Machine Intelligence* 34(5) (2011): 972–986.

Boykov, Yuri, and Gareth Funka-Lea. "Graph cuts and efficient ND image segmentation." *International Journal of Computer Vision* 70(2) (2006): 109–131.

Boykov, Yuri Y., and M.-P. Jolly. "Interactive graph cuts for optimal boundary & region segmentation of objects in ND images." In: *Proceedings of the Eighth IEEE International Conference on Computer Vision. ICCV 2001*. Vol. 1, IEEE, 2001.

Boykov, Yuri, and Vladimir Kolmogorov. "An experimental comparison of min-cut/max-flow algorithms for energy minimization in vision." *IEEE Transactions on Pattern Analysis and Machine Intelligence* 26(9) (2004): 1124–1137.

Boykov, Yuri, Olga Veksler, and Ramin Zabih. "Fast approximate energy minimization via graph cuts." *IEEE Transactions on Pattern Analysis and Machine Intelligence* 23(11) (2001): 1222–1239.

Chen, Can, et al. "Light field stereo matching using bilateral statistics of surface cameras." In: *Proceedings of the IEEE Conference on Computer Vision and Pattern Recognition*, 2014.

Cho, Donghyeon, Sunyeong Kim, and Yu-Wing Tai. "Consistent matting for light field images." In: *European Conference on Computer Vision*, Springer, Cham, 2014.

Fiss, Juliet, Brian Curless, and Rick Szeliski. "Light field layer matting." In: *Proceedings of the IEEE Conference on Computer Vision and Pattern Recognition*, 2015.

Gortler, Steven J., et al. "The lumigraph." In: *Proceedings of the 23rd Annual Conference on Computer Graphics and Interactive Techniques*, 1996.

Greig, Dorothy M., Bruce T. Porteous, and Allan H. Seheult. "Exact maximum a posteriori estimation for binary images." *Journal of the Royal Statistical Society: Series B (Methodological)* 51(2) (1989): 271–279.

Gupta, Anjali, and Gunjan Pahuja. "Hybrid clustering and boundary value refinement for tumor segmentation using brain MRI." In: *IOP Conference Series Materials Science and Engineering*, Vol. 225, no. 1, IOP Publishing, 2017.

Horn, Daniel Reiter, and Billy Chen. "Lightshop: Interactive light field manipulation and rendering." In: *Proceedings of the 2007 Symposium on Interactive 3D Graphics and Games*, 2007.

Jarabo, Adrian, et al. "How do people edit light fields?" *ACM Transactions on Graphics (Proc. SIGGRAPH)* 33(4):1–11, (2014).

Kolmogorov, Vladimir, and Ramin Zabih. "Multi-camera scene reconstruction via graph cuts." In: *European Conference on Computer Vision*, Springer, Berlin, Heidelberg, 2002.

Kowdle, Adarsh, Sudipta N. Sinha, and Richard Szeliski. "Multiple view object cosegmentation using appearance and stereo cues." In: *European Conference on Computer Vision*, Springer, Berlin, Heidelberg, 2012.

Levoy, Marc, and Pat Hanrahan. "Light field rendering." In: *Proceedings of the 23rd Annual Conference on Computer Graphics and Interactive Techniques*, 1996.

Lin, Haiting, et al. "Depth recovery from light field using focal stack symmetry." In: *Proceedings of the IEEE International Conference on Computer Vision*, 2015.

Lumsdaine, Andrew, and Todor Georgiev. "The focused plenoptic camera." In: *2009 IEEE International Conference on Computational Photography (ICCP)*, IEEE, 2009.

Maeno, Kazuki, et al. "Light field distortion feature for transparent object recognition." In: *Proceedings of the IEEE Conference on Computer Vision and Pattern Recognition*, 2013.

Mendrik, Adriënne M., et al. "MRBrainS challenge: Online evaluation framework for brain image segmentation in 3T MRI scans." *Computational Intelligence and Neuroscience* 2015 (2015).

Nagahashi, Tomoyuki, Hironobu Fujiyoshi, and Takeo Kanade. "Video segmentation using iterated graph cuts based on spatio-temporal volumes." In: *Asian Conference on Computer Vision*, Springer, Berlin, Heidelberg, 2009.

Ng, Ren, et al. "Light field photography with a hand-held plenoptic camera." *Computer Science Technical Report CSTR* 2(11) (2005): 1–11.

Oliveira, Gustavo Casagrande, Renato Varoto, and Alberto Cliquet Jr. "Brain tumor segmentation in magnetic resonance images using genetic algorithm clustering and AdaBoost CLASSIFIER." *BIOIMAGIN*, 2, 77–82 (2018).

Osher, Stanley, and James A. Sethian. "Fronts propagating with curvature-dependent speed: Algorithms based on Hamilton-Jacobi formulations." *Journal of Computational Physics* 79(1) (1988): 12–49.

Platt, John. "Probabilistic outputs for support vector machines and comparisons to regularized likelihood methods." *Advances in Large Margin Classifiers* 10(3) (1999): 61–74.

Rother, Carsten, Vladimir Kolmogorov, and Andrew Blake. "'rabCut' interactive foreground extraction using iterated graph cuts." *ACM Transactions on Graphics (TOG)* 23(3) (2004): 309–314.

Saeed, Soobia, and Afnizanfaizal Bin Abdullah. "Investigation of a brain cancer with interfacing of 3-dimensional image processing." In: *2019 International Conference on Information Science and Communication Technology (ICISCT)*, IEEE, 2019.

Saeed, Soobia, and Afnizanfaizal Abdullah. "Recognition of brain cancer and cerebrospinal fluid due to the usage of different MRI image by utilizing support vector machine." *Bulletin of Electrical Engineering and Informatics* 9(2) (2020): 619–625.

Saeed, Soobia, Afnizanfaizal Abdullah, and N. Z. Jhanjhi. "Analysis of the Lung Cancer patient's for Data Mining Tool." *IJCSNS* 19(7) (2019a): 90.

Saeed, Soobia, Afnizanfaizal Abdullah, and N. Z. Jhanjhi. "Implementation of Fourier transformation with brain cancer and CSF images." *Indian Journal of Science and Technology* 12(37) (2019b): 37.

Saeed, Soobia, and Raza Jafri. "Estimation of brain tumor using latest technology of mobile phone." *Journal of Information and Communication Technology (JICT)* 9(1) (2015): 32–09.

Wanner, Sven, and Bastian Goldluecke. "Globally consistent depth labeling of 4D light fields." In: *2012 IEEE Conference on Computer Vision and Pattern Recognition*, IEEE, 2012.

Wanner, Sven, Stephan Meister, and Bastian Goldluecke "Datasets and benchmarks for densely sampled 4D light fields." *VMV* 13, 1–12, 2013.

Wanner, Sven, Christoph Straehle, and Bastian Goldluecke. "Globally consistent multi-label assignment on the ray space of 4d light fields." In: *Proceedings of the IEEE Conference on Computer Vision and Pattern Recognition*, 1–12,2013.

Xu, Yichao, et al. "Transcut: Transparent object segmentation from a light-field image." In: *Proceedings of the IEEE International Conference on Computer Vision*, 1–8, 2015.

10

Patient Report Analysis for Identification and Diagnosis of Disease

Muralidharan C., Mohamed Sirajudeen Y., and Anitha R.

CONTENTS

10.1 Introduction 130
10.2 Data Variability 131
    10.2.1 Structured Data.. 132
        10.2.1.1 Human Generated Data 132
        10.2.1.2 Machine Generated Data 132
    10.2.2 Semi-Structured Data 133
    10.2.3 Unstructured Data 133
    10.2.4 Comparison of Structured, Unstructured Data, and
        Semi-Structured 134
10.3 Data Collection of Diseases 135
    10.3.1 EMR Data Collection through eHealth Devices 135
    10.3.2 Semantic Data Extraction from Healthcare Websites.............. 136
    10.3.3 Patient Chatbots 136
    10.3.4 Structured Data.. 137
    10.3.5 Consistency and Quality of Structured Data 137
10.4 Predictive Models for Analysis.. 138
    10.4.1 Regression Techniques 139
    10.4.2 Machine Learning Techniques 140
    10.4.3 Algorithms.. 141
        10.4.3.1 Naïve Bayes.. 141
        10.4.3.2 Support Vector Machine 142
        10.4.3.3 Logistic Regression 142
        10.4.3.4 Decision Trees 142
    10.4.4 Use Cases 142
        10.4.4.1 Cleveland Clinic.. 142
        10.4.4.2 Providence Health 143
        10.4.4.3 Dartmouth Hitchcock 143
        10.4.4.4 Google... 143
10.5 Semi-Structured Data... 144
    10.5.1 Semantic Extraction.. 144
    10.5.2 Web Mantic Extraction... 144
    10.5.3 Use Cases 145

10.6 Unstructured Data.. 145
    10.6.1 Finding Meaning in Unstructured Data 145
    10.6.2 Extraction of Data 146
        10.6.2.1 Text Extraction.. 146
        10.6.2.2 Image Extraction 146
        10.6.2.3 Challenges of Data Extraction from PDFs.................. 147
        10.6.2.4 Video Extraction... 152
        10.6.2.5 Sound Extraction.. 153
    10.6.3 Algorithms... 153
        10.6.3.1 Natural Language Processing...................................... 153
        10.6.3.2 Naïve Bayes.. 154
        10.6.3.3 Deep Learning.. 154
        10.6.3.4 Convolutional Neural Network 154
        10.6.3.5 Phenotyping Algorithms 155
    10.6.4 Use Cases 155
10.7 Conclusion 156
References.. 156

10.1 Introduction

Healthcare is an important field where the health of living beings is improved or maintained through diagnosis, prevention, and treatment of diseases. The costs for the healthcare have been increasing constantly and on the other hand, the quality of care given to the patients has seen considerable improvements. Several researchers in health care industry have come up with a study which shows that after the incorporation of current healthcare technologies, the mortality rate, cost, and complications have been reduced a considerable amount.In 2009, the US government created a Health Information Technology for Economic and Clinical Health Act (HITECH) which includes an incentive scheme worth around 27 billion US dollars for use of Electronic Medical Records. The advances in the IT industry include the ability to collect healthcare data that exists in various forms. Data seems to be an integral part of the healthcare field. A report by Google comments on big data (Luo et al. 2016) indicates that existing healthcare data has the potential worth of 300 billion US dollars because of the advancements in the technologies that enables the sensing and acquisition of data. Healthcare institutions or organizations and hospitals are collecting patients' healthcare data. Advanced analytical techniques need to be developed for better understanding and knowledge of the healthcare data, as it may transform the existing data to meaningful information (Sharmila et al. 2017). Data analysis forms a critical component of these emerging computing technologies. The solutions that are observed from the analysis are then applied to the available healthcare data which have the potential for transforming healthcare from a reactive state to a proactive state (Mohan and Sarojadevi 2018). It has been predicted that for several years healthcare analysis will grow more and more. Typically, the underlying patterns of several diseases can be observed and understood by analyzing health data. This allows the physicians to build a personalized patient profiles which can support the physician for computing accurate diagnoses for the individual patients who are likely to suffer diseases. Healthcare data are the most valuable data and can be derived from a variety of sources such as sensors, clinical notes, images, text from biomedical literatures, or traditional electronic records (Jutel 2011). These different types of data are collected from different sources seem to be heterogeneous in nature, which requires several challenging processes for analysis. Various techniques are needed for analyzing the different forms of data. Due to the heterogeneous nature the data integration seems more challenging. In many of the cases the insights are obtained from diverse data types that cannot be collected from single source. Hence, high potential integrated data analysis methods are needed (Razia et al. 2017). The healthcare field observes many advances that are coming from diverse disciplines such as data mining, databases, information retrieval, healthcare practitioners, and medical researchers. This booming interdisciplinary nature adds richness to the healthcare field, but it also adds challenges for making significant advances. This is because researchers from the computer science field will not have previous exposure to domain-specific medical concepts. Likewise, practitioners and researchers of medical fields will have had limited exposure to the statistical and mathematical concepts that are required for data analytics (Vinitha et al. 2018). This understood to be a critical situation for creating the coherent body of work in this field, even though the available analysis techniques can process the available data. This diversity results in forming an independent line of work that is based on two completely different perspectives. As a result, this chapter aims to provide better understanding about healthcare data and its different forms with some possible algorithms and uses cases.

The chapter has been organized so that Section 10.2 examines the data variability; Section 10.3 focuses on data collection; Section 10.4 describes the structured data; Section 10.5 describes the semi-structured data; Section 10.6 briefly explains the unstructured data; and Section 10.7 concludes the chapter.

10.2 Data Variability

Put simply, data is something that provides valuable information by analyzing it. Data are of different sizes and formats. For example, data information that are provided in a resume will be about a particular person and will include educational details, working experience, personal interests, address, etc. Small sized data can be easily analyzed or understood. But in recent times, the size of digital data has increased tremendously. This may include different forms of data that need to be collected and analyzed for extracting information. Digital data can come in different forms such as structured, unstructured, and semi-structured.

10.2.1 Structured Data

Structured data are organized or labeled data that can be analyzed easily and effectively. They are well organized data that are formatted in a repository such as a database. This includes all the data that are stored in an SQL database as rows and columns. Usually, a database has relational keys with which the fields can be easily mapped, hence accessibility and searching information is too easy in such type. They are comparatively too simple for storing, retrieving, and analyzing, but are strictly defined in terms of field type and field name. Nowadays, these types of data seem to the be most processed, as it is simpler for information processing, but they represent only 10% of all the informatics data. Thus, it is not be sufficient to extract the information by analyzing the data. An example is relational data.

The data source can be from two different sources such as:

1. Data generated by humans
2. Data generated by machines

10.2.1.1 Human Generated Data

These data are generated by humans by making an interaction with machines. **Examples include:**

Input data: Input data are fed to a machine by a human. For example, to understand customer behavior data like their name, sex, age, income, and survey responses (which are non-free) and so on will be collected.

Click stream data: This data can be generated from websites whenever a link is clicked. This might be analyzed for acquiring valuable information.

Gaming-related data: In games every move made by the gamer will be recorded for understanding the behaviors of the different users so that the game can be updated.

10.2.1.2 Machine Generated Data

These data are generated automatically without any interaction by the human.

Examples include:

Sensor data: this includes RFID tags, healthcare devices, smart meters, GPS data, etc. These can be used in the inventory control and supply chain management.

Log data: the behavior of the applications, servers, and networks will be recorded every now and then while they operate. These behavioral logs are called log data. These logs will be in huge forms which can be used to predict the security breaches that occur and other changes in the service level agreements.

Point-of-sale data: the product related information can be generated when the bar code of the product is scanned while it is purchased.

Financial data: systems used in financial sectors are automated through predefined rules. For example, trading data which contains the symbol of the company and its dollar value.

10.2.2 Semi-Structured Data

Semi-structured data are structured data formed in an unorganized way. This type of data has the properties related to an organization but will not reside in the relational database and can be processed easily. By making changes in the process, it can be stored in the relational database. Since it does not have the formal structure as a relational database or any other form of data tables, it needs tags or other form of markers for separating the semantic elements, hierarchies, and fields that exist within the data. Examples include the data in websites such as JSON files, .csv files, XML files, and delimited text files. Since this type of data are in unorganized forms it is difficult to store, retrieve, and analyze.

10.2.3 Unstructured Data

The data that is in unorganized formats or that do not have data models are said to be unstructured data. Therefore, it will not fit the relational database in a predefined manner. Thus, for these types of data, alternative advanced tools (software, etc.) will be used for storing, accessing, and managing the data. This type will be most prevalent in IT systems for varieties of business intelligence, and for different analytics applications for predicting valuable information. Examples include Word files, PDFs, images, videos, audio, text, web pages, emails, and other streaming data.

Examples of unstructured data (generated by machines) include:

- **Satellite data:** data collected from satellites such as surveillance imagery, weather, etc.
- **Scientific data:** atmospheric data which are collected by sensors and machines.

- **Photographs and video:** surveillance footage, traffic monitoring videos, etc.

Examples of unstructured data (generated by humans):

1. **The internal text of enterprises:** this includes documents, logs, and e-mails that are maintained for an organization. The information of the enterprise seems to generate the largest text information.
2. **Social media data:** data generated from social media outlets such as Youtube, LinkedIn, Flickr, etc.
3. **Mobile data:** data collected from mobile devices include location information, text messages, user logs, etc.
4. **Website content:** the data that are collected from any website will be in unstructured format. This may include data gather from Twitter, and Instagram, etc.

10.2.4　Comparison of Structured, Unstructured Data, and Semi-Structured

Table 10.1

TABLE 10.1

Comparison of Structured, Semi-Structured, and Unstructured Data

Field	STRUCTURED DATA	SEMI-STRUCTURED DATA	UNSTRUCTURED DATA
Technology	Relational database	XML/RDF	Binary data
Management of Versions	Versioning can be done over rows, tuples, tables.	Versioning is possible through graph or tuples	Versioning as the whole
Management of Transactions	Transaction is matured and uses concurrency Techniques	Transaction is based on DBMS and are not matured.	No concurrency and transaction management
Scalability of data	Low	Medium	High
Flexibility of data	Flexibility is low and is schema dependent	Flexibility is higher than structured data and lower than unstructured data	More Flexible and no schema dependency
Robustness	Highly robust	Not very spread as it is new technology	—
Performance of Query	Queries are Structured which allows joining of complex data	Anonymous nodes can be queried	Query over text is alone possible

10.3 Data Collection of Diseases

Data collection is defined as the process of collecting, analyzing, and interpreting different types of information relating to a particular disease or healthcare need. Traditional patient records are collected from sources like personal surveys, handwritten prescriptions, and hardcopies of the patient's records from local hospitals. Prior to the evolvement of digital data, the healthcare records come in physical form. Thus, the data are collected and managed within the hospital itself. But following the recent IT advancements, patient records are collected in a digital format (Kaur and Siri 2006). Some of the examples of digital data used in the field of medicine are digital scan reports, videos shot on laparoscopic cameras, digital X-ray reports, endoscopy videos, and ultrasonic records. These medical data are fast growing data in the digital world. As per the survey conducted by DELL EMC. (2018) the healthcare data growth rate has increased by 878% since 2016. It also claims that the total amount of healthcare data will have reached 20,000 petabytes by 2020. In addition to that, more healthcare applications and databases are developed every day that work with healthcare data.

An important source of electronic medical records are electronic health (eHealth) devices and communication-supported health devices. These collect data at frequent intervals from patients though eHealth devices and store it in cloud storage. If the data are collected from patients through electronic devices directly, then the data are called Patient-Generated Healthcare Data (PGHD). The Cloud Service Provider (CSP) maintains the patient's clinical data like demographics, progress notes, problems, and medications on cloud storage. Patients' medical records are digitalized and assist in ensuring data is accurate. Electronic Medical Records (EMR) data collection can be classified as both quantitative and qualitative data collection. In quantitative data collection, the data are collected in the form of numeric variables. In other words, the information is collected from the patient as numeric values, such as count, number, and percentage. Qualitative data collection methods collect patient data in a non-numeric fashion. This type of data is collected through methods of observation, one-to-one interviews, and online surveys. Qualitative data are also known as categorical data.

The important ways of collecting the Electronic Medical Records (EMR) are eHealth devices, semantic data collection, and patient chatbots.

10.3.1 EMR Data Collection through eHealth Devices

eHealth devices are also called self-monitoring healthcare devices. They use sensors and wireless communication design to measure the patient's health and transfer it to cloud storage. This allows the patient, as well as the physicians, to measure and monitor the patient's health remotely. Some of the available healthcare monitoring eHealth devices in the market are temperature devices, heartbeat tracking devices, glucometers, oximeters, pulsometers, and blood pressure devices. These IoT-based healthcare devices are considered to be an important advancement in the field of healthcare management. As the use of cloud computing and wireless technology increases, the demand for eHealth devices is also rapidly growing. It is predicted that in 2020, eHealth devices will account for 80% of wireless devices. The main advantage of these devices are mobility and accessibility of smartphones and tablets.

10.3.2 Semantic Data Extraction from Healthcare Websites

Semantic extraction of healthcare information extracts information related to a particular disease, medical facts, attributes from a website, or unstructured data. The purpose of semantic data extraction in healthcare is to enable analysis of the unstructured content, electronic prescriptions, medical text documents, emails, digital images, and patient reports. The main objective of semantic analysis is to structure the unstructured data (Wu et al. 2018).

Semantic data extraction on websites has two major approaches: rule matching data collection and machine learning data collection

Rule matching data collection: this collects the information related to a particular word or phrase from websites. A rule-based matching algorithm is used on raw medical websites to gather the information about a particular disease. They also provide access to the tokens within the document and their relationships.

Machine learning–based data collection: this is a statistical analysis of the content, the potential compute-intensive application that can benefit from using Hadoop. This approach derives the relationship from statistical co-occurrence within the website.

10.3.3 Patient Chatbots

To deliver quality services to the patients, medical informatics entities are using recent technologies like Artificial Intelligence and predictive technologies in the healthcare application. It is impossible for a patient to get advice from physicians in an emergency situation. To provide "round the clock" medical advice to patients, healthcare industries are investing a lot in the creation of automated medical chatbots. Medical chatbots are conversational software available for smartphone applications. They provide a more immediate service for patients. They are adequate enough to communicate and gather information from the patients. The collected information is fed to the deep learning algorithms to improve the intelligence of the chatbots. These medical chatbots are a recent trend in the healthcare industry. Some of the most popular chatbots are related to the healthcare industry.

10.3.4 Structured Data

Medical data exists in different forms such as laboratory test results, notes by physicians, lifestyle data of patients, vital signs, and various forms of imagery data such as Magnetic Resonance Imaging (MRI), radiology, ultrasonography, pathology slides. etc. There is no proper standard for encompassing the medical data, hence it is important to understand the information of the data before processing it.

Structured data are organized and consistent in nature. Structured data can be analyzed easily. A few examples of medical data include numerical values such as blood pressure, height and weight, and categorical values, such as blood type, diagnostic stage of disease, etc. It is a non-homogenous and non-monolithic category as the data will be in structured form and it doesn't mean that it makes sense with the data as it is in structured form. Furthermore, we cannot say that the data with no formal structure cannot be interrupted easily.

10.3.5 Consistency and Quality of Structured Data

The structured data consists of two main parts – the value and the variable name. Consider the height of patients. In electronic medical records of patients, the height of the patient might be stored as "height: 64". This depicts the height of the patient in inches. It is also possible to store the value in meters as "height: 1.625m" or it might be stored in terms of yards as "1.77 yards" and so on. The variable might also be stored in different forms.

Logical Observation Identifiers Names and Codes (LOINC) is a universal and database standard developed for identifying the medical laboratory reports. Health Level 7 is an international standard for transferring administrative and clinical data between the application which are used by various medical providers. The Fast Healthcare Interoperability Resources (FHIR), is a drafting standard for elements, data formats, and API for exchanging the medical data.

Usually structured patient generated data is collected from devices that are held with the consumers and it may not be an FDA approved device, hence the data from these devices cannot be compared to each other although they are in structured format. For example, when using an accelerometer the number of steps walked by a consumer is measured but there is no standard algorithm for converting this raw data. Though this data is inconsistent, the clinician still uses it to find the relative improvement of patient for a period of time, conditionally the patient should use the same electronic device for the entire period. But the direct patient comparison wiould be implausible. To overcome these issues standardized devices should be used.

10.4 Predictive Models for Analysis

The predictive models that exist in the data analytics provide a valuable score for measurable medical data elements. These can also predict and provide the probability of diseases that can affect the patient in the near future. It may also provide the likelihood of a patient defaulting on a disease based on his or her personal history or characteristics. Statistical models are also available for predicting the type of disease and prevention of diseases.

The context of applying predictive analytics is quite diverse. The expected outcomes may vary from binary values such as "yes/no" or "true/false" for fake prediction to predict the real numerical values of medical field (Asif et al. 2018). Here, different classes of predictive techniques have been discussed which will support the reader to understand the various models that are prevalent.

1. **Managing the Data Sources:** for managing the data sources, the quality and operational pathways need to be understood. The data may come from different sources such as a staging platform, warehouse, or a "data mart" which is owned by an application. The most important thing for the production is change management. This is because while upstreaming the data sources the change tolerance or anticipation and is important and must not be restricted by the coming changes. To get into the main data, it is suggested to have an engine related to the medical field for the parsing and use of the structured data in the form of Extract, Transform, and Load (ETL).

2. **Metadata Management:** data about the data is metadata. An example can be seen in that the codes of ICD-10 will have different meanings, but with these diagnostic codes the risk cannot be well understood anf it will not be sufficient. The biggest risks are the most expensive diseases; dangerous patient health conditions which come from the concomitant interactions and an understanding of the disease relationship is almost a prediction. For organization which are not capable of understanding these relationships, specifications such as the CMS-DRG codes can be used.

3. **Population Segmentation:** almost all the medicare predictive analytics need to create the population segments. Even to evaluate the goal of the provider, having an understanding of the populations is important. Thus, population segments are one of the core capabilities for healthcare analytics. An important element is the physiological state of the patients and this is known from the primary data source. Segmenting the population is also important for responding to interventions.

4. **Data Manipulation:** using most of the ETL functions, the data can be processed, transformed, compared, and managed with more aggressive capabilities for natural language processing. The tools for manipulation are available as free resources, and the terminology engines seem to be more sophisticated as these capabilities are embedded within them.

5. **Predicting Healthcare Facts:** this is the core capability of the whole process. It is important that the solution from the prediction supports the system to act upon the human health. Integrating the predictions with the systems that are exposed to customers must be more simplified for convenience (Chen et al. 2017).

Predictive analytics can be classified into two major learning methods: supervised and unsupervised. In supervised learning the target variable is easily acquired using traditional techniques. The trained data can be used to create a model that can reveal the correlations between target and input variable. Whereas in unsupervised learning, patterns and trends in the data need to be discovered without any pre-defined assumptions. Attribute-based algorithms can be constructed through this learning process by determining the association and clusters in the data.

Predictive analytics can be grouped into two major groups: regression and machine learning techniques.

10.4.1 Regression Techniques

Regression analysis is one of the predictive modeling techniques which predict the dependency between the target variables. It is used to predict sales trends, and the possibility of churns or fraudulent transactions. It focuses on forming the mathematical equation for capturing the interactions between the different targets, thereby reducing the overall error in the predicted model

Linear regression is one type of regression model that can be used to predict the response variable in a linear manner. The parameters can be adjusted or learned so that the addition of squared residuals is minimized.

Logistic regression assigns probabilities for the possible outcomes. A binary outcome variable can be converted to an unbounded continuous variable from which a regular multivariate model is estimated.

Time series models are used for predicting the future behavior of the variables when the internal structures such as trends, auto correlation, etc. is available. They are capable of analysing the components such as seasonal and trends through which better models can be produced. A few time series models include: the Moving Average Model, the Auto Regressive Model. A combination of these two models is called an Auto Regressive Moving Average and Auto Regressive Integrated Moving Average.

Decision trees is a model which sees the collection of defined rules based on variables in the dataset, where the rules are defined so as to obtain the best split for differentiating the observations that belong to different target classes. Rules are explanatory and are preferred by the data analysts.

10.4.2 Machine Learning Techniques

Machine learning–based models are another form of predictive analytics that are used for applications such as diagnosing medical conditions, or fraud detection, and more. However, unlike classification or regression trees, this model remains a black box without considering the relationship between the predictor variables, and it sufficiently predicts the dependent variable.

Among the various existing machine learning models, neural networks are the model which is inspired by the human nervous system. It has become increasingly popularity in recent times as it is capable of learning complex relationships among the predictor variables. For classification there exists a wide variety of neural network models. The earlier neural network models used only three layers – the input, hidden, and output layer – and the deep neural model has gained popularity by using more than one hidden layer. Large numbers of neurons and the interconnections between them are capable of modeling non-linear relationships between input and output variables.

Some of the most commonly used neural networks that are suitable for prediction tasks are:

1. Multilayer Perceptron

   This neural network uses more than one hidden layer of neurons. It is also known as "deep feed forward neural networks".

2. Convolutional Neural Networks

   This type of neural network performs convolutions between the input data and desired filter. They are more efficient in learning hierarchal features from the data by extracting the relationships between the neighbors.

3. Recurrent Neural Network

   These types of neural network have hidden layer neurons which have self-connections for helping the neuron to possess memory. These types of networks are suitable for text processing as the interpretation of the text will be dependent on neighboring words or contexts. Thus, these types of neural network models the interrelationships of words by considering their sequence.

4. Long-Short Term Memory Network

   This type of network are extensions of recurrent neural networks in which each hidden layer neuron will be incorporated with a memory cell. They are good at finding long-distance relationships. These types of networks can be applied for analyzing any kind of sequential data.

10.4.3 Algorithms

Figure 10.1 shows the algorithms that are used for analyzing the healthcare data. The algorithms used for analyzing structured data are discussed below.

10.4.3.1 Naïve Bayes

Naïve Bayes is a classifier method used for categorization of text, and for solving the problem of document judging so as to identify the category to which it belongs to. The Naïve Bayes classifier considers that one particular feature of the class will be unrelated to other features. Even though the features of a class are independent, all its properties will independently contribute its probability for a certain category. It is one of the most efficient classification algorithms that has been successfully applied for many medical related problems.

1. Support Vector Machine

2. Neural Networks

3. Discriminant Analysis

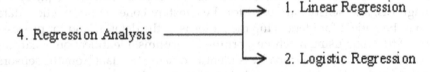

4. Regression Analysis ⟶ 1. Linear Regression

⟶ 2. Logistic Regression

5. Random Forest

6. Naïve Bayes

7. Decision Tree

8. Nearest Neighbor

FIGURE 10.1
Algorithms used for health care analysis.

10.4.3.2 Support Vector Machine

Support Vector Machines (SVM) can be applied for both classification and regression, but this algorithm is widely used in classification-related problems which divides the dataset into two different classes through a hyperplane. The goal of using the hyperplane is to find the greatest distance between the hyperplane or possible margin at any point within the training data, through which the new data can be correctly classified. In SVM, the solution will always be the global optimum as it deals with the convex optimization problems. They are extensively used in identifying cancer, cancer prediction and diagnosis, detection of neurological diseases, and in general for classifying datasets with imbalanced values.

10.4.3.3 Logistic Regression

Logistic regression is one of the multivariable algorithms which is used for analyzing dichotomous outcomes. The procedure of logistic regression is nearly the same as that of multiple linear regression, but the only difference is that the response variable will be binomial. When compared to linear regression, the confounding effects are avoided by analyzing the variables' association. In the healthcare field, it is widely used to solve classification-related problems and for predicting the event probability.

10.4.3.4 Decision Trees

Decision trees are mostly used in the diagnosis of illnesses in the medical field. In some cases, constant monitoring of auto neuropathy is required for diagnosis, and sensors are used for the constant collection of medical data from the patient for identifying the patterns in the datasets and for processing of this data using machine learning algorithms. Identification of cardiovascular autonomic neuropathy is identified using the data from the sensors by understanding the signs of diabetes. This analysis further supports the development of advanced diet and treatment plans for the patient.

10.4.4 Use Cases

10.4.4.1 Cleveland Clinic

Cleveland Clinic aims to evaluate the quality of providers by creating risk adjustment score. For evaluating the quality of the care delivered, it is impossible to create an "apples to apples" comparison. To solve this problem, a risk adjustment score is created for all the individuals who have suffered with similar but unique situations, this allows the statistical models to be predictive. Using sparsely annotated procedure codes, the Cleveland Clinic compares the factors that are not related to the patient's physiology using the annotated procedure codes. This study has the ability to compare the employers, health plans, and institutions while also accounting for the represented populations. This innovation uses simple data that can be availed of from administrative records.

10.4.4.2 Providence Health

Providence Health demonstrates the management of high-risk patients by collaborating multidisciplinary values. This disease care management program can be used in relation to heart failure, diabetes management, asthma, coronary disease, and COPD. It assesses the risk of the patient based on type of emergency. Care teams collaborated with data scientists and felt that working with simple and elegant solutions is more sufficient, as more complex data mining is not possible.

10.4.4.3 Dartmouth Hitchcock

Dartmouth Hitchcock predicts readmission risk. It includes the creation of readmission predictive models which are culled from Epic Clarity's data warehouse, and it has been found that Dartmouth remains one of the 22% of American hospitals that avoids readmission penalties which are levied by the Centers for Medicare and Medicaid Services. For congestive heart failure, pneumonia, heart attacks, lung ailments such as chronic bronchitis, and knee or hip replacements, the avoidance of unnecessary readmissions the Dartmouth is in the top 2% of hospitals. This has shown that Dartmouth is a place which ensures that patients are healing after they leave the hospital.

10.4.4.4 Google

Google uses unlikely data sources to predict where the locations of flu and dengue, which is semi-real time in nature. The team of data scientists collaborate with the epidemiologists from all over the world to parse the search streams in order to predict, in real time, the whereabouts of flu and dengue. In the case of the flu, they used surveillance data to validate the findings. In the case of dengue, the epidemiological data from many developing countries are collected via Google. Based on the search stream, Google predicts the presence of flu, and after few months the team validates the predictions through further surveillance methods. In this case, a fundamental epidemiological breakthrough took place which reduces the wait time as the disease trend is achieved. In few years, this type of outside-the-box thinking will be determining the extents to which healthcare systems dominate in a new place, where the predictions will be embedded into administrative and clinical software.

10.5 Semi-Structured Data

Semi-structured data comes in the form of structured data which does not rely on the formal structure of data models that are associated with relational databases or any other forms of data tables. It includes tags or markers for separating semantic elements. It enforces the hierarchy of fields and records that exist within the data. This can also be called the self-describing data model. Here, the entities which belong to single class will have different attributes. Another important fact is that the attribute order is not important. These types of data seem to increasingly occur since the emergence of the internet. Semi-structured data are often found in object-oriented databases.

10.5.1 Semantic Extraction

Semantic extraction is a processing technique that is used to extract and identify entities such as organizations, animals, locations, etc. for populating meta data. The purpose of this model is to analyze unstructured data such as text documents, images, emails, reports, and other business content. The semantic analysis of unstructured data seems to be an important technique as the unstructured data can be converted into structured data. The accuracy of this model seems to be critical, because without a considerable level of accuracy there is the risk of feeding the decision makers with non-actionable or misleading insights.

Semantic extraction is based on one of two approaches:

- **Rule-Based Matching:** this requires a greater number of vocabularies, which is similar to the entity extraction.
- **Machine Learning:** if the data seem to be in substantial form, the statistical analysis can be computed for intensive application. Machine learning uses the corpus with which it derives the relationships of the data.
- **Hybrid Approach:** this is a statistically driven approach but it can be enhanced through vocabulary. If the content set seems to be a specific area, then it seems to be the most suitable approach.

10.5.2 Web Mantic Extraction

Web Mantic extraction is the extraction that converts a HTML page into an XML document. Tables and lists are the two structures which are used to represent the information of the web pages. It includes few steps, such as:

- A tree generator is used to represent the structures that are stored in web pages. The lists and tables in the pages create a tree structure.

- For converting HTML to XML, it is the rule generator module where the data represented in tree form that will be used for generating rules that represent the important information that has to be translated. Then, the XML tags are defined by the user.
- The subsumption module is used to generalize the rules which are defined when an XML tag created will represent the same concept.
- The XML Parser module creates the XML document. Header files of the XML are automatically written. Semantic generator rules will be executed sequentially for preprocessing.

10.5.3 Use Cases

- **Website Management:** in website management the designers tend to have concern for the management of content, structure, and graphical presentation simultaneously. As a result, it is difficult to restructure the websites. This is because integrity constrains enforcement, and the possibility of creating multiple sites with same data and updating of the websites. It can be managed by specifying the structure of the website in a declarative manner as a website exists over an integrated collection of data. Several systems can be built such as: Strudel, Araneus, YAT, Autoweb, and Tiramisu.
- **Test of XML:** XML (Extended Markup Language) is emerging as a standard for exchanging data over the Web. It enables separation of the content (XML) and separation of presentation (such as XSL). Document Type Descriptors (DTDs) provide spatial schemas for XML documents. All the application then needs is to manage the XML data. Here, attributes, objects, and atomic values are taken as tags, elements, and character respectively for extraction of data.

10.6 Unstructured Data

Unstructured data, on the other hand, lacks the organization and precision of structured data. Examples in this category include physician notes, x-ray images, and even faxed copies of structured data. In most cases, unstructured data must be manually analyzed and interpreted.

10.6.1 Finding Meaning in Unstructured Data

It is a great challenge to analyze and interpret unstructured data than structured data. Free texts and images cannot be categorized easily in the same way. For example, straightforward code can be used to interpret blood pressure readings (such as normal, elevated, or hypertensive). While considering the physician's notes the interpretation of such as "chest pain, gen fatigue, trouble breath" will also suggest hypertension. However, abbreviations and spelling errors need to be decoded through human interpretation.

Imagery presents challenges when similar images (such as x-rays and pathology slides) are indecipherable for all except well-trained professionals and, even though the clinicians are experienced a second opinion is often required for validating the diagnosis or interpretation. The unstructured data is largely analyzed in the medical industry as most of the medical data requires images to diagnose.

With the advancements of Artificial Intelligence and machine learning techniques, the unstructured data can be transformed as needed. A natural language processing tool can be used for decoding the physician's note, and the above example then can be interpreted as "chest pain, general fatigue, trouble breathing". A machine learning decision support tool might be used for suggesting that these symptoms are related to hypertension

Data scientists are working with large amounts of data from repositories for training the machine learning models for pattern recognition of medical images thereby providing automated secondary opinion for interpretation or diagnosis of disease.

10.6.2 Extraction of Data

10.6.2.1 Text Extraction

Step 1: it is impossible to analyze the entire text manually, hence a random or stratified sample is needed to build a dictionary.

Step 2: for capturing the true essence of the available text, the data needs to be cleaned. For example, "Sathish's, Sathish, and Satish" should be considered as one word. Another important thing is to remove the stop words.

Step 3: after cleaning the text, the most frequently occurring words are extracted. Manual identification of the frequently occurring words can also be conducted. This will form the dictionary.

Step 4: entire datasets has been cleaned which will make sure that the created dictionary will work on the entire dataset.

Step 5: with this dictionary, every transaction statement can be categorized.

Step 6: once the tags on each transaction statement are created, the entirety of the data can be summarized for gaining business strategies and insights.

10.6.2.2 Image Extraction

In the healthcare field, computer vision plays a major role. It is used to analyze medical-related images and medical research-related PDFs for different purposes, such as drug development processes, patient care systems, etc. With computer vision, unusual patterns can be analyzed using AI algorithms for registration, segmentation, and fusion of images.

Data extraction can be taken from two different types of healthcare data such as:

1. **Data from X-rays, CT Scans, MRIs, etc.:** the growth rate of such types of data has been estimated as at 300% each year. These types of medical data can be used for training computer vision algorithms for deriving the insights faster to imrpove the patient care. With the support of AI algorithms, new cures can be realized. It also finds hidden patterns of diseases and the physicians can thus find more causes and make more diagnoses of disease.

2. **Data from Medical Publications:** this includes medical-related theses and information about ongoing medical research and clinical trials. Usually these types of data will be available as PDF. These types of scanned images cannot be analyzed manually as it is too time-consuming. Hence, systematic analyzation visualization is necessary.

10.6.2.3 Challenges of Data Extraction from PDFs

Data that are used by the medical researchers will be available on the web in different formats. It is impossible to extract all the important and relevant information from PDFs and image files. Though the computer vision uses AI techniques, it is more challenging to extract data from text images and PDFs because the document may be in different forms such as single or double columns, layout variations, multiple fronts, pie charts, and other varying formats (Rosenbloom et al. 2011).

PDFs are scanned images, hence it is hard to read the text and the text extraction of PDF includes footnotes removal, exclusion of graphs, and so on. To overcome this problem, optical character recognition is used for differentiating the symbols and formats, etc., for enabling the efficient readability of the scanned document (Wu et al. 2018). The feature extraction steps are shown below with an example:

1. **Original image of Vessel Extraction from Digital Retinal Images**

   A sample image is shown in Figure 10.2 for the image analysis discussion.

2. **Forming Identity Kernel**

   The identity kernel will not change the given original image and are seen as a black and white form as shown in Figure 10.3.

3. **Edge Detection (Horizontal Form)**

   The changes in the horizontal direction of the image can be seen in Figure 10.4. We can observe that the light that occurs from the lighting beam is filtered off.

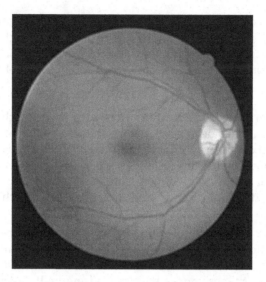

FIGURE 10.2
Original image of retina.

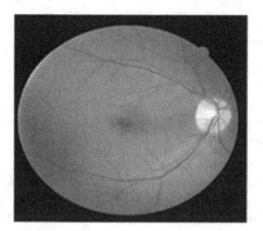

FIGURE 10.3
Identity kernel formation.

4. **Edge Detection (Vertical)**

   The changes will be made in the vertical direction of the images. It is observed that the light beam has been returned in blurred form in the natural image, as shown in Figure 10.5.

5. **Edge Detection (Gradient Magnitude)**

   The square root of summed value is needed in order to get the gradient magnitude as shown in Figure 10.6.

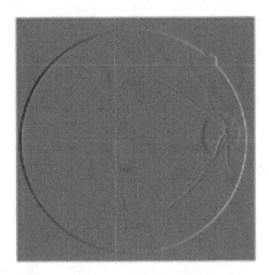

FIGURE 10.4
Edge detection in horizontal form.

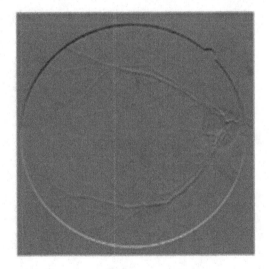

FIGURE 10.5
Edge detection in vertical direction.

6. **Edge Detection (Gradient Direction)**

    Using the arc tangent function, the gradient direction can be obtained, as shown in Figure 10.7.

7. **The Sobel Filter (Gradient Magnitude)**

    Now let us consider the Sobel filter used for getting the gradient magnitude as shown in Figure 10.8.

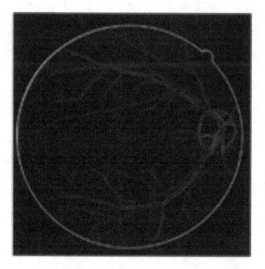

FIGURE 10.6
Edge detection in gradient magnitude.

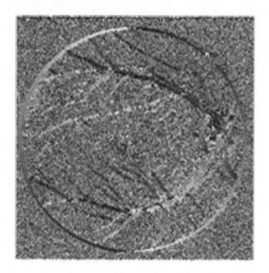

FIGURE 10.7
Edge detection in gradient direction.

8. Sobel Filters (Gradient Direction)

For gradient directions, the Sobel filter is again used and it can be found that the roots are clear, as shown in Figure 10.9.

9. Gaussian Blur

Using the Gaussian filter the image is blurred as shown in Figure 10.10 which is called a Gaussian blur.

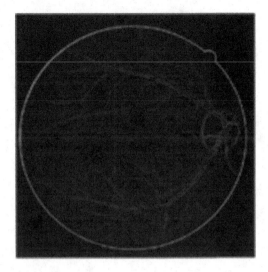

FIGURE 10.8
Sobel filters in gradient magnitude.

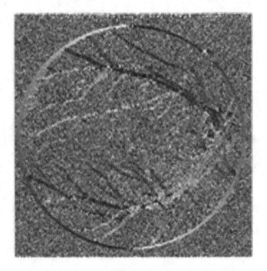

FIGURE 10.9
Sobel filters in gradient direction.

10. **Sharpening the Edges**

The images can be sharpened by finding the edges of the images as shown in Figure 10.11.

11. **Emboss**

With this tool, the images can be viewed with a shadow effect. This results in forming a "bump map" of the image.

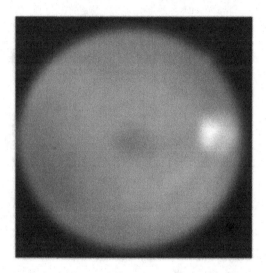

FIGURE 10.10
Gaussian blur.

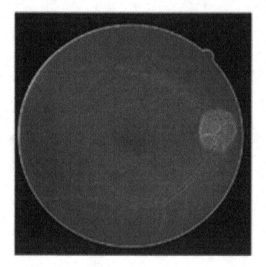

FIGURE 10.11
Image with sharpened edges.

10.6.2.4 Video Extraction

The video data model is the representation of video data and its content. The idea behind the model is segmentation or annotation of video. Mining of video data requires a good data model for the representation. Various models have been proposed by different authors. Petkovic et al., (2000) proposed a content-based data retrieval model which includes four layers. They are:

1. A raw video data layer that includes a sequence of frames, as well as some of the attributes of the video.
2. A feature layer which consists of domain independent features extracted from the raw data. It also characterizes the colors, shapes, motion, and textures.
3. An object layer holds the entities which are characterized by prominent spatial dimensions and are then assigned to all the regions across the frames.
4. An event layer holds the entities which are characterized by a prominent temporal extent which describes the interactions and movements of different objects in a spatial-temporal manner.

10.6.2.5 Sound Extraction

Vacher et al., (2006) state that the everyday sounds that exists around us can be divided into different classes. The criteria used for this categorization includes statistical probability of occurrence of sound in the everyday life, alarm sounds (maybe a scream) for priority, sound duration (unalarming sounds are considered to be short and impulsive). These classes can be related to two different categories:

- Normal sounds that happen which are related to the usual activity of patients such as doors closing or being locked, walking sounds, phones ringing, the sound of dishes being moved, and human sounds such as coughing, and sneezing.
- Abnormal sounds that can be interpreted as a kind of alarm include breaking glasses, human screams, the sound of someone falling, and more. If it is recognized, the sound analysis system will transmit an alarm to the application used for medical supervising. The decision to call the emergency department is made by this data fusion system.

The signal detection seems to be more important because once an event is lost, it will be lost forever. On the other hand, with the best conditions the start and stop time of sounds must be established accurately for using the classification steps. Unlike fast fourier transform, wavelet transform seems to be more adapted for signaling which have more localized features than time independent wave like signals such as door slap, breaking of glasses, step sound etc.

10.6.3 Algorithms

10.6.3.1 Natural Language Processing

In the healthcare industry, the clinical information comes in the form of written text which will be in huge forms, such as laboratory reports, physical examination reports, operation notes of patients, discharge related summaries, etc. These are usually in unstructured forms and are not comprehensible for the computer-based programs as they need special models for processing the text (Luo et al. 2016). The Natural Language Processing model provides a solution to these issues by identifying a series of keywords that are relevant to the disease in the patient notes based on the existing databases, thereby enriching the structured data for supporting clinical decision making.

10.6.3.2 Naïve Bayes

The Naïve Bayes classifier is a probabilistic method used for categorizing the text, and solving the problem of document predictions for finding the category to which it belongs to. The Naïve Bayes classifier considers that one particular feature of the class will be unrelated to other features. Even though the features of a class are independent, all its properties will independently contribute its probability for a certain category. It is one of the most efficient probabilistic classification algorithms that are successfully applied for many of the medical related problems.

10.6.3.3 Deep Learning

Deep learning belongs to the machine learning family and it is based on the artificial neural network techniques, as it is a neural network with an increased number of layers. When compared to traditional machine learning algorithms, the more complex non-linear patterns can be learned using the deep learning algorithms in the data. Modules are pipelined and are trainable. It is a scalable approach and the automatic feature extraction of data can be performed.

In healthcare applications, these types of algorithms handle both the tasks such as machine learning and language processing. The predominantly used deep learning algorithms are convolution neural networks, deep belief networks, the multilayer perception model, and recurrent neural networks. It remains one of the most effective classification algorithms and is successfully used in addressing many healthcare-related problems, such as healthcare report classification and journal classification.

10.6.3.4 Convolutional Neural Network

Convolutional neural networks (CNNs) are developed to handle high dimensional data or data with an increased number of traits. As proposed by LeCun et al., (1995), the pixel values that are rectified with the normalization of images will be the inputs. Convolutional networks were inspired by medical processes, and thus the connectivity pattern that exists between the neurons with separate cortical neurons (which respond to the stimuli in the region) is restricted. However, the whole visual field is covered as the receptive field of various neurons will overlap. The CNN then transfers the weighted pixel values of the image in the convolution layers and sampling is done in the subsampling layers. The final output will be a recursive function of the input values.

10.6.3.5 Phenotyping Algorithms

Phenotyping algorithms are implemented using the samples of the diseases on the EHR data that are usually collected from healthcare units for diagnosing the diseases. The data may be in an unstructured form which contains large amount of texts from the physicians' reports, various diagnostics of diseases, and different vital signs. A phenotyping algorithm is a different form of special model that is carried through various numbers of medical data points with specific codes for radiology results, billing, and natural language processing where different forms of texts are extracted from the physicians. Machine learning algorithms with supported vector machines can be applied for identifying arthritis in a combination of patient's prescription records for improving the accuracy of predictive models of disease. For example, the prevalent condition of diabetic patients can be suggested by examining the usage of hypoglycemic agents that are collected from the prescription records.

10.6.4 Use Cases

1. **Automated Trigger:** an automated trigger for sepsis clinical decision support using ML has been created. It involves the extraction of text and vital signs for predicting the life-threatening infection that may affect the patients. Natural Language Processing (NLP) is used for extracting the data from the clinical text. It has been found that the area under the curve value is 0.667 without using the NLP and 0.86 when the NLP is used. It was also seen that the accuracy of the model is increased when the language processing algorithm is used.

2. **Patient Risk Prediction:** this is an important process as it is used for making decisions. It assists the physicians in making valuable predictions. The predicted test result values will be used to ensure that the particular treatment which was undergone is useful or not. It has been found that out of the total predictive rules used, 97% of them seem to be more sensible when the NLP is used. There are other cases where the physician's prediction ability is seen to be poor. For this instance, oncologists found that only 20% accuracy is achieved while predicting the survival rates of ill patients.

3. **Cohort Building:** this can be done by leveraging the oncology department's electronic health record data. A demonstration of non-small cell lung cancer is done using the structured as well as

unstructured data. It is found that 8,324 patients are affected with non-small cell lung cancer by using both the type of data. Out of the 8,324 patients, more than 2,000 patients were found with the cohort which was formed by structured data. In addition to this, 1,090 patients would be further included in the cohort if only the structured data is used. It was found that more than 1,000 patients did not match with the parameters of the study. Hence, only the patients affected with non-small cell lung cancer that are more than 2,000 in number were found to be the true cohort that can be used for analysis. This analysis highlights the importance of analyzing both structured and unstructured data.

10.7 Conclusion

This chapter has outlined that there is a consequential need for the improvement of structured, semi-structured, and unstructured healthcare data for storing, analyzing, and interpreting. Though powerful tools already exist for analysis – one that might help the analysts to analyze the data well – there is a lack of standardization which continues to impede the overall process. Machine learning, language processing, and Artificial Intelligence have the potential to streamline the way that the unstructured data can be utilized, but we fail to capture the point that the machines are making the critical decisions instead of traditional decision-making physicians. Regardless, all patients should aexpect and look forward for improved medical or health outcomes as the technological advancements continue to improve the way health data are used. Thus, this chapters elaborates on the different forms of healthcare data with examples of relevant algorithms and use cases, thereby supporting users to understand the basic concepts of healthcare data analysis.

References

Asif, Muhammad, H. F. M. C. M. Martiniano, A. M. Vicente, and F. M. Couto "Identifying disease genes using machine learning and gene functional similarities, assessed through Gene Ontology". *PLoS One* 13(12) (2018): 12.

Ba, Mohan, and H. Sarojadevi "Disease diagnosis system by exploring machine learning algorithms". *International Journal of Innovations in Engineering and Technology* 10(2) (2018): 14–21.

Chen, Min, et al. "Disease prediction by machine learning over big data from healthcare communities". *IEEE Access* 5 (2017): 8869–8879.

Istrate, D., E. Castelli, M. Vacher, L. Besacier, and J.-F., Serignat. Information Extraction From Sound for Medical Telemonitoring. Information Technology in Biomedicine, IEEE Transactions on, 2006, 10(2), pp. 264–274. ffhal-00419915f

Jutel, Annemarie "Classification, disease, and diagnosis". *Perspectives in Biology and Medicine* 54(2) (2011): 189–205.

Kaur, Harleen, and Siri Krishan Wasan "Empirical study on applications of data mining techniques in healthcare". *Journal of Computer Science* 2(2) (2006): 194–200.

Y, LeCun and Y. Bengio, Convolutional networks for images, speech, and time series, The handbook of brain theory and neural networks 3361 (10) 1995.

Luo, Jake, M. Wu, D. Gopukumar, and Y. Zhao "Big data application in biomedical research and health care: A literature review". *Biomedical Informatics Insights* 8 (2016): BII-S31559.

Petkovic, M., and Jonker, W. *An Overview of Data Models and Query Languages for Content-based Video Retrieval.* (2000).

Razia, Shaik, et al. "A review on disease diagnosis using machine learning techniques". *International Journal of Pure and Applied Mathematics*, 117(16), (2017): 79–85.

Rosenbloom, S. Trent, et al. "Data from clinical notes: A perspective on the tension between structure and flexible documentation". *Journal of the American Medical Informatics Association JAMIA* 18(2) (2011): 181–186.

Sharmila, S., C. Leoni, Dharuman, and P. Venkatesan "Disease classification using machine learning algorithms-A comparative study". *International Journal of Pure and Applied Mathematics* 114(6) (2017): 1–10.

Vinitha, S., et al. "Disease prediction using machine learning over big data". *Computer Science & Engineering: Anais an International Journal (CSEIJ)* 8 (2018): 1.

Wu, Honghan, et al. "SemEHR: A general-purpose semantic search system to surface semantic data from clinical notes for tailored care, trial recruitment, and clinical research". *Journal of the American Medical Informatics Association JAMIA* 25(5) (2018): 530–537.

11

Statistical Analysis of the Pre- and Post-Surgery in the Healthcare Sector Using High Dimension Segmentation

Soobia Saeed, Afnizanfaizal Abdullah, N. Z. Jhanjhi,
Memood Naqvi, and Mamoona Humayun

CONTENTS

11.1 Introduction...159
11.2 Methodology 161
    11.2.1 Sampling Techniques...162
    11.2.2 Sample Data and Size...162
    11.2.3 Light Field Toolbox for MATLAB..162
    11.2.4 High Dimensional Light Field Segmentation Method............163
11.3 Support Vector Machine (SVM)...163
    11.3.1 4-Dimentional SVM Graphs..166
11.4 Statistical Technique...166
11.5 Result and Discussion...168
11.6 Conclusion 170
11.7 Future Work...171
References...171

11.1 Introduction

Cerebrospinal fluid (CSF) is the fluid that travels through the brain's ventricles (cavities or voids) and around the surface of the brain and spine. CSF is one of the most challenging neuro-chirurgical complications (Saunders et al. 2018).

CSF leakage is a condition that occurs when the CSF leaks through a deformity in the dura or head and exits through the nose or ear. CSF leakage is the result of a hole or tears of the dura and is the most extreme layer of meningitis. The causes behind the hole or tear can damage the head and the functionality of the brain or breast. CSF slots can occur in the same way in the lower back, in what is also called spinal cord or spinal anesthesia. A CSF leak can occur without restriction in a similar manner without a known cause (Suman et al. 2017). The cells that make up these interfaces are also sites of integrated exchange mechanisms (vectors) that control the entry and exit of the brain into a wide range of molecules (Shree, Varuna, and Kumar, 2018). An important mechanism for controlling the distinctive synthesis of interstitial fluid in the brain is the secretion of cerebrospinal fluid by the placental plexus, which flows through the ventricular system and exchanges materials between the cerebrospinal fluid and the brain (Shree and Kumar 2018). It is necessary to understand how complex the barrier mechanisms are to assess the effects of inflammatory conditions in the brain, both in adults and during development. The exhaustion of the cerebrospinal fluid may occur through a leakage, a shunt, inadequate production, or very rapid absorption (Abdullah et al. 2011). There are also some similar syndromes in which intracranial compliance is very high; they cause similar symptoms when the brain shrinks when standing up and floats. Cerebrospinal fluid is widely targeted to detect molecules for cancer detection. This research examines current scientific knowledge about the biochemical factors in CSF that have been reported in brain cancer literature (Saeed, Abdullah, and Jhanjhi 2020).

A brain tumor is a mass of unwanted abnormal cells growing in the brain. Your skull is very rigid in order to protect your brain. Any growth can cause problems in this narrow space (Lavanyadevi et al. 2017). Cancerous (malignant) or non-cancerous (benign) cells can be found in brain tumors. They may increase intracranial pressure when tumors grow, both benign and malignant (Abdullah, Afnizanfaizal, et al, 2011). This can cause damage to the brain and endanger life. Tumors of the brain are classified as either primary or secondary (Li et al. 2015).

Many primary tumors of the brain are beneficial. Secondary brain tumors, also known as diffuse brain tumors, occur when other organs, such as the lung or breast, spread cancer cells to the brain (Lee et al. 2005). Brain and spinal cord is uncontrollable groups of abnormal cells in the brain or spinal cord (Saeed, Afnizanfaizal and Jhanjhi 2019a). It is very important to distinguish between benign (non-cancerous) tumors and malignant (cancerous) tumors in most other parts of the body. Tumors do not grow in nearby tissues or spread to remote areas, so they do not endanger life in other parts of the body (Saeed and Abdullah 2020). One of the major causes of malignant tumor severity is that it can spread all over the body. Section one provides the overview on detection of brain cancer and CSF as an image segmentation process and an abstract definition of all kinds of segmentation (Saeed and Abdullah 2019). This research closes with a discussion of the challenges of the deep learning method in the context of medical imaging and research issue (Khotanlou et al. 2009). The researcher describes the background of brain cancer using Interfacing of MRI-4-dimensional image segmentation (Liang et al. 2018). The researcher describes the details of brain cancer and explains cerebrospinal fluid (CSF) leakage with the aim of treating cancer and show the experimental result after the implementation of segmentation process and K-NN algorithm as well. Section two presents the methodology used in the detection of brain cancer using Interfacing of MRI-4D Images. The sampling techniques and tools will generate experimental result after the implementation of the statistical analysis. Section three explains the Support Vector Machine (SVM) results and SVM linear equation. Section four describes the method used in Statistical Technique. The framework can identify cancer damage areas or isolated tumors and non-tumors well by using 4D image light field segmentations. Initially, the MRI processes the pre-processed image method with the final target selected to adjust the image for the rest of the procedures. Section five provides the details of results and discussion with comparison of previous result to new achievements. Section six presents the conclusion, describes the contributions made by this study, and suggests future directions. This chapter also presents the achievements of the set objectives and the comparative performance evaluations and simulation of experimental results. One of the contributions of this research is presenting the results of statistical data. The researcher analyzes the all results in 2D and 3D formats, but we didn't find any available work on 4D platform to analyze the statistical data of patients. In addition, this research differs from previous work by presenting MRI tool analysis in detail.

11.2 Methodology

The proposed research aim is to acquire statistics related to the detection of most brain cancers (because of growing via CSF leakage) with the interface of MRI high dimensional images. The researcher discusses the damaged cells of the mind due to the abnormalities of the mobile. This is a qualitative research study. Therefore, it is a part of a large number and uses secondary sources, which includes comparative research studies from a global perspective. The primary aim of our work is to build up a framework that understands the tumor area. At first, the data MRI picture is preprocessed with a specific stop aim to restore the photo for relaxation of the procedures with the help of light subject toolbox of excessive dimensional and their graphical illustration.

The sampling collections are used for the have a look at consists of clinical mind snap shots for human being. The researcher will almost implement and simulate the experiments of (4D picture segmentation procedure) to the testing on human being and their mind tissues (animal mind pattern) randomly from Malaysia. The major goal of our proposed model is to broaden a gadget that could come across the CSF leakage inside the brain and tumors place or can separate between tumors and non-tumors patient. Data are accrued thru various assets, which are applying the necessary research equipment.

SVM tool is one of the important equipment to for you to teach the facts and tested the original sampling records. The SVM technique is one of the not unusual approaches to satisfy this requirement and boom the margin among classes, so that the overall overall performance is generally higher. Regarding the usage of more than one classes in SVM, comparison assessment is used. Thus, the researcher uses SVM to decide the objectivity of the classifications. This version identifies the most cancers at very early degree. Moreover, the clinical nice of relevant literature could be checked through important appraisal tools for higher evaluation.

11.2.1 Sampling Techniques

Sampling techniques are usually collected from the 4D light field segmentation process. The purpose of this study is to detect brain cancer through MRIs of the brain, for example, using supervised machine learning in relation to 4D light field segmentation, and SVM (support vector machine) tools for training and testing of datasets. The SVM approach is one of the most common ways to meet this requirement. SVMs increase the margin between categories so that the overall performance is generally higher. Regarding the use of multiple categories in SVM, comparability is used and SVM is used to determine the objectivity of the classifications.

11.2.2 Sample Data and Size

The sampling data is based on human tissue and scans images from MRIs. The sample size population is more than 200 (for the damaged brain cell after the CSF leakage and selecting the sample for human brain images or CSF sample images as well). The data was entered and analyzed using SPSS version 19.0. The main areas found to be ones of concern were the importance of using brain language and time management, and identifying the main area of patient concerns.

11.2.3 Light Field Toolbox for MATLAB

The purpose of using a set of tools to work with light field images (also known as plenoptic images) in MATLAB is to decode, calibrate correct, correct color, filter basic images, and visualize light field images. There are several ways to represent the 4D lighting field segmentation. The researcher adopted the Lumigraph method to clarify the rays in the three-dimensional space. The intersection points with "u-v" and "x-y" are defined in the 3D coordinates of the beam (rays). The radius can be represented as a point at a 4D distance such as p = (u, v, x, y), and the intensity of p is represented. The representation lumigraph can be converted to multiple representations that contain a viewpoint level, an image plane, and vice versa. In multi-point display, the U-V and X-Y models, respectively, correspond to the artifact s width and image. In this thesis, the researcher explains the multifactorial method in a way that is easy to understand.

11.2.4 High Dimensional Light Field Segmentation Method

The purpose of selection of a light field is basically a 4D structure. Most of the sounds of each pixel corresponding to the ray, the two dimensions determine the position of that ray, while the other two determine its direction. In the case of images measured by a camera, based on a camera lens such as Lytro, the two dimensions choose a lens image. The remaining two of them choose pixels within the image of this lens to maintain the resolution of the segmentation.

Table 11.1 shows that the original images of 3D images of the CSF leakage in the spinal cord. This is converted in to the 4D image images and create the histogram for finding the accuracy and size of CSF leakage in the spinal cord and, additionally, the graphical representation has been programmed as you can see in the second image of the CSF.

Leakage here is more prominent in the area of the tumor when compared to the previous image. After implementation of the 4D image process, the image is converted into grayscale and it clearly displays the size of the CSF tumor – which is 0 – so it means that the statistical graph shows the size of the tumor is 2,550. Here another value of maximum intensity (max_c) represents the intensity of the CSF-tumor which is 15,023 and shows the appearance of CSF leakage. Image 2 show the size of the CSF-tumor which is still in 0 but the value of statistical graph is different at 2,550. This shows that the situation of CSF leakage – which is slowly increasing in the brain and damaging the brain cell – and the max_c of Image 2 is 887. Image 3 also shows that the size of the CSF-tumor is 0 and the statistical graph shows the size of tumor value is 2,550 but that the max_c is 2,621 which represent the tumor shell in hard form after the CSF has been deposited in the brain. This is basically the leakage from initial to final stage of the tumor in the spinal cord which can be seen in Table 11.1.

11.3 Support Vector Machine (SVM)

The SVM monitors a learning algorithm based on the theory of statistical learning. In view of the sample data, the named dataset (training set), D = {Q, p,x class}, SVM tries to calculate the function 'y' f designation as f(x) = y for all samples in the dataset. The assignment function describes the relation between data samples and their class labels; new, unknown data are classified. In the context of the SVM, classification is carried out using the following classification function (a process called the advanced stage). The

TABLE.11.1

4-Dimention Size of CSF Leakage in Spine

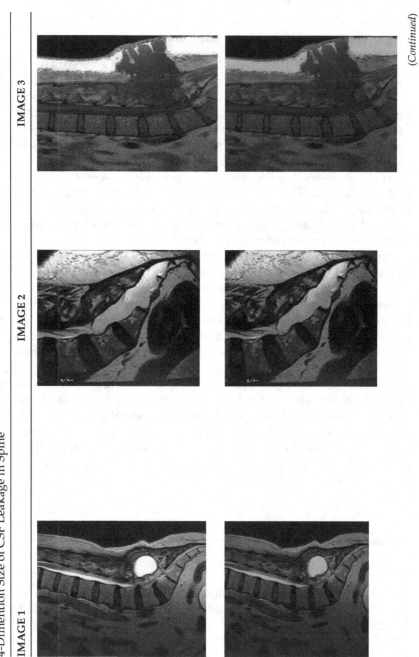

(Continued)

TABLE.11.1 (CONTINUED)

4-Dimention Size of CSF Leakage in Spine

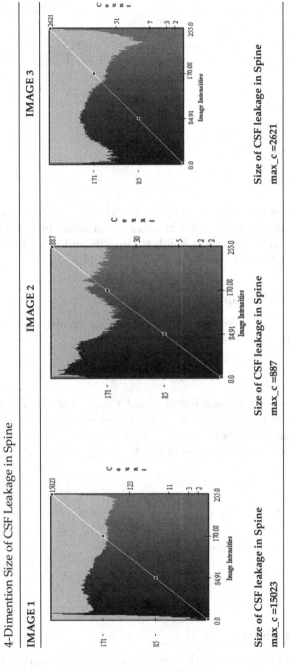

IMAGE 1

Size of CSF leakage in Spine
max_c =15023

IMAGE 2

Size of CSF leakage in Spine
max_c =887

IMAGE 3

Size of CSF leakage in Spine
max_c =2621

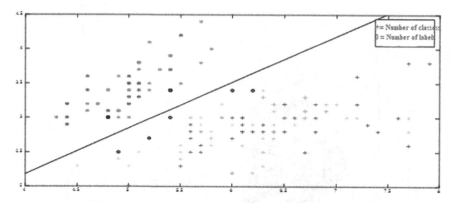

FIGURE 11.1
Statistical graph of SVM.

purpose of support vector machine is to explore the idea of transforming an input field into a high-dimensional space in order to optimize the best classification function, otherwise, and SVM is able to run RBF and view multiple layers. Figure 11.1 presents SVM graph.

11.3.1 4-Dimentional SVM Graphs

Here we show the experimental results of SVM classification after the training and testing of the given dataset.

$$y = X * x + Y \tag{11.1}$$

Here X represents the value of trained datasets and Y represents the value of testing datasets after the implementation of SVM classification techniques. The values of X and Y are given below:

Coefficients variable values of data sets of SVM:

$$X = 0.29308$$

$$Y = 1.062$$

Norm of residuals = 2.0304

11.4 Statistical Technique

Google gathered the data source, which is developed, structured, and verified by the American Cancer Society and multiple cancer and CSF surgery-related hospitals. The data was collected across the period of 2018–19 and, afterwards, responses were feed into the SPSS "Statistical Package for computational research" for further analysis. In SPSS the researcher used a t-test on collected data for evaluation. In this study, data was analysed through SPSS. SPSS is a statistical tool which is commonly used by many researchers. The t-test was applied to find the relationship between MRI sequences for brain cancer with CSF leakage. The t-test is used for finding the significant ratio, probability, and accuracy of MRI sequence results. The results of pre- and post-surgery are given more priority than normal test results. T-tests estimate the results involving all the above-mentioned independent variables with the dependent variable. This model shows strong relationship between dependent and independent variables based on the probability of findings; the outputs are interpreted. Since the result is based on a two-tailed approach, this indicates that there will be difference between the means, but the direction of the difference can't be predicted (Table 11.2).

Figure 11.2 shows the statistical results in terms of graphical representation as the authors list the complete details of pre- and post-surgery of patient results, and their tool usage. As we can see that the values of all tools are mentioned, as is the accuracy of MRI significant tools. The same situation varies for Table 11.3 after the implementation of SPPS test results and

TABLE 11.2

Statistical Results of Pre- and Post-Surgery Data

	Group Statistics				
	Surgery	N	Mean	Std. Deviation	Std. Error Mean
	Pre-Surgery	22	.73	.456	.097
	Post-Surgery	22	.00	.000	.000
RAVLT	Pre-Surgery	22	.36	.492	.105
	Post-Surgery	22	.14	.351	.075
TrailA	Pre-Surgery	22	.91	.294	.063
	Post-Surgery	22	.55	.510	.109
TrailB	Pre-Surgery	22	.91	.294	.063
	Post-Surgery	22	.55	.510	.109
HPTR9	Pre-Surgery	22	.86	.351	.075
	Post-Surgery	22	.50	.512	.109
HPTL9	Pre-Surgery	22	.91	.294	.063
	Post-Surgery	22	.55	.510	.109
COWAT	Pre-Surgery	22	.45	.510	.109
	Post-Surgery	22	.23	.429	.091
WDRT	Pre-Surgery	22	.91	.294	.063
	Post-Surgery	22	.55	.510	.109
mwalk10	Pre-Surgery	22	.86	.351	.075
	Post-Surgery	22	.55	.510	.109

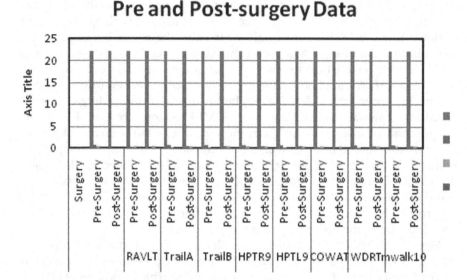

FIGURE 11.2
Graphical results of pre- and post-surgery data.

also when finding the significant values through using a t-test. Figure 11.3 shows the graphical results of independent samples of pre- and post-surgery patient data and also shows the range of the majority samples result.

11.5 Result and Discussion

The aim of this research is to construct a proposed framework that can identify cancer damaged areas or be isolated from tumors and non-tumors and leakage of CSF. By using HD image light field segmentation with two different forms, the MRI processed the pre-processed image method with the final target selected to adjust the image for the rest of the procedures. The basis of this study is the detection of brain cancer and CSF leakage through to the process of interfacing the 4D image segmentation process. Therefore, it consists of primary and secondary sources after a research study, followed by MATLAB software modelling techniques with the use of original medical sample images to measure the range of brain damage cells deep inside of CSF.

In this study, the researcher proposes a HD modulation method that supervises the light field that can be used to emit light. Depending on the user's input and using SVM to maintain the HD frequency (redundancy) light fields. The researcher uses the technique for editing the brain skull damaged

TABLE 11.3

Statistical Results of Independent Sample Test

		Independent Samples Test							
		Levene's Test for Equality of Variances		T-test for Equality of Means					95% Confidence Interval of the Difference
		F	Sig.	T	Df	Sig. (2-tailed)	Mean Difference	Std. Error Difference	Lower	Upper
NART	Equal variances assumes	80.640	.000	7.483	42	.000	.727	.097	.531	.923
	Equal variances do not assume			7.483	21.000	.000	.727	.097	.525	.929
RAVLT	Equal variances assumes	13.644	.001	1.763	42	.085	.227	.129	−.033	.487
	Equal variances not assumes			1.763	37.978	.086	.227	.129	−.034	.488
Trail A	Equal variances assumes	40.000	.000	2.898	42	.006	.364	.125	.110	.617
	Equal variances not assumes			2.898	33.600	.007	.364	.125	.109	.619
Trail B	Equal variances assumes	40.000	.000	2.898	42	.006	.364	.125	.110	.617
	Equal variances not assumes			2.898	33.600	.007	.364	.125	.109	.619
HPTR9	Equal variances assumes	23.579	.000	2.748	42	.009	.364	.132	.097	.631
	Equal variances not assumes			2.748	37.192	.009	.364	.132	.096	.632
HPTL9	Equal variances assumes	40.000	.000	2.898	42	.006	.364	.125	.110	.617
	Equal variances not assumes			2.898	33.600	.007	.364	.125	.109	.619
COWAT	Equal variances assumes	8.090	.007	1.600	42	.117	.227	.142	−.059	.514
	Equal variances not assumes			1.600	40.810	.117	.227	.142	−.060	.514
WDRT	Equal variances assumes	40.000	.000	2.898	42	.006	.364	.125	.110	.617
	Equal variances not assumes			2.898	33.600	.007	.364	.125	.109	.619
mwalk10	Equal variances assumes	22.120	.000	2.411	42	.020	.318	.132	.052	.584
	Equal variances not assumes			2.411	37.277	.021	.318	.132	.051	.585

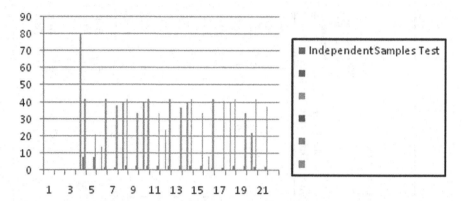

FIGURE 11.3
Graphical results of independent samples

images of brain cancer samples. These findings show the effectiveness of our approach to light editing applications. These light field methods can be useful for improving the quality of the segmentation of application editing and the composite light field pipeline, as they reduce boundary artefacts. The statistical data show the accuracy of pre and post-surgery results of brain cancer with CSF leakage.

11.6 Conclusion

The research closes with a discussion of the challenges of the deep learning method in relation to medical imaging and the research problem. The researcher describes the statistical results of brain cancer through an interface of MRI-four-dimensional photo segmentation. The researcher mentions the details of brain cancer and explains the cerebrospinal fluid (CSF) leakage with the concept of treating cancer so as to assist the experimental end result after the implementation of segmentation process and Tt-checking out of massive consequences as well.

The researcher also mentions the pre- and post-surgical results with the usage of SPSS tests and shows the substantial testing of the results. Some of the tumor's characteristics are detected and will be useful in medical applications. The findings of statistical data are one of the most important aspects of our study. The researcher analyzes all findings in the both 2D and 3D context. However, we have not found any work in the literature on the 4D system to be used to analyze patient data statistics. Furthermore, the researcher creates the novelty of MRI images tools and compare the previous work on MRI tools is available.

11.7 Future Work

Future work is suggested to include segmenting and detecting more images with more features that help classify multiple tumor types.

References

Abdullah, Afnizanfaizal, et al. "An improved local best searching in particle swarm optimization using differential evolution". In: *2011 11th International Conference on Hybrid Intelligent Systems (HIS)*. IEEE, Malaysia2011.

Abdullah, Afnizanfaizal, et al. "Cerebrospinal fluid pulsatile segmentation-a review". In: *The 5th 2012 Biomedical Engineering International Conference*. IEEE, 2012.

Abdullah, Afnizanfaizal, et al. "An improved swarm optimization for parameter estimation and biological model selection". *PLoS One* 8(4) (2013): 4.

Das, Suman, et al. "Detection and area calculation of brain tumour from MRI images using MATLAB". *International Journal* 4 (2017): 1.

Gamage, P. T., and Dr Lochandaka Ranathunga "Identification of brain tumor using image processing techniques". *Faculty of Information Technology, University of Moratuwa* (2017). https://www. researchgate. net/publication/276133543.

Gelb, Sivan, et al. "Mechanisms of neuropsychiatric lupus: The relative roles of the blood-cerebrospinal fluid barrier versus blood-brain barrier". *Journal of Autoimmunity* 91 (2018): 34–44.

Gupta, Anjali, and Gunjan Pahuja. "Hybrid clustering and boundary value refinement for tumor segmentation using brain MRI". In: *IOP Conference Series: Materials Science and Engineering*, Vol. 225, No. 1. IOP Publishing, 2017.

Heinen, Rutger, et al. "Robustness of automated methods for brain volume measurements across different MRI field strengths". *PLoS One* 11(10) (2016): 10.

Jian, Wen-xuan, et al. "Potential roles of brain barrier dysfunctions in the early stage of Alzheimer's disease". *Brain Research Bulletin* 142 (2018): 360–367.

Kant, Shawn, et al. "Choroid plexus genes for CSF production and brain homeostasis are altered in Alzheimer's disease". *Fluids and Barriers of the CNS* 15(1) (2018): 34.

Khan, A. Raouf, Noor Zaman, and Saira Muzafar "Health hazards linked to using mobile cellular phones". *Journal of Information and Communication Technology* 2(2) (2008): 101–108.

Khotanlou, Hassan, et al. "3D brain tumor segmentation in MRI using fuzzy classification, symmetry analysis and spatially constrained deformable models". *Fuzzy Sets and Systems* 160(10) (2009): 1457–1473.

Kinaci, Ahmet, et al. "Effectiveness of dural sealants in prevention of cerebrospinal fluid leakage after craniotomy: A systematic review". *World Neurosurgery* 118 (2018): 368–376.

Lavanyadevi, R., et al. "Brain tumor classification and segmentation in MRI images using PNN". In: *2017 IEEE International Conference on Electrical, Instrumentation and Communication Engineering (ICEICE)*. IEEE, 2017.

Lee, Chi-Hoon, et al. "Segmenting brain tumors with conditional random fields and support vector machines". In: *International Workshop on Computer Vision for Biomedical Image Applications*. Springer, Berlin, Heidelberg, 2005.

Lee, Su Yeon, et al. "Regulation of tumor progression by programmed necrosis". *Oxidative Medicine and Cellular Longevity*, 2018, 1–28,(2018).

Li, Guodong, et al. "Automatic liver segmentation based on shape constraints and deformable graph cut in CT images". *IEEE Transactions on Image Processing : A Publication of the IEEE Signal Processing Society* 24(12) (2015): 5315–5329.

Liang, Fan, et al. "Abdominal, multi-organ, auto-contouring method for online adaptive magnetic resonance guided radiotherapy: An intelligent, multi-level fusion approach". *Artificial Intelligence in Medicine*, 90 (2018): 34–41.

Liu, Jia, et al. "A cascaded deep convolutional neural network for joint segmentation and genotype prediction of brainstem gliomas". *IEEE Transactions on Bio-Medical Engineering* 65(9) (2018): 1943–1952.

Mendrik, Adriënne M., et al. "MR BrainS challenge: Online evaluation framework for brain image segmentation in 3T MRI scans". *Computational Intelligence and Neuroscience* 2015, Nagoya, Japan, 18.(2015).

Miller, Kimberly. *Cancer Treatment & Survivorship Facts & Figures*. American Cancer Society, pp.1–44, 2016.

Moeskops, Pim, et al. "Automatic segmentation of MR brain images with a convolutional neural network". *IEEE Transactions on Medical Imaging* 35(5) (2016): 1252–1261.

Oliveira, Gustavo Casagrande, Renato Varoto, and Alberto Cliquet Jr. "Brain tumor segmentation in magnetic resonance images using genetic algorithm clustering and adaboost classifier". *BIOIMAGING.2*, 77–82. (2018).

Prahl, Louis S., et al. "Glioma cell migration in confined microchannels via a motor-clutch mechanism". *bioRxi 1(2), 1 -12*, (2018): 500843.

Saeed, Soobia, and Afnizanfaizal Bin Abdullah "Investigation of a brain cancer with interfacing of 3-dimensional image processing". In: *2019 International Conference on Information Science and Communication Technology (ICISCT)*. IEEE, 2019.

Saeed, Soobia, and Afnizanfaizal Abdullah "Recognition of brain cancer and cerebrospinal fluid due to the usage of different MRI image by utilizing support vector machine". *Bulletin of Electrical Engineering and Informatics* 9(2) (2020): 619–625.

Saeed, Soobia, Afnizanfaizal Abdullah, and N. Z. Jhanjhi "Analysis of the Lung Cancer patient's for Data Mining Tool." *IJCSNS* 19(7) (2019a): 90.

Saeed, Soobia, Afnizanfaizal Abdullah, and N. Z. Jhanjhi "Implementation of Fourier transformation with brain cancer and CSF images". *Indian Journal of Science and Technology* 12(37) (2019b): 37.

Saeed, Soobia, and Raza Jafri "Estimation of brain tumor using latest technology of mobile phone". *Journal of Information and Communication Technology (JICT)* 9(1) (2015): 32–09.

Saeed, Soobia, and Shahbaz Ahmed Noor "Analysis of a brain tumour due to the usage of mobile phone". *Mehran University Research Journal of Engineering & Technology Journal* 36(3): 609–620, July 2017.

Saunders, Norman R., et al. "Physiology and molecular biology of barrier mechanisms in the fetal and neonatal brain". *The Journal of Physiology* 596(23) (2018): 5723–5756.

Shree, N. Varuna, and T. N. R. Kumar "Identification and classification of brain tumor MRI images with feature extraction using DWT and probabilistic neural network". *Brain Informatics* 5(1) (2018): 23–30.

Usman, Khalid, and Kashif Rajpoot "Brain tumor classification from multi-modality MRI using wavelets and machine learning". *Pattern Analysis and Applications* 20(3) (2017): 871–881.

van der Kleij, Lisa A., et al. "Fast CSF MRI for brain segmentation; Cross-validation by comparison with 3D T1-based brain segmentation methods". *PLoS One* 13(4) (2018): 4.

12

Machine Learning in Diagnosis of Children with Disorders

Lokesh Kumar Saxena and Manishikha Saxena

CONTENTS

12.1 Introduction 175
    12.1.1 Down Syndrome (DS) 176
    12.1.2 Sensory Processing Disorder (SPD) 176
    12.1.3 Autism Spectrum Disorder (ASD)... 176
    12.1.4 Aims and Organisation 177
12.2 Existing Tools for Diagnosis of DS, SPD, and ASD............................. 178
    12.2.1 Existing Tools of DS Diagnosis 178
    12.2.2 Existing Tools of SPD Diagnosis... 179
    12.2.3 Existing Tools for ASD Diagnosis 179
12.3 Machine Learning Applied for Diagnosis of DS, SPD, and ASD 180
12.4 Machine Learning Case Studies of DS, SPD, and ASD....................... 180
    12.4.1 Machine Learning (ML) Case Study for DS............................. 180
    12.4.2 Machine Learning Case Study of SPD...................................... 182
    12.4.3 Machine Learning Case Study for ASD 182
12.5 Conclusion 183
References.. 183

12.1 Introduction

Sustainable development refers to a development fulfilling the present needs of the world and preserving the resources for future generations (Bruntland 1987). It has three pillars: economic, social, and environment (Elkinton 2004). The European Commission has taken it on as a fundamental objective (Commission 2009). Now, industries are pressured to include sustainable development in their business goals, but the social dimension has been left unaccounted for by industry (Seuring 2013; Lokesh et al. 2016, 2018a,b, 2020). The European Commission declared in its agenda for 2014–2020 that its prime goal is to foster economic growth with regional development, coupled with job creation. To participate in economic growth, the people must have appropriate education and training, as well as adequate health. A particular section of society, are known as disabled children (or people who did not get opportunities due to a lack of appropriate education, training, and health and therefore did not contribute in the economic growth of nation, society, or themselves). These children had a disorder that developed either during pregnancy (prenatal) or after birth. These disorders prevent them getting appropriate education, training, and wellbeing. In recent years, the number of children with disabilities has increased at an exponential rate. Common disabilities include neurodevelopmental disorders such as Down's syndrome (DS), Autism spectrum disorder (ASD), and sensory processing disorder (SPD).

12.1.1 Down Syndrome (DS)

More than 1 in 1,000 newborn babies have DS, a disability requiring considerable social, monetary, and legal help. Almost 85% infants with Down's syndrome live past their first year, and about 50% of survivors have a life expectancy of over 50 years. DS is a major chromosomal disability in fetuses. It has an 8% share in all congenitally abnormal newborn babies (Koivua et al. 2018).

12.1.2 Sensory Processing Disorder (SPD)

SPD is a clinical state which makes it difficult to modulate and organize sensory inputs and employ them adequately. About 16% children in the United States suffer with SPD (Parabases et al. 2019). Children who have SPD usually lack the skills needed for educational achievement in schools. Owing to the sensory processing disruption, a lot of children who have SPD show late language and motor development progress. These are shown clearly over time with higher complexity. Thus, children who have SPD usually face educational, emotional, and social obstacles. It includes poor self-concept, anxiety, inattention, aggression, dysgraphia, and educational failures.

Furthermore, there are some children with SPD who also have common sensory problems such as hyper- or hypo-sensitivity to sound and touch. These children might show other behavioral conditions like ASD and attention deficit hyperactivity disorder (ADHD). Most children who have SPD do not display social communication problems as often found in ASD. But, up to 92% of persons with ASD display hyper- or hypo-sensitivity. ADHD indicaors are usually found in more than 40% children who have SPD, such as acute inattention and/or hyperactivity (Payabvash et al. 2019a).

12.1.3 Autism Spectrum Disorder (ASD)

ASD is a neuron development-related disorder which limits communication, social transactions, and behavior. It is a rapidly growing in the world. Its causes are associated with genetics and neurologic factors. It is mainly detected by utilizing non-genetical factors such as communication, repetitive behaviors, social transactions, play, and imagination. Almost 1.5% the world population is thought to be on the Autistic spectrum. Recent studies have reported a 3:1 ratio of male-to-females with ASD. In the US, about 1 in 59 children, are reported to have ASD.

ASD prevalence in US children has grown by 120% since the year 2000. ASD has been listed among the fastest-growing developmental disabilities. It costs about $250 billion per year in for US healthcare (Center for Disease Control and Prevention 2014). ASD may vary in severity ranging from mild, to somewhat limiting of normal life, to a severe disability requiring institutional care. Unfortunately, at present, no one single diagnostic test is able to identify ASD accurately. Instead, diagnosis is usually made by special experts through a comparative evaluation of a person's abnormal behaviors when compared to other children of the same age (Lord and Jones 1994, 2000). ASD is a lifelong disability. Thus, early identification to treat is very important in order to enhance the life of child and their family, and to decrease the financial burden on society.

ASD affects the day-to-day life of the individual. It creates considerable stress for their families. The traits are usually displayed when the child is three. Environment and genetics-related factors are supposed as a major causal factor for ASD. An important autistic characteristic is difficulties in social interactions. Here, the autonomic nervous system plays a key role. Other autistic traits include having limited interests and rigid or repetitive behaviors. The main communication gap can sometimes be seen through no or unsteady eye contact, slow or no response to somebody speaking, placing all focus on a favorite subject without caring for others' interests, an unusual voice tone, and the inability to understand other people's activities. People with ASD can also exhibit echolalia or repetitive behaviors. They can exhibit keen interest in some topics, sometimes facts or numbers. They tend to be upset by tiny changes in daily routine. They may have less or more sensitivity than other people to sensory inputs such as light or noise, etc. Autistic people may also possess many strengths, which sometimes include such things as extremely improved memory, learning ability for the finer details of things, advanced visual or auditory comprehension, or to excel in sciences, or mathematics, or music.

12.1.4 Aims and Organisation

This chapter is aims to provide the following insights:

1. To provide a short overview of research with the hope of motivating engineering and medical professionals to conduct collaborative research and develop technological solutions for diagnosis and the medical care of children/persons with disabilities using machine learning.

2. To identify the machine learning tools needed for such collaborative research.

3. To report on existing research with novel application of machine learning to the prenatal and postnatal early diagnosis of some disabilities such as Down's syndrome, Autism disorder, and Sensory Processing Disorder to prevent occurrence and/or to provide early medical care to facilitate children in getting the education and training needed to become productive contributors in the growth of themselves, the nation, and world.

This chapter is organized into five sections. Section 1 comprises of a preamble and introduction. Section 2 shows existing tools for diagnosis, and problems facing DS, SPD, and ASD. Section 3 describes machine learning applied for diagnosis of DS, SPD, and ASD. Section 4 describes machine learning case studies of DS, SPD, and ASD. Section 5 offers a conclusion.

12.2 Existing Tools for Diagnosis of DS, SPD, and ASD

This section discusses existing diagnostic tools for DS, SPD, and ASD.

12.2.1 Existing Tools of DS Diagnosis

Risk screening of first trimester for Down's syndrome (also known as trisomy 21, or T2) is usually done by examining maternal attributes and many biomarkers, e.g. FhCGβ (maternal serum free human chorionic gonadotropin β-subunit); PAPP-A (pregnancy associated plasma protein-A); and NT (ultrasound nuchal translucency). A first trimester test with above three markers is known as a combined test (Cuckle and Maymon 2016).

The existing pre-natal screening software for DS risk evaluation – e.g. LifeCycle™ from PerkinElmer, Waltman, MA, USA – uses the multi-variable based Gaussian models. Risk evaluation methods use a risk evaluation engine to compute the risk amounts. Basic building elements in protocol are some functions in the protocol. The marker results obtained from the model of risk are first normalized, and then the required rectifications are included for MoM (modified multiple of median) values of every marker. Then, the probability of T21 is computed as a ratio an affected likelihood to unaffected likelihood. The likelihood for effected and unaffected situations are found using a multi-variable GDF (Gaussian density function). GDF employ the population measures for each marker i.e. mean, SD (standard deviation), and marker correlation for given gestation and computed MoM value of every marker. For LifeCycle™ version 4.0, the population measures were taken from the study by Wald et al. (2003).

12.2.2 Existing Tools of SPD Diagnosis

The diffusion tensor imaging (DTI) micro structural is used for SPD diagnosis. In DTI, correlates/matrices of SPD for identification of children are MD (mean diffusivity), FA (fractional anisotropy), AD (axial diffusivity), and RD (radial diffusivity).

DTI research in SPD children found defective microstructures of white matter primarily in the commissural tracts and backward projection along-with reduction in FA and increase in RD (Owen et al. 2013; Chang et al. 2015). DTI metrics from water diffusivity are employed for integrity and connectivity of white matter. This denotes spatially mean characteristics over voxels. These consist of many discontinuous, usually components with opposite and directional nature (Mukherjee et al. 2008). Probabilistic tractography develops streamlines structure of diffusion fiber tracks considering the directionality trait for movements of water molecules. Therefore, it frames a map of track density (TD). These can give more insights about changes in white matter micro structural (Calamante et al. 2010; 2012a, b). In the human brain, the complex neuron network may be examined by employing graph theory. Here, subcortical and cortical gray matter zones can be denoted by nodes. White matter interconnective pathways can be represented by links or edges (Bullmore and Sporns 2009). Edge density imaging (ED) facilitates a structure to denote the spatial structure, by inserting such connectomic edges in white matter (Owen et al. 2015; Greene et al. 2017). For full characterization of the neural network correlation of SPD, one can investigate white matter's diffusion properties by employing DTI measures to FA, RD, MD, and AD. Furthermore, probabilistic tractography can be employed to create maps of ED and TD for comparison of the white matter connectivity in children who have SPD with other children.

12.2.3 Existing Tools for ASD Diagnosis

ASD diagnostic techniques employ medical experts to perform an evaluation of the person's development involving various factors (such as self-care, communication, behavior, social skills). This is known as a Clinical Judgment approach (CJ) (Wiggins et al. 2014). An Autism Diagnostic Interview (ADI) and Autism Diagnostic Observation Schedule (ADOS) are frequent evaluation approaches for diagnosis (Lord et al. 1994, 2000). An Autism Diagnostic Interview (ADI) is an interview-based approach with 93 items. It is usually performed by a recognized expert in collaboration with the person's guardian. An ADOS has four parts. Each part is applied to a pre-specified development age group, that is implemented along dimensions ranging from non-verbal persons to verbally fluent persons. People are evaluated by their reported traits and/or observed traits according to a developmental task set in each module(Lord et al. 2000).

In addition to the CJ approach, self-evaluation approaches are also defined, such as Childhood Autism Rating Scale (CARS), Child Behavior Checklist

(CBCL), Autism Spectrum Quotient (AQ) (Baron-Cohen et al. 2001), Autism Behavior Checklist (ABC), etc. (Thabtah et al. 2018). These approaches are usually performed by care experts, teachers, parents, or the person themselves. These need to be filled out with replies to various questions that results in many inefficient responses (Thabtah et al. 2018). Therefore, there is a need to reduce the number of variables in these approaches to make them more efficient.

12.3 Machine Learning Applied for Diagnosis of DS, SPD, and ASD

This section identifies machine tools applied in some noteworthy research on Down's syndrome, Sensory Processing Disorder, and Autism spectrum disorder. Table 12.1 shows the machine learning application for disorder characterization.

12.4 Machine Learning Case Studies of DS, SPD, and ASD

This section presented case studies with a focus on machine learning application for DS, SPD, and ASD diagnosis.

12.4.1 Machine Learning (ML) Case Study for DS

Koivu et al. (2018) presented a study with a focus on machine learning applications for DS diagnosis. Prenatal screening yields a huge amount of data to predict risk of various disorders based on multiple clinical variables. Authors applied ML to augment results of the first three months filtration of DS. ML appears to be an adjustable option to generate better models for risk evaluation using the existing variables in clinical practice. This research used two existing datasets with multiple classification algorithms such as deep neural networks, the support vector machine model, and a risk evaluation business software. Deep neural networks yield a 0.96 area value under the curve, and 78% value of detection rate, with 1% value of false positive rate for the data. Support vector machine yields 0.95 area value under the curve, and 61% value of detection rate with 1% value of false positive rate for the data. Support vector machine yields some poorer results. Deep neural networks yield greater rate of detection having similar rates of false positives or same rates of detection and far lower rates of false positive.

TABLE 12.1

Machine Learning Applied for Diagnosis of DS, SPD, and ASD

Disorder	Authors	Machine learning tools	Description
DS	Grossi et al. 2016	Artificial neural network	Artificial neural networks have been investigated to develop model to predict autism.
	Williams et al. 1999	logistic regression, NN, classification and regression-tree methods	For prenatal screening, Williams et al. proposed logistic regression / linear discriminant.
	Uzun et al. 2013	Probabilistic classifiers, machine learning algorithms, including Decision Tree, SVM, k-Nearest Neighbor (KNN), and Multilayer Perceptron	Authors examined various probabilistic classifiers to identify DS, aimed at decreasing invasive test numbers. They reported SVM and multilayer perceptron i.e. feed forward ANN as the best performing options.
	Koivu et al. 2018	Deep neural network, Support vector machine	Authors applied these algorithms to enhance identification performance of DS using the existing clinical variables and a commercial risk assessment software.
	Neocleous et al. 2018	Feed forward neural network	Neocleous et al. 2018 examined the application of a feed forward neural network for an euploidies forecasting during the first three month of pregnancy from data of Prenatal Non-invasive Testing.
	Catic et al. 2018	Neural network (NN)- recurrent, feed forward and feedback	Authors examined neural network (NN) the data of multiple genetic defects, e.g. DS.
SPD	Payabash et al. 2019c, a	stepwise penalized logistic regression, Naïve Bayes, random forest, support vector machine (SVM)	These were utilized to detect independent measures to forecast AOR, as possible imaging marker for AOR.
	Tavassoli et al. 2019	support vector machine, Naïve Bayes, random forest, neural networks.	These were applied to identify children with SPD using DTI measures.
ASD	Allison et al. 2012	Discriminant index (DI)	DI decreased variables in the AQ approach from 50 to 10 variables, and, in Q-CHAT from 25 parameters to 10.
	Wall et al. 2012a,b	Alternating Decision TreeClassifier algorithm (ADTree) using WEKA	AD Tree decreased the variables/ items in ADOS-R to 8.
	Duda et al.2016	Logistic Regression, decision tree classifiers Random Forest	Decreased the time required for ADOS and Social Responsiveness Scale.
	Kosmicki et al. 2015	Backward step-wide feature selection for machine learning	Reduced the variables/items in ADOS part 2 and 3.

(Continued)

TABLE 12.1 (CONTINUED)

Machine Learning Applied for Diagnosis of DS, SPD, and ASD

Disorder	Authors	Machine learning tools	Description
	Jin et al. 2015	Multi-kernel support vector machine classification	For ASD-induced defects within 24 months after birth, authors proposed a novel classification framework using the connectivity measures and diffusion measures diffusivity.
	Payabash et al. 2019b	support vector machines, random forest, Naïve Bayes, neural networks	These are used to detect ASD children with ASD using DTI metrics.
	Thabtah et al. 2018, 2017	RIPPER, Decision Tree (C4.5) Va is programmed in Java and interfaced with WEKA 3.9.1 to classify ASD.	reduced the items in AQusing Variable Analysis (Va) to correlate items in three AQ approaches with normalised scores of Chi-Square (CHI) and Information Gain (IG) approaches.

12.4.2 Machine Learning Case Study of SPD

Payabash et al. (2019c) presented a study with a focus on machine learning applications for SPD diagnosis. It employed machine learning algorithms to identify children with SPD using DTI/ tractography metrics. This research considered 44 SPD0affected children and 41 "typically" developing other children (DOC) for MRI scanning. It used DTI measures- FA, MD, RD, and AD. This research also used probabilistic tractography to produce ED and TD employing DTI maps. Support vector machine, random forest, Naïve Bayes, and neural networks were used to identify the children with SPD. The study found accurate rates of classification from measures such as FA, MD, AD, RD, TD, and ED. This study found that SPD-affected children possess fewer FA, ED, and TD values, and greater M and RD values in comparison to DOC, mainly in backside tracts of white matter composed of backside corona radiata, backside thalamic radiation, backside body, and splenium of corpus callosum. The average TD of the splenium (p < 0.001) was found as a single independent measure identifying SPD-affected children from ODC using stepwise penalized logistic regression. This research found defective microstructural and connectivity/connectomic integrity in SPD affected children, mainly in backside tracts of white matter. It also found decreased TD for splenium of corpus callosum, representing the significant detectable pattern for identifying children with ASD. It may be applied to design imaging markers of neurodevelopmental defects.

12.4.3 Machine Learning Case Study for ASD

Thabtah et al. (2018) presented a study with a focus on machine learning applications for ASD diagnosis. ASD is among the most rapidly growing developmental disabilities. Most people are not aware of ASD attributes. Therefore, they do not go for diagnostic services or contact their doctor. Thus, there is need for a simple tool that employs variables/traits of ASD for affect families, so that they may increase the probability of seeking expert evaluation. It is critical to detect and treat ASD as early as possible. The machine learning algorithms used in this research are RIPPER and C4.5. Variable Analysis (Va) is programmed in Java and interfaced with WEKA 3.9.1 to classify ASD. In this study, the authors reduced the items in AQ using the Va to correlate items in three AQ approaches with normalized scores of Chi-Square (CHI) and Information Gain (IG) approaches. The results shows that the Va had shown the ability to reduce the features required for screening approaches from children, adolescents, and adults. This method also maintained a good level of accuracy, specificity, and sensitivity.

12.5 Conclusion

Among sustainable development gaols, the social dimension is the most neglected. More focus and work should be carried out in this area. One important area of the social dimension that is highly neglected in developing countries, such as India, is the care of children with disabilities.

This chapter has contributed to the area of developmental care of children/persons with disorders as follows:

1. It presented examples of methods to identify persons with disabilities using machine learning.
2. It identified the machine learning tools for such research.
3. It also reported on the existing research with novel application of machine learning in the prenatal and postnatal early diagnosis of some disabilities such as Down's syndrome, Autism spectrum disorder, and Sensory Processing Disorder to prevent occurrences and/or to provide early medical care to affected children to facilitate them to get the right education and training they need to become productive contributors in the growth of themselves, the nation, and world.

References

Allison C, Auyeung B, Baron-Cohen S (2012) Toward brief "Red flags" for autism screening: The short Autism Spectrum Quotient and the short quantitative checklist for autism in toddlers in 1,000 cases and 3,000 controls [corrected]. *J. Am. Acad. Child Adolesc. Psychiatry* 51(2):202–212.

Baron-Cohen S, Wheelwright S, Skinner R, Martin J, Clubley E (2001) The autism spectrum quotient (AQ): Evidence from Asperger syndrome/high-functioning autism, males and females, scientists and mathematicians. *J. Autism Dev. Disord.* 31(1):5–17.

Bruntland G H (1987) *World Commission on Environment and Development in: Our Common Future*, United Nations, Oxford University Press, 8–9.

Bullmore E, Sporns O (2009) Complex brain networks: Graph theoretical analysis of structural and functional systems. *Nat. Rev. Neurosci.* 10(3):186–198.

Calamante F, Tournier J D, Jackson G D, Connelly A (2010) Track-density imaging (TDI): Super-resolution white matter imaging using whole-brain track-density mapping. *Neuroimage* 53(4):1233–1243.

Calamante F, Tournier J D, Kurniawan N D, Yang Z, Gyengesi E, Galloway G J, Reutens D C, Connelly A (2012a) Super-resolution track-density imaging studies of mouse brain: Comparison to histology. *Neuroimage* 59(1):286–296.

Calamante F, Tournier J D, Smith R E, Connelly A (2012b) A generalised framework for super-resolution track-weighted imaging. *Neuroimage* 59(3):2494–2503.

Catic A, Gurbeta L, Kurtovic-Kozaric A, Mehmedbasic S, Badnjevic A (2018) Application of neural networks for classification of patau, edwards, down, turner and klinefelter syndrome based on first trimester maternal serum screening data, ultrasonographic findings and patient demographics. *BMC Med. Genomics* 11(1):19.

Centers for Disease Control and Prevention (2014) Prevalence of autism spectrum disorder among children aged 8 years autism and developmental disabilities monitoring network, 11 sites, United States, 2010. *Morb. Mortal. Wkly Rep. Surveill. Summ.* 63(2):1–21.

Chang Y S, Gratiot M, Owen J P, Brandes-Aitken A, Desai S S, Hill S S, Arnett A B, Harris J, Marco E J, Mukherjee P (2015) White matter microstructure is associated with auditory and tactile processing in children with and without sensory processing disorder. *Front. Neuroanat.* 9:169.

Commission E (2009) Communication from the Commission to the European Parliament the Council the European Economic and Social committee and the Committee of the Regions Mainstreaming Sustainable Development into EU Policies: 2009 Review of the European Union strategy for sustainable development brussels.

Cuckle H, Maymon R (2016) Development of prenatal screening: A historical overview. *Semin. Perinatol.* 40(1):12–22. doi:10.1053/j.semperi.2015.11.003.

Duda M, Ma R, Haber N, Wall D (2016) Use of machine learning for behavioral distinction of autism and ADHD. *Transl. Psychiatry* 9(6):732.

Elkinton J (2004) Enter the triple bottom line. In: Henriques and J.Richardson(Eds) *The Triple Bottom Line: Does It All Add Up? Assessiong the sustainability of business andCSSR*, London: Earthscan Publications Ltd., 1–16.

Greene C A, Cieslak M, Grafton S T (2017) Effect of different spatial normalization approaches on tractography and structural brain networks. *Netw. Neurosci.* 3:1–43.

Grossi E, Veggo F, Narzisi A, Compare A, Muratori F (2016) Pregnancy risk factors in autism: A pilot study with artificial neural networks. *Pediatr. Res.* 79(2):339–347.

Jin Y, Wee C Y, Shi F, Thung K H, Ni D, Yap P T, Shen D (2015) Identification of infants at high-risk for autism spectrum disorder using multi parameter scale white matter connectivity networks. *Hum. Brain Mapp.* 36(12):4880–4896.

Koivua A, Ko Korpim T, Kivel P, Pahikkal T, Sairanen M (2018) Evaluation of machine learning algorithms for improved risk assessment for Down's syndrome. *Comput. Biol. Med.* 98:1–7.

Kosmicki J, Sochat V, Duda M, Wall D (2015) Searching for a minimal set of behaviors for autism detection through feature selection-based machine learning. *Transl. Psychiatry* 5:514.

Lokesh K S, Jain P K, Sharma A K (2018a) Tactical supply chain planning for Tyre remanufacturing considering carbon tax policy. *Int. J. Adv. Manuf. Technol.* 97(1–4):1505–1528. doi:10.1007/s00170-018-1972-03.

Lokesh K S, Jain P K, Sharma A K (2018b) A fuzzy goal programme with carbon tax for Brownfield tyre remanufacturing supply chain planning. *J. Cleaner Prod.* 198:1–17. doi:10.1016/j.jclepro.2018.07.005.

Lokesh, K., Jain, P. K. (2016) Tyre- remanufacturing supply chain management practices: an exploratory study to improve competitiveness and environmental friendliness. EBSCC 2016 Conference, IIT Kharagpur, India, 12–14 February 2016.

Lokesh K S, Jain P K Sharma A K (2020) A fuzzy goal programme based sustainable Greenfield supply network design for tyre retreading industry. *International Journal of Advance Manufacturing Technology,* 108, 2955–2980.

Lord C, Risi S, Lambrecht L, Cook E H, Leventhal B L, DiLavore P C, Pickles A, Rutter M (2000) The autism diagnostic observation schedule generic: A standard measure of social and communication deficits associated with 1the spectrum of autism. *J. Autism Dev. Disord.* 30(3):205–223.

Lord C, Rutter M, Le Couteur A (1994) Autism diagnostic interview-revised: A revised version of a diagnostic interview for caregivers of individuals with possible pervasive developmental disorders. *J. Autism Dev. Disord.* 24(5):659–685.

Mukherjee P, Berman J I, Chung S W, Hess C P, Henry R G (2008) Diffusion tensor MR imaging and fibertractography: Theoretic underpinnings. *AJNR Am. J. Neuroradiol.* 29(4):632–641.

Neocleous A C, Syngelaki A, Nicolaides K H, Schizas C N (2018) Two-stage approach for risk estimation of fetal trisomy 21 and other aneuploidies using computational intelligence systems. *Ultrasound Obstet. Gynecol. Offic. J. Int. Soci. Ultrasound Obstet. Gynecol.* 51(4):503–508.

Owen J P, Chang Y S, Mukherjee P (2015) Edge density imaging: Mapping the anatomic embedding of the structural connectome within the white matter of the human brain. *Neuroimage* 109:402–417.

Owen J P, Marco E J, Desai S, Fourie E, Harris J, Hill S S, Arnett A B, Mukherjee P (2013) Abnormal white matter microstructure in children with sensory processing disorders. *NeuroImage Clin.* 2: 844–853.

Payabvash S, Palacios E, Owen J P, Wang M B, Tavassoli T, Gerdes M R, Brandes Aitken A, Mukherjee P, Marco E J (2019a) White matter connectome correlates of auditory over-responsivity: Edge density imaging and machine-learning classifiers. *Front. Integr. Neurosci.* 29:10.

Payabvash S, Palacios E M, Owen J P, Wang M B, Tavassoli T, Gerdes M, BrandesAitken A, Marco E J, Mukherjee P (2019b) Diffusion tensor tractography in children with sensory processing disorder: Potentials for devising machine learning classifiers. *NeuroImage Clin.* 23:1018.

Payabvash S, Palacios E M, Owen J P, Wang M B, Tavassoli T, Gerdes M, Brandes Aitken A, Cuneo D, Marco E J, Mukherjee P (2019c) White matter connectome edge density in children with autism Spectrum disorders: Potential imaging biomarkers using machine-learning models. *Brain Connect.* 9(2):209–220.

Seuring S (2013) A review of modelling approaches for sustainable supply chain management. *Decis. Support Syst.* 54(4):1513–1520.

Tavassoli T, Brandes-Aitken A, Chu R, Porter L, Schoen S, Miller L J, Gerdes M R, Owen J, Mukherjee P, Marco E J (2019) Sensory over-responsivity: Parent report, direct assessment measures, and neural architecture. *Mol. Autism* 10:4. doi:10.1186/s13229-019-0255-7.

Thabtah F (2017) Autism spectrum disorder screening: Machine learning adaptation and DSM-5 fulfillment. In: *Proceedings of the 1st International Conference on Medical and Health Informatics 2017 Taichung City Taiwan ACM*, pp. 1–6.

Thabtah F, Kamalov F, Rajab K (2018) A new computational intelligence approach to detect autistic features for autism screening. *Int. J. Med. Inform.* 117:112–124.

Uzun O, Kaya H, Gürgen F, Varol F G (2013) Prenatal risk assessment of trisomy 21 by probabilistic classifiers. In: *21st Signal Processing and Communications Applications Conference (SIU)*, Vol. 2013, pp. 1–4. doi:10.1109/SIU.2013.6531604.

Wald N J, Rodeck C, Hackshaw A K, Walters J, Chitty L, Mackinson A M (2003) First and second trimester antenatal screening for Down's syndrome: The results of the serum, urine and ultrasound screening study (suruss). *Health Technol. Assess.* 7:1–77 (Winchester, England).

Wall D, Dally R, Luyster R, Jung J, Deluca T (2012a) Use of artificial intelligence to shorten the behavioural diagnosis of autism. *PLoS One* 7(8):43855.

Wall D, Kosmiscki J, Deluca T, Harstad L, Fusaro V (2012b) Use of machine learning to shorten observation-based screening and diagnosis of autism. *Transl. Psychiatry* 2:52–58.

Wiggins L, Reynolds A, Rice C, Mody E, Bernal P, Blaskey L, Rosenberg S, Lee L, Levy S (2014) Using standardized diagnostic instruments to classify children with autism in the study to explore early development. *J. Autism Dev. Disord.* 45(5):1271–1280.

Williams C J, Lee S S, Fisher R A, Dickerman L H (1999) A comparison of statistical methods for prenatal screening for down syndrome. *Appl. Stoch. Model Bus. Ind.* 15(2):89–101. doi:10.1002/(SICI)15264025(199904/06)15:2¡89::AIDASMB36 6¿3.0.CO;2-K.

13

Forecasting Dengue Incidence Rate in Tamil Nadu Using ARIMA Time Series Model

S. Dhamodharavadhani, R. Rathipriya

CONTENTS

13.1 Introduction 187
13.2 Literature Review 190
    13.2.1 Findings 190
13.3 Methods and Materials 190
    13.3.1 Study Area 190
    13.3.2 Snapshot for Dataset 190
    13.3.3 Proposed Model 193
    13.3.4 Estimate and Develop the Model 193
13.4 Results and Discussions 194
13.5 Conclusion 201
13.6 Acknowledgment 201
References 201

13.1 Introduction

Mosquitoes are one of India's toxic insects. They have the ability to carry and spread disease to humans and this causes millions of deaths every year. In the year 2015, there 10,683 outbreaks of India Similarly, the worldwide incidence of dengue has risen 30-fold in the past 30 years, and an increasing number of countries are reporting their first outbreaks of the disease. The Aedesa Aegypti mosquito transmits Mosquito-Borne Disease (MBD) such as chikungunya, dengue, yellow fever, and zika virus to humans. Sustained and effective mosquito control efforts are necessary to avoid outbreaks of such diseases (Yong-Su Kwon 2015).

In India, the challenge MBD poses is serious because the increases in geographic distribution of vectors and MBD have the potential to affect 90% of the population. MBD is mostly an urban public health problem; however, outbreaks are being increasingly documented in rural areas too (Dhamodharavadhani and Rathipriya 2016).

Geographical Factors of Dengue:

1. Water
2. Housing
3. Climate change
4. Poverty
5. Air Travel
6. Health System

Climate change has had substantial consequences in the global distribution of MBD. Climate change often impacts dengue transmission, as mosquitoes grow faster in higher temperatures and bite more often. Researchers have developed a tool that can forecast the possibility of dengue outbreaks in different parts of India on the basis of environmental conditions; a development that can help to take preventive measures against deadly infection (Descloux 2012).

A climate-based model of dengue prediction will assist health authorities in assessing disease intensity in a country or region. On this basis, authorities may have systematic a plan for disease control well in advance and optimize the use of available resources for the same reason (Descloux 2012).

Dengue has been known in India since the 1940s, but the spread of the disease was previously very limited. The most important MBDs that affect humans are dengue viruses. According to the World Health Organization (WHO), dengue is divided into two: types 1 and type 2. Type 1 is a common form dengue that leads to dengue fever, Dengue Hemorrhagic Fever (DHF) is type 2. Four types of Dengue Hemorrhagic Fever exist: DHF1, DHF2, DHF3, and DHF4. Infection of dengue is one of the world's fastest spreading MBDs – a viral disease that accounts for nearly 50 million cases annually (Allard 1998).

- The rate of dengue virus transmission is dangerously high due to global warming, climate change, rapid urbanization, unsuitable sanitation, insufficient public health services, and migratory populations.

- Regions such as East Mediterranean, Latin America, South East Asia, and Western Pacific, and Africa are all susceptible to recurrent dengue fever outbreaks.

Figure 13.1 indicates that in 2017 the dengue cases had been the highest in a decade. In dengue cases, an increase of more than 300% occurred in 2009, and the total MBD-related death cases in 2017 was the highest in the last decade. According to data from the National Program for Vector Borne Disease Control (NVBDCP) and National Health Profile of 2018, dengue

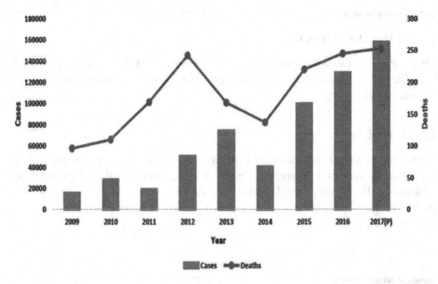

FIGURE 13.1
Dengue cases and deaths in India.

cases rose to 188,401 in 2017 a than a 300% leap from less than 60,000 cases in 2009. It is more than a 250% jump compared to the 75,808 events in 2013 (Chiung Ching Ho 2015).

For example, Tamil Nadu has seen Dengue cases rise to 20,945 in 2017 and Puducherry's union territory has registered 4,507 dengue cases for the same year. This means that 2% of the entire population of Puducherry has been affected by dengue.

Other southern states like Kerala and Karnataka have been badly affected by this huge dengue outbreak. Kerala showed a dramatic rise from 7,439 cases of dengue in 2016 to 19,638 in 2017. In Karnataka, 16,209 people were affected by it which translates as 260% higher than in 2016 (Chandran and Azeez 2015).

As such, successful monitoring and prediction of the incidence rate of MBD is important in preventing disease spread. Passive, preventive, and reactive monitoring systems are used to monitor the MBD outbreaks and incidence rate in Tamilnadu (Dhamodharavadhani and Rathipriya 2020[a]). Nonetheless, these programs face problems such as preference for eradication over surveillance, difficulty in interpreting findings, and most importantly, lack of coordination between MBD eradication units and MBD monitoring units (Karnaboopathy and Venkatesan 2018).

As a result of the above factors, there is a compelling case for alternative forms of MBD tracking and forecasting. Therefore, this chapter proposed an approach based on ARIMA time-series model for forecasting MBD incidence rate using meteorological data.

13.2 Literature Review

This section provides a state-of-the-art ARIMA models as used in the literature for predictive analytics. Table 13.1 presents the comparative analysis of various works.

13.2.1 Findings

From this study, it is clear that efficient and effective dengue forecast tool with higher accuracy a pressing need in order to control and prevent such outbreaks all over the world. This study reveals that time series model using meteorological data has been successful aimed to forecast of specific transmissible diseases.

13.3 Methods and Materials

13.3.1 Study Area

In this research, two datasets are taken to predict the dengue incidence rate using meteorological data in Tamil Nadu. Dataset 1 contains weekly dengue cases data for the periods 1990–2009 of Tamil Nadu. Dataset 2 contains weekly minimum temperatures, maximum temperatures, average temperatures, rainfall, and precipitation for the period of 1990–2009 in Tamil Nadu District (Yong-Su Kwon 2015)

13.3.2 Snapshot for Dataset

Dataset 1

week_start_date	total_cases
4/30/1990	4
5/7/1990	5
5/14/1990	4
5/21/1990	3
5/28/1990	6
6/4/1990	2
6/11/1990	4
6/18/1990	5
6/25/1990	10
7/2/1990	6
7/9/1990	8

TABLE 13.1

Comparative Analysis

Technique	Description	Dataset	Recommendation/Prediction
Exponential smoothing ARIMA	STL decomposition forecasts trend and seasonal patterns in a better way. (Chiung Ching Ho 2015)	Malaysian Open Data Portal	To study the impact of the out-of-sample data on the models and integrate correlation studies with meteorological data. Prediction: Dengue fever outbreaks in Malaysia (Sahanaa and Mishra 2018)
Trend of morbidity and mortality	Tamil Nadu has been witnessing a fall in the morbidity trend over the past five years, and dengue deaths since 2015. Nevertheless, cases of dengue morbidity are increasing and median mortality is rising from 2012 to 2016, nationally.	Morbidity and dengue-related mortality at Puducherry and Tamil Nadu, India (2012–2016).	This work had assessed the Dengue in Puducherry and Tamil Nadu and proposed the model to reduce and eradicate the dengue outburst Prediction: early detection of the dengue outbreak, in fact prediction of dengue outbreak (Sahanaa and Mishra 2018)
Statistical analysis and modeling; Time series analysis, Bivariate analysis, Multivariate analysis.	Dengue cases in Noumea were basically driven by climate during the last forty years. (Descloux 2012)	Epidemiological data: January 1971– December 2010 Meteorological data: January 1971 to December 2010 Entomological surveillance data: since 1997	(Earnest 2012) (Elodie Descloux 2012) Prediction: Climate-based Dengue Epidemic Models for Understanding and Forecasting
support vector machine (SVM), classification and regression tree (CART), and random forest (RF).	To examine the spatial and temporal variations in the frequency of urban mosquitoes and the relationships with meteorological and habitat conditions such as type of land use.	Mosquito data collected from 2011 to 2012 at 12 locations, and environmental data (Yong-Su Kwon 2015).	Applied for the efficient control of urban mosquitoes. Prediction: Mosquito Occurrence (Yong-Su Kwon 2015).

(Continued)

TABLE 13.1 (CONTINUED)

Comparative Analysis

Technique	Description	Dataset	Recommendation/Prediction
Auto Regressive Integrated Moving Average (ARIMA) Model.	The trend in forecast dengue cases for the years 2018 to 2025 shows that there is a stable growth of Dengue cases, which is of serious concern.	Dengue cases in Tamil Nadu 1997–2017.	(Karnaboopathy and Venkatesan 2018) To avoid the disease from becoming endemic, new interventions with increased intensity of existing interventions and help from the international community together with the WHO are essential in order to stop the epidemics. Prediction: Number of cases till December 2025
Seasonal Autoregressive Integrated Moving Average (SARIMA) models	To model the monthly number of dengue fever (DF) cases in Dhaka, Bangladesh, and forecast the dengue incidence using time series analysis (Zamil Choudhurya and Banu 2008).	Dengue fever (DF) cases in Dhaka Bangladesh monthly data January 2000 to October 2007 (M.A.H. Zamil Choudhurya and Banu, 2008).	Separate modelling approaches for DF, DHF and DSS would provide better information to policy-makers and planners Prediction: forecast for the period November 2007 to December 2008.

Dataset 2

week_start_date	TMAX	TMIN	TAVG	RAINFALL	PRCP
4/30/1990	28.78571	21.74286	25.25714	7.042857	1.428571
5/7/1990	29.11429	21.58571	25.32857	7.528571	3.014286
5/14/1990	27.92857	21.65714	24.78571	6.271429	7.314286
5/21/1990	28.4	21.1	24.72857	7.3	3.985714
5/28/1990	28.32857	21.28571	24.82857	7.042857	2.242857
6/4/1990	28.17143	20.71429	24.45714	7.457143	4.285714
6/11/1990	28.41429	21.44286	24.95714	6.971429	2.3
6/18/1990	27.77143	21.12857	24.47143	6.642857	2.571429
6/25/1990	28.48571	21.6	25.04286	6.885714	0.657143
7/2/1990	27.85714	21.28571	24.57143	6.571429	4.9
7/9/1990	27.38571	21.65714	24.52857	5.728571	3.271429

13.3.3 Proposed Model

Time series analysis Brockwell (2013) may be classified as linear and non-linear (Dhamodharavadhani Rathipriya2020b). Extremely specific techniques are used for the study of time series ARIMA, such as the Box-Jenkins multivariate and Holt winter exponential smoothing (single, double, and triple). ARIMA models are traditional forecasting models that require historical empirical data as evidence to make predictions (Dhamodharavadhani and Rathipriya 2019). This model is a simple statistical framework that can be used as the basis for mathematical models. These three order variables (a, b, c) describe the process of fitting the ARIMA model to the Box-Jenkins system (Sahanaa and Mishra 2018).

The Figure 13.2 shows the methodology of time series forecasting using ARIMA model. The first step of the ARIMA model is preprocessing the data. Time series data are plotted and its patterns and irregularities are examined. Next, the outliers and missing values are removed. The second step is to decompose the data and then to stationary the series and after that to calculate the autocorrelation by choosing the model order based on the process to fit the ARIMA model, then to evaluate and improve the model. The following Table 13.2 describes the steps to fit the ARIMA to a dengue forecasting model and its mathematical format.

13.3.4 Estimate and Develop the Model

The prediction is iterated in two ways to enhance the forecast. One is to add the seasonal variable to be removed earlier. Another solution would be to require (A, B, C) components to be included in the model; refitting the model on the same results, so that its silent ability is determined by a particular seasonal trend in the sequence, with the seasonal aspect defined in AR (1) (Dalinina 2017). The parameters (a, b, c) have also been modified to include the seasonal variable. Once the same process of analyzing the residual model has been done, the ACF/PACF plots change the structure as appropriate. For

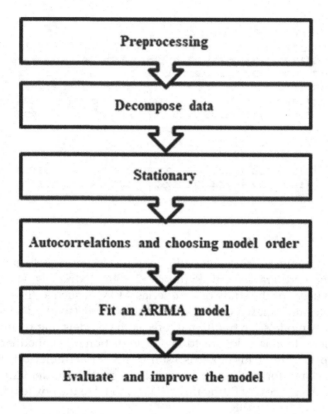

FIGURE 13.2
Workflow of proposed model.

example, finding the same higher-order evidence is present in auto correlations with lag 7, which indicates a higher-order component may be required.

13.4 Results and Discussions

By plotting the data, the outliers, randomness, or irregularities can be found as shown in Figure 13.3. In this case, dengue cases show a lot of variations from one week to another. Despite this, these variations do have a pattern. For example, the number of dengue cases is less in the winter months and a higher number dengue cases are observed in the summer months.

In total the number of dengue cases decreased less than 100 on the first week and to over 400 on the following week as shown in Figure 13.4. These are alleged outliers that by skewing the statistical summaries may distort the model. A preprocessing method is used to remove time series outliers. This

TABLE13.2

Proposed Model Description

Model	Mathematical Equations	Model parameter
Preprocessing using Moving Average (MA(c))	$m = 2k + 1$	c = number of terms in model m = series average Y k = period point
ARIMA model	$R_t = c + \alpha_1 R_{bt-1} + \alpha_a e_{bt-a} + \dots$ $+ \alpha_1 e_{t-1} + \alpha_a e_{a-1} + e_t$	R_b is R differenced b times c = constant e_t = error a = alpha
Decomposition	$x_t = T + S + R$ $x_t = T * S * R$ $Y = S_t * T_t * E_t$	T = Trend S = seasonal R = Random of series $x_t = x$ differenced t times Y = total number of dengue cases St = seasonal variable T_t = pattern and cycle E_t = rest of the error
Stationary	$Y_{d_t} = Y_t - Y_{t-1}$ $Y_{d2_t} = Y_{dt} - Y_{dt-1} = (Y_t - Y_{t-1}) - (Y_{t-1} - Y_{t-2})$ $Y_{d2_t} = Y_{dt} - Y_{dt-1} = (Y_t - Y_{t-1}) - (Y_{t-1} - Y_{t-2})$	$d = 2$ Y = total number of dengue cases t = times point
Autocorrelations	$r_k = \dfrac{\sum_{t=k+1}^{n}(y_t - y')(y_t - k^{-y'})}{\sum_{t=1}^{n}(y_t - y')^2}$	rk = lag k autocorrelation k = the time lag n = total number of dengue cases
Fitting Dengue ARIMA Model	$\hat{Y}_{d_t} = 0.4551 Y_{t-1} - 0.3496 e_{t-1} + E$	Y = total number of dengue cases t = times point E = error original dengue cases differentiates from order 1

will identify and remove outliers with time series smoothing and decomposition. This process is effective in passing missed values to the array.

The more varied the gap of the moving average, the smoother the original series develops. For Tamil Nadu's dengue dataset, the weekly moving average is considered for smoothing the series.

The Figure 13.5 shows decomposition of data into different components. They are: data variables represented as weekly data; trend variable is complete pattern series; seasonal variable denotes that fluctuations in the data related to calendar cycles; and remainder elements consisting of decreasing or increasing non-seasonal trends.

Figure 13.6 shows that the left panel is stationary, where data values oscillate with a constant variance around the average of 1. The right side of the

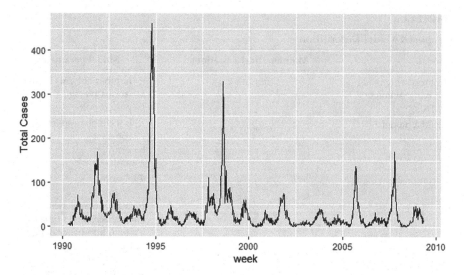

FIGURE13.3
weekly dengue cases in Tamil Nadu.

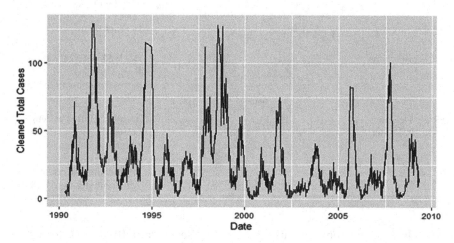

FIGURE 13.4
Cleaned data.

plot displays a non-stationary sequence; thus the series mean value will differ across various time periods. Figure 13.6 shows stationary and non-stationary series

The meteorological data is non-stationary; the total number of cases of dengue varies over time, and shifts in scales. A proper ADF test does not reject the non-stationary null hypothesis which confirms graphical representation.

In Figure 13.7 ACF shows correlation between a series and its lags. ACF plots can assist in taking responsibility for MA(b) (Dalinina 2017) order in

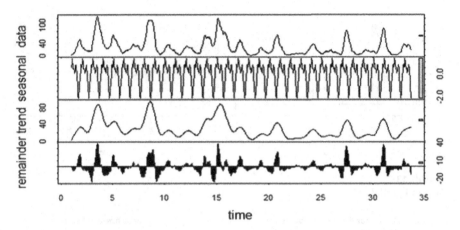

FIGURE 13.5
Decomposition of data. Left panel.

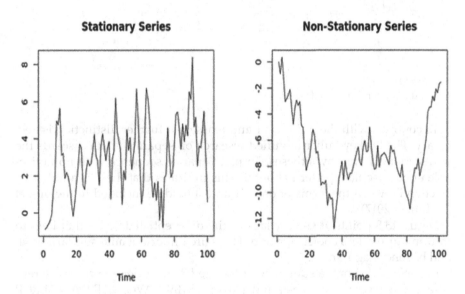

FIGURE 13.6
Stationary and non-stationary series.

addition to recommending the order of variation. PACF denotes that a relationship between a variable and its lags that could not be explained by previous lags. It useful to fit the AR(a) order model.

As blue dotted lines, the plots are borders of 95% importance. There are important meteorological data auto-correlations with many lags, as shown in the ACF map. It is possible to the transfer effect after the initial lags, as shown in the PACF point at lags (1,7,7).

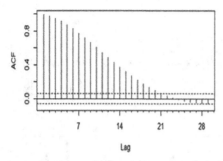
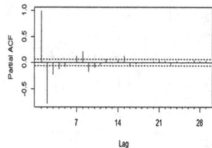

FIGURE 13.7
ACF and partial ACF.

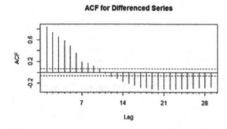
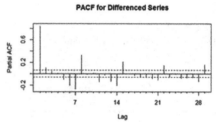

FIGURE13.8
ACF and PACF for differenced series.

To continue with the order d = 1 and reassess if further distinction is necessary. The Dickey-Fuller modified research on separated data discards the non-stationary null hypotheses. To plot Separate sequence with no noticeable effect, oscillate pattern about 0. This indicates that there is ample distinction between the terms of order 1 and should be included in the model (Dalinina, 2017).

Figure 13.8 points at similar lags of the differentiated series that help to inform our model's choice of a or b. There are important auto similarities at, and beyond, Lag 1 and 2.

In Table 13.3 shows a summary of the model. Total dengue cases are represented as response variables and TMAX, TMIN, TAVG, RAINFALL, PRCP are represented as predictors.

Figure 13.9 indicates plots for configuration residuals of ACF and PACF. Parameters of the model's order and construction are correctly defined, so there are no major autocorrelations to predict.

Forecasting (ARIMA [1,1,7]) using a fitted model to determine forward forecast horizon h intervals for full predictions, and using the fitted model to produce such predictions as shown in Figure 13.10.

The light blue line indicates the fit given by the model in Figure 13.11, and how the model will work in Tamil Nadu in future dengue cases. One

TABLE 13.3

Dengue ARIMA Model

Model = total dengue cases ~TMAX+TMIN+TAVG+ RAINFALL+PRCP			
Deviance Residuals	**Min**	**MEDIAN**	**MAX**
	−50.72	−9.82	419.70
Null Deviance	2146476 on 789 degree of freedom		
Residual Deviance	1992815 on 784 degree of freedom		
AIC	84		

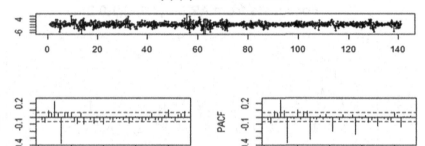

FIGURE 13.9
ACF and PACF for model residuals.

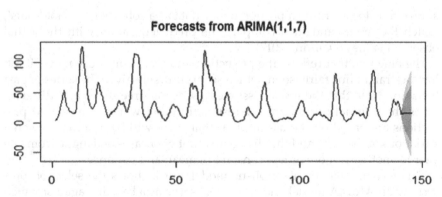

FIGURE 13.10
Forecasts from ARIMA (1,1,7).

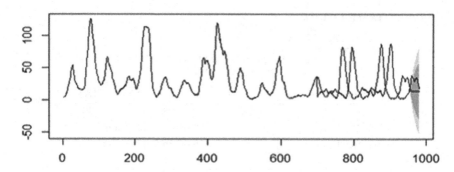

FIGURE13.11
Forecast compare to the actual values.

Forecasts from ARIMA(3,1,4)(1,0,2)(7)

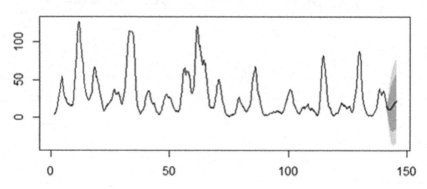

FIGURE13.12
Improving Forecasts from ARIMA.

approach is to substitute a portion of our data as a collection of "hold-outs", match the model and then compare the predicted values with the actual observed values (Dalinina 2017)

The blue line that reflects the projection, though, seems very naive: it follows a straight line fairly soon, which seems unlikely given the series of past behavior. Note that the model assumes a seasonal-free series and differentiates the original non-stationary results. In other words, the plotted predictions are based on the assumption that there will be no other seasonal variations in the data, and the change in number of cases of dengue from one year to another is more or less constant in mean and variance.

This forecast may be a simplistic model, but it shows the selection process for an ARIMA model and could also serve as a baseline against which to assess when more complex models are designed. All estimates are given confidence boundaries for Figure 13.12. 80% trust boundaries are shaded in darker blue (Dalinina 2017) and 95% in lighter blue. Longer-term predictions will usually have more volatility as the formula will return to future Y on expected values. In this case, this is reflected in the outline of the trust limits, as they begin to grow with rising horizon. The trust boundaries trend may point to the need for a more reliable model. Looking at the forecast limits, the estimated error associated with point predictions is very important.

13.5 Conclusion

In this chapter, the time series proposed ARIMA models are used to predict the number of dengue cases in Tamil Nadu. The result of the ARIMA model is more accurate. This model provides significant benefits in predicting dengue incidence rate in advance. It may help health officials to take effective timely preventative measures which saves time, cost, and human lives.

13.6 Acknowledgment

The first author acknowledges the UGC- Special Assistance Programme (SAP) for the financial support to her research under the UGC-SAP at the level of DRS-II (Ref.No.F.5-6/2018/DRS-II [SAP-II]), 26 July 2018 in the Department of Computer Science, Periyar University.

References

Allard, R. (1998). Use of Time-Series Analysis in Infectious Disease Surveillance. *Bulletin of the World Health Organization*,76(4), 327–333.

Brockwell, P. D. (2013). *Time Series: Theory and Methods*. Springer Science & Business Media.

Chandran, R., Azeez, P. (2015). Outbreak of Dengue in Tamil Nadu, India. *Research Communications*. 109(1):171–176.

Chiung Ching Ho, T. C. (2015, November 17–19). Time Series Analysis and Forecasting of Dengue Using Open Data. In: *4th International Visual Informatics Conference, IVIC 2015*. Bangi, Malaysia: Advances in Visual Informatics.

Dalinina, R. (2017, January 10). Introduction to Forecasting with ARIMA in R. Retrieved from Oracle Data Science Blog: https://blogs.oracle.com/datascience/introduction-to-forecasting-with-arima-in-r

Dhamodharavadhani, S., Rathipriya, R. (2016). A Pilot Study on Climate Data Analysis Tools and Software. In: *2016 Online International Conference on Green Engineering and Technologies (IC-GET)*. IEEE Xplore Digital Library. *Coimbatore.*

Dhamodharavadhani, S., Rathipriya, R. (2019). Region-Wise Rainfall Prediction Using MapReduce-Based Exponential Smoothing Techniques. In: *Advances in Big Data and Cloud Computing Coimbatore*. Springer (pp. 229–239).

Dhamodharavadhani, S., Rathipriya, R. (2020a). Enhanced Logistic Regression (ELR) Model for Big Data. In: F. Garcia Marquez (Ed.), *Handbook of Research on Big Data Clustering and Machine Learning* (pp. 152–176). IGI Global.

Dhamodharavadhani, S., Rathipriya, R. (2020b). Variable Selection Method for Regression Models Using Computational Intelligence Techniques. In: P. Ganapathi, & D. Shanmugapriya (Eds.), *Handbook of Research on Machine and Deep Learning Applications for Cyber Security, IGI global* (pp. 416–436).

Earnest, A. T.-S. (2012). Comparing Statistical Models to Predict Dengue Fever Notifications. *Computational and Mathematical Methods in Medicine*.1:1–6.

Elodie Descloux, M. M.-C.-P. (2012). Climate-Based Models for Understanding and Forecasting Dengue Epidemics. *PLOS Neglected Tropical Diseases*.6(2)e1470.

Karnaboopathy, R., Venkatesan, D. V. (2018). Forecasting Dengue Incidence in Tamil Nadu, India: An Time Series Analysis. *Journal of Comprehensive Health*. 6(2),62–66.

Sahanaa, C., Mishra, A. K. (2018). Trend of Morbidity and Mortality of Dengue in Tamil Nadu and Puducherry, South India. *International Journal of Community Medicine and Public Health*, 5(1)322–325.

Yong-Su Kwon, M.-J. B.-R. (2015). Modeling Occurrence of Urban Mosquitos Based on Land Use Types and Meteorological Factors in Korea. *International Journal of Environmental Research and Public Health*. 12(10), 13131–1314.

Zamil Choudhurya, M. A. H., Banu, S. (2008). Forecasting Dengue Incidence in Dhaka, Bangladesh: A Time Series Analysis. *Dengue Bulletin*. 32, 29–37.

Index

AdaBoost, 8
ARIMA, 189
Artificial Intelligence, 4
Association Rule, 33
Autism Spectrum Disorder, 176

Biosignals, 69
Boltzmann Entropy, 47
Brain Cancer, 54

Cancer, 56
Categorical Data, 20
Classification, 1
Clustering, 33
Convolutional Network, 103
Cutting, 88, 115

Data Uncertainty, 2
Decision Entropy-based Logistic
       Regression, 47
Decision Making, 41
Decision Tree, 6
Deep Learning, 27, 100
DFL Algorithm, 42
Diagnosis of Disease, 29, 146
Diagnosis of Special Children, 175
Dimensions of Big Data, 3
Disease Identification, 146
Down Syndrome, 176

Electroencephalography
       (EEG), 69
Electromagnetic Radiation, 55
Electronic Sensors, 22
Entropy, 42

Feature Extraction, 71
Filter and Wrapper, 42
Forecasting Model, 193

Glioma, 56
Graph, 87
Graph-119

Health Information System Framework, 27
Healthcare Analysis, 131
Healthcare Professionals, 21
High Dimension, 87, 119
High Dimension Fractionation, 159
Hospital Operational Management, 18

Image Analysis, 31
Imaging Data, 20

Keras based Deep Learning, 102

Light Field, 84, 119
Linear regression, 6
Liver Cancer, 100, 107
Logistic Regression, 42

Machine Learning in Healthcare, 26
Machine learning, 1, 42, 180
Medical Data, 19
Medical Information System, 17
Meningioma, 56
Metaheuristic Algorithm for
       Healthcare, 32
Metaheuristic, 32
MIS Data, 21
MRI, 160

Neural Network, 30, 103

Parkinson's Disease, 30
Patient Report Analysis, 129
Pattern Recognition, 1
Pre-and Post-operative Operations, 159
Prediction, 1
Predictive Model, 42

Radio Frequency Waves, 55
Readmission Prediction, 42

Sensory Processing Disorder, 176
Shannon Entropy, 47
Spatial Channel, 69

Supervised Learning, 6
Support Vector Machine (SVM), 6

TensorFlow, 108
Textual Data, 20

Transportation Cost, 35
Tumor, 86, 125
Tumor Identification, 160

Unsupervised Learning, 9

Printed in the United States
By Bookmasters